"*Yemen: Poverty and Conflict* is an outstand[illegible] profound knowledge of the country and will e[illegible] all interested in the future of Yemen."

Dr Noel Brehony, *Honor[illegible]*
Chair[illegible]

"Lackner has written another valuable and perceptive book on Yemen. Focusing on politics, economics and society, this book is a well-informed, sober and insightful account based on facts and experience gained during her long periods of being in the field. It provides fresh insights into one of the most neglected crises in world affairs."

Marieke Brandt, *Institute for Social Anthropology, Austrian Academy of Sciences, and author of* Tribes and Politics in Yemen: A History of the Houthi Conflict

Yemen

Focusing on the fundamental reasons underlying the lasting crisis of the Yemeni Civil War, this book frames contemporary Yemen and assesses prospects beyond the conflict, identifying the factors which will determine its future internal and international characteristics.

Building on Helen Lackner's profound experience in Yemen, this volume discusses Yemen's history and state formation, the main political institutions emerging since the Republic of Yemen was established and their role in the war, including the significance of current fragmentation. The volume goes on to discuss climate change, including the water scarcity issue, in the context of resource constraints to economic development and the role of migration. Rural and urban life, as well as the impact of international development and humanitarian aid, are also covered, together with Yemen's international relations – its interaction with its neighbours as well as Western states. Looking forward, this volume suggests the type of policies able to give Yemenis the conditions needed for a reasonable standard of living.

Thanks to analysis of determining events, the book will appeal to politicians, diplomats, humanitarian organizations, security analysts, researchers on the Middle East and those generally interested in Yemen. It will also be an essential text for students of international relations, political economy, failing states, development studies and contemporary Middle Eastern history.

Helen Lackner is Associate Researcher, Middle East Institute, SOAS, and Visiting Fellow at the European Council for Foreign Relations (ECFR).

The Contemporary Middle East
Edited by Professor Anoushiravan Ehteshami
Institute for Middle Eastern and Islamic Studies, *University of Durham, United Kingdom*

For well over a century now, the Middle East and North Africa countries have formed a central plank of the international system. **The Contemporary Middle East Series** provides the first systematic attempt at studying the key actors of this dynamic, complex, and strategically important region. Using an innovative common format – which in each case study provides an easily-digestible analysis of the origins of the state, its contemporary politics, economics and international relations – prominent Middle East experts have been brought together to write definitive studies of the MENA region's key countries.

Iran
Stuck in Transition
Anoushiravan Ehteshami

Israel
Ilan Pappé

Afghanistan
Politics and Economics in a Globalising State
Niamatullah Ibrahimi and William Maley

Egypt
A Fragile Power
Eberhard Kienle

Yemen
Poverty and Conflict
Helen Lackner

For more information about this series, please visit:
https://www.routledge.com/The-Contemporary-Middle-East/book-series/CME

Yemen

Poverty and Conflict

Helen Lackner

Routledge
Taylor & Francis Group
LONDON AND NEW YORK

Cover image: © Helen Lackner

First published 2023
by Routledge
4 Park Square, Milton Park, Abingdon, Oxon OX14 4RN

and by Routledge
605 Third Avenue, New York, NY 10158

Routledge is an imprint of the Taylor & Francis Group, an informa business

British Library Cataloguing-in-Publication Data
A catalogue record for this book is available from the British Library

Library of Congress Cataloging-in-Publication Data
A catalog record has been requested for this book

ISBN: 978-0-367-18049-2 (hbk)
ISBN: 978-0-367-18050-8 (pbk)
ISBN: 978-0-429-05931-5 (ebk)

DOI: 10.4324/9780429059315

Typeset in Times New Roman
by Newgen Publishing UK

Contents

Maps

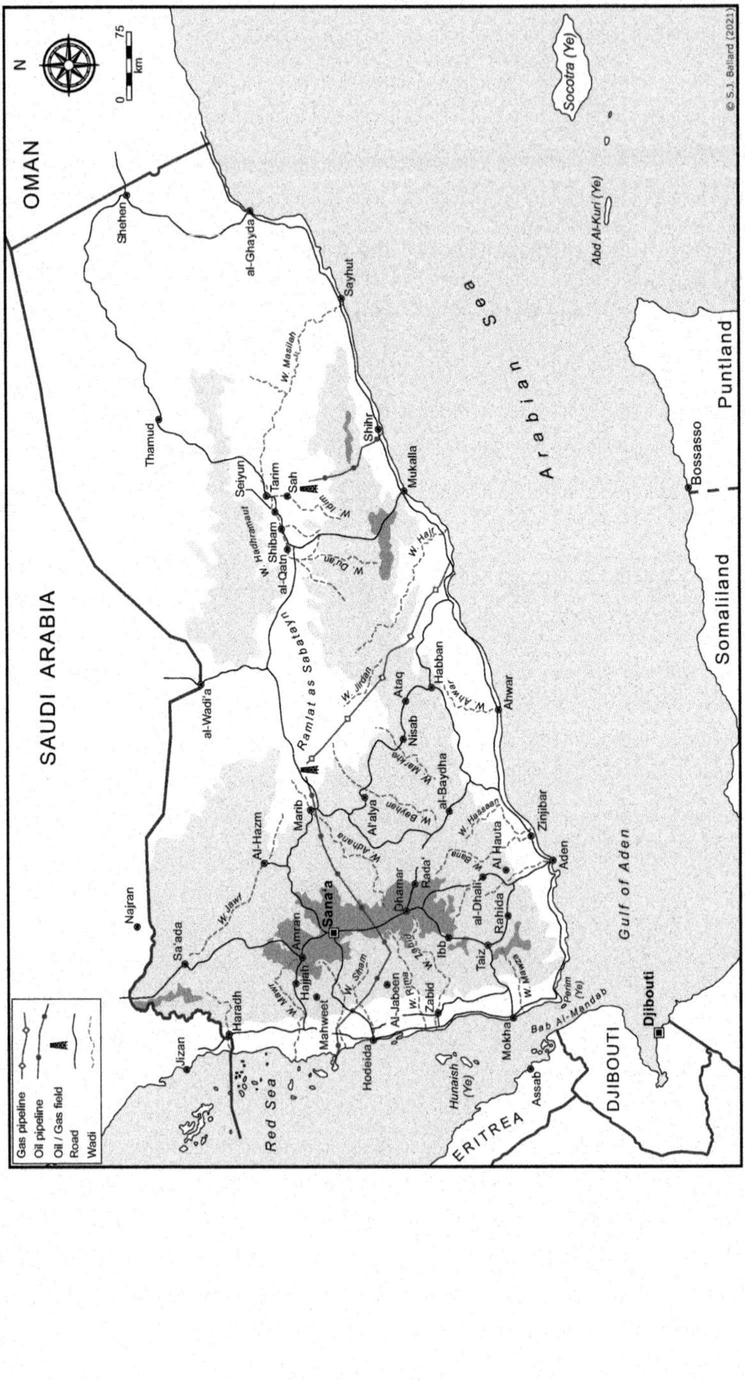

Map 1 Topography and infrastructure of the Republic of Yemen
© S J Ballard

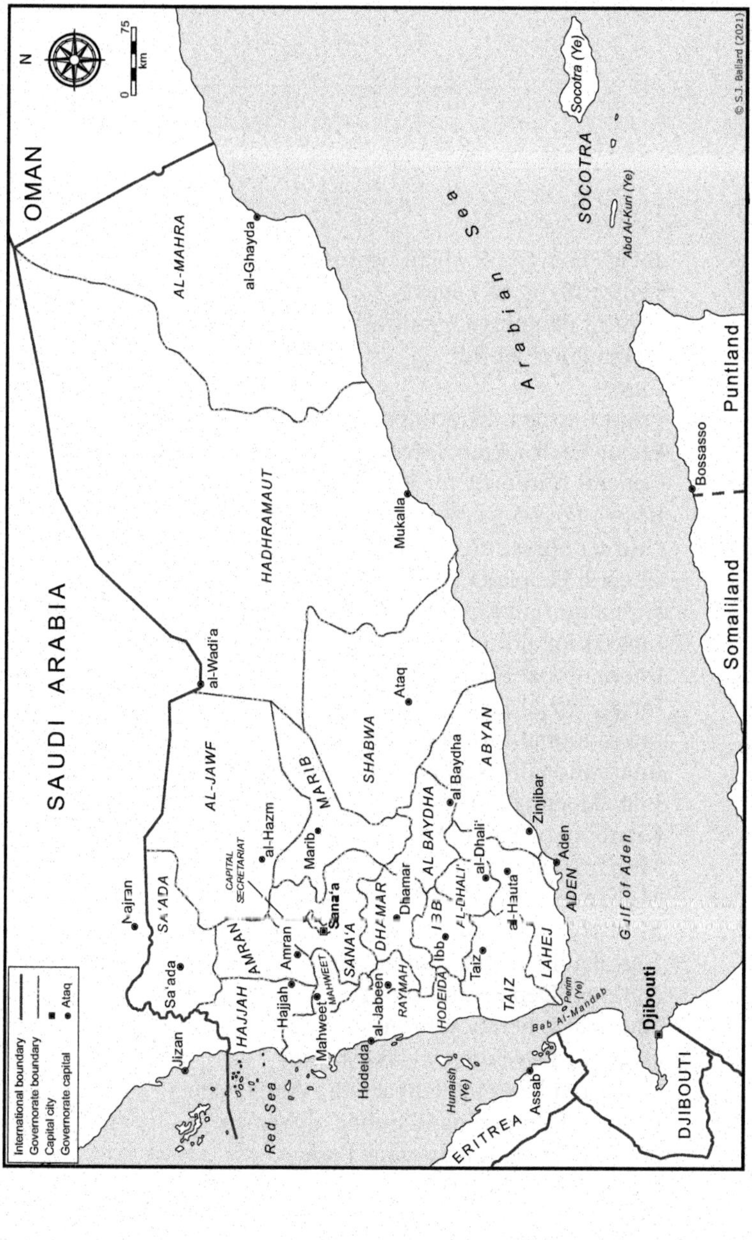

Map 2 Governorates of the Republic of Yemen
© S J Ballard

Abbreviations

AQAP	al Qaeda in the Arabian Peninsula
CBY	Central Bank of Yemen
CPO	Central Planning Organization
DPW	Dubai Ports World
EUR	Euro
FLOSY	Front for the Liberation of Occupied South Yemen
FTS	Financial Tracking Service
GARWSS	General Authority for Rural Water Supply and Sanitation
GBP	British Pound Sterling
GCC	Gulf Cooperation Council
GPC	General People's Congress
HRP	Humanitarian Response Plan
IFAD	International Fund for Agricultural Development
IFI	International Financial Institution
ILO	International Labour Organization
IMF	International Monetary Fund
IRG	Internationally Recognised Government
JMP	Joint Meeting Parties
KSA	Kingdom of Saudi Arabia
MBS	Mohammed bin Salman
MBZ	Mohammed bin Zayed
MOPIC	Ministry of Planning and International Cooperation
NDC	National Dialogue Conference
NDF	National Democratic Front
NLF	National Liberation Front
ODA	Overseas Development Assistance
PNPA	Peace and National Partnership Agreement
PDRY	People's Democratic Republic of Yemen
PRSP	Poverty Reduction Strategy Paper
PWP	Public Works Project
RALP	Rainfed Agriculture and Livestock Project
RoY	Republic of Yemen
SFD	Social Fund for Development

SPC	Supreme People's Council (parliament of the PDRY)
SPC	Supreme Political Council (in Huthi-controlled area since 2016)
SR	Saudi Riyal
STC	Southern Transitional Council
UAE	United Arab Emirates
UNSC	United Nations Security Council
UNVIM	United National Verification and Inspection Mechanism
WB	World Bank
WFP	World Food Programme
YAR	Yemen Arab Republic
YR	Yemeni Riyal
YSP	Yemeni Socialist Party

Chronology

Date	*Event*
700 000 BC	First signs of human presence in Wadi Du‘an
7000 BC	Oldest rock paintings in Sa‘ada, Neolithic stone tools in Rub‘ al Khali, Khawlan, domestication of livestock
3300–1200 BC	Bronze Age: highland-enclosed villages, irrigated agriculture, earliest idols
1200–700 BC	Ancient south Arabian language, first appearance of writing in southern Arabia, first mention of Saba in ancient Assyrian texts, first stone architecture, first monumental inscriptions
700–110 BC	Caravan kingdoms, Sabaean hegemony; first Hadhramaut domination, Qa‘taban dynasty, early south Arabian coins; high period of south Arabian art, Arab tribes arrive in Jawf, emergence of Himyarite era
100–300 AD	Sabaean restoration, Abyssinians occupy western Yemen, Hadhramaut Empire success, Himyarite kings take Saba
300–500	Himyarite Empire, control all south Arabia, Marib dam restored
500–570	Christian and Jewish kingdoms; Abyssinian domination, including Abraha who transfers the capital to Sana‘a; construction of the Sana‘a cathedral; final repairs of Marib dam
575–632	Abyssinian king overthrown by Persian domination
628	Islam arrives in Yemen
625–75	Abyssinian occupation of Yemen
630–32	Yemen joins the Islamic state established by Mohammed in Medina
800–1200	Ibadhi domination in Hadhramaut, Zuraydi dynasty in Aden
820	Zabid founded
898	Zaydi imamate founded in Yemen, lasts until 1962

Date	*Event*
1045–1138	Sulayhids
1173–1222	Ayyubids
1229–1454	Rasulids
1454–1526	Tahirids
1528–1636	Ottoman domination in parts of Yemen
1636–1849	Zaydi imamate dominates parts of Yemen
1839	Britain occupies Aden
1850–78	Hadhramaut wars between Kathiri and Qu'ayti
1849–1918	Ottomans occupy Yemen
1904	Mutawakkilite Imam Yahya comes to power in Sana'a
1905	Anglo-Ottoman treaty on the borders, ratified in 1914
1911	Treaty of Da'an between Imam Yahya and Ottomans giving the Imam almost full independence
1934	Treaty of Taif, between King Abdul Aziz ibn Saud and Imam Yahya, agrees on timed contract basis Yemen's northern border, giving the Kingdom of Saudi Arabia control over Asir, Najran and Jizan for 40 years
	Border agreement between Imam Yahya and the British
1944	Establishment of the Free Yemeni movement
1945	Yemen joins the Arab League
1947	Legislative council established in Aden
1948	Imam Yahya assassinated, Imam Ahmad takes over, sacking of Sana'a, Ahmed moves capital to Taiz; major labour strikes in Aden
1952	Egypt: free officers overthrow monarchy; two years later Gamal Abdul Nasser becomes leader
1958	Mutawakkilite imamate in Sana'a joins Egypt and Syria to form the United Arab States, dissolved in 1961
1959	Creation of the Federation of South Arabian Emirates
1962	Death of Imam Ahmad; revolution of 26 September creates the Yemen Arab Republic; establishment of South Arabian Federation with the inclusion of Aden
1962–70	Civil war between royalists supported by Saudi Arabia and UK against the republicans supported by Nasser's Egypt, republic survives
1963–67	Anti-colonial armed struggle in Aden and the Protectorates
1967	June War, Egypt defeated, Aden uprising against UK, independence of the PRSY
1967–68	Siege of Sana'a by royalists fails to dislodge republicans
1969	Left of the National Liberation Front wins power struggle in the PRSY

Date	*Event*
1970	PRSY renamed People's Democratic Republic of Yemen; Saudi military attacks; Agrarian reform in PDRY
1972	First intra-Yemeni war, leads to unity agreement
1974	Ibrahim al Hamdi leads 'coup', becomes president of the YAR
1976	Establishment of Diplomatic relations between PDRY and KSA
1977	Ibrahim al Hamdi assassinated prior to travel to PDRY to announce unity
1978	President al Ghashmi assassinated, Ali Abdullah Saleh becomes president of YAR; President Salmine in Aden executed, establishment of the Yemeni Socialist Party (YSP)
1979	Second intra-Yemeni war, leads to unity agreement
1980	Ali Nasser Mohammed becomes president and secretary general of YSP, in addition to his earlier position as prime minister in PDRY, Abdul Fattah Ismail goes into exile
1982	YAR: General People's Congress (GPC) created
1984	YAR: Commercial quantities of oil discovered in Marib
1985	PDRY: Abdul Fattah Ismail returns to Aden from Soviet Union; power struggle
1986	PDRY:13 January 'events', short civil war, Ali Nasser Mohammed and supporters, including Abdu Rabbu Mansour Hadi exiled in Sana'a; Ali Salem al Beedh becomes Secretary General of YSP
1990	22 May: Unification of PDRY and YAR into the Republic of Yemen (RoY); Ali Abdullah Saleh president, Ali Salem al Beedh vice president
	Iraq invades Kuwait; ROY votes against use of force at UNSC; leads to loss of international development aid and return of 800 000 Yemenis from GCC states; creation of Islah party
1991	Zaydi revival movement starts in far north of RoY; commercial quantities of oil discovered in Hadhramaut;
1993	Parliamentary elections
1994	Civil war: Al Beedh announces re-establishment of separate state in Aden; defeated by Saleh forces aided by former exiles. RoY constitution amended to increase presidential power

Date	*Event*
1995	RoY accepts IMF advice, introduces structural adjustment policies; foreign aid returns
1999	Presidential elections; Ali Abdullah Saleh elected
2000	RoY and Saudi Arabia sign Jeddah treaty agreeing permanent borders; USS Cole attacked in Aden port by al Qa'eda
2001	First elections of local councils; after 9/11 Saleh rushes to support Bush's 'war against terror'
2003	Formation of Joint Meeting Parties (JMP), by Islah, YSP, Nasserites, Popular Forces, Baath party and al Haq party; second parliamentary elections
2004	First Huthi war: Husayn Badr al-Din al Huthi killed
2006	Formation of the Southern Military Retirees Organisation
2011	Popular uprisings demanding downfall of Saleh regime, jobs, dignity and end to corruption; UNSC resolution 2014 supports Gulf Cooperation Council (GCC) initiative on transfer of power
2012	Abdu Rabbu Mansour Hadi elected president for two-year transitional period; Saleh remains head of GPC; International community pledges USD 8.4 billion development aid
2013–14	National Dialogue Conference agrees 1800 'outcomes'; Presidential Committee agrees on six-region federation; Huthi movement expands its geographical control
2014	Huthi movement take Sana'a thanks to support from Saleh; Peace and National Partnership Agreement signed between transitional government and Huthis; new government formed
2015	Huthi full take-over in Sana'a; Hadi announces Aden Temporary Capital, Huthi–Saleh forces attack Aden, leading to Hadi escaping to Riyadh, Saudi-led Coalition launches 'Decisive Storm' operation to restore government to power; UAE and local troops expel Huthi–Saleh forces from Aden; UNSC votes resolution 2216 limiting its mediation potential
2016	Kuwait failed peace negotiations last three months; Huthi–Saleh establish Supreme Political Council and Government of National Salvation in Sana'a; Hadi appoints Ali Mohsen as vice president; deadliest air strike on the Great Hall in Sana'a kills more than 140

Date	*Event*
2017	Formation of UAE-supported Southern Transitional Council (STC) in Aden, challenges authority of Hadi's Internationally Recognised Government (IRG); Huthis kill Saleh in Sana'a; Yemen first described by UN as the 'worst Humanitarian crisis in the world'
2018	Coalition offensive on Hodeida interrupted by international intervention; UN-sponsored Stockholm Agreement leads to Hodeida cease-fire
2019	STC expel IRG from Aden; Saudis negotiate the Riyadh Agreement between the two factions; UAE 'withdraws' most troops from Yemen; increase in Huthi missile attacks on Saudi Arabia; largest UN Humanitarian support financed (USD 3.9 billion)
2020	Huthi offensive in north-east breaks lasting stalemate; a year after Riyadh agreement, new government formed and arrives in Aden, but differences between STC and IRG remain active; UN Humanitarian plan receives half of requirement (USD 2 billion); humanitarian situation worsens throughout the country
2021	Huthis renew offensive on Marib; Biden administration appoints special envoy, announces interruption of arms sales to Saudi Arabia and UAE; UN appoints new special envoy

Preface

The inclusion of this volume in the Contemporary Middle East Series is a reminder to all that Yemen is, indeed, part of the Middle East, however defined. This is important as the country is so often ignored in discussions of the region, whether cultural, economic, political or historical. This neglect in both Western and Arab discourse is surprising: a country with 30 million Arabic speaking people, a millennial history, an extraordinarily varied geography and diverse landscapes, and control of one of the world's major international sea routes, should receive more attention, despite not being a significant hydrocarbon exporter. Even the current conflict, which as of 2022 Yemenis have been suffering for more than seven years, has received so little international attention that, when mentioned, it is frequently described as 'the forgotten war'. This is the case despite the UN, since 2017, stating that the war has caused the world's worst humanitarian crisis.

Reader, welcome to Yemen. Despite the subtitle of this book being eminently apt, given that the country has been riven by conflict for decades, even centuries, and is by far the poorest in the Middle East, those who have had the opportunity of visiting Yemen and meeting its people know that it is beautiful with a long history and culture, unique in the Arabian Peninsula and the Middle East. Yemenis are generous and hospitable despite the extraordinarily difficult physical, economic and political environment in which they have survived throughout history. This book, focused on politics, economics and society, has unfortunately little room for many of the most wonderful features of the country, but I hope that understanding these aspects will encourage you to follow up and investigate the country's archaeology, music, poetry, architecture and other elements of its culture, which will reveal Yemen's most agreeable features. I also hope that, in the not-too-distant future, you will be able to travel there and visit the multiplicity of sceneries, towns, villages, ancient sites and Islamic monuments dispersed throughout the country and to meet Yemenis.

My work on this book has benefitted enormously from help, advice and information from and discussions with a number of people, most of whom prefer to remain anonymous. They know who they are and how grateful I am for all the help given. As is customary, I remain responsible for any errors and all interpretations of events. Transliteration primarily uses the more common English usage of names and has no pretence to being scientific; only ‘ayn is represented as here. Hopefully this makes the book easier to read. Good reading.

Oxford, November 2021

Introduction

In 2021, in addition to the Huthi military offensive in Marib in the north-east of the country, the main claim to fame for Yemen is its official position as the UN's 'worst humanitarian crisis', a concept widely questioned by experts, as it is based on unreliable estimates using even less reliable baselines (Sana'a Centre for Strategic Studies, 2021). According to the new UN Under-Secretary General for Humanitarian Affairs (until recently the UN Special Envoy to Yemen) in August 2021 'about 5 million people are just one step away from succumbing to famine and the diseases that go with it. Ten million more are right behind them. Famine isn't just a "food problem"' (OCHA, 2021). There is no doubt that the humanitarian situation has been bad and getting worse for the last four years, in particular with respect to people's ability to obtain the food they need for survival. However, neither the UN nor any Yemeni power holder has declared a famine, and it is doubtful that such a stage has been reached. Regardless, the humanitarian situation is disastrous and primarily the responsibility of the Yemeni politico-military leadership, the regional coalition members, while the internationally financed humanitarian sector has failed to fully prevent widespread hunger.

What excuse do the Yemeni leaders on all sides have? Discussing the issues involved in the food security crisis requires addressing many aspects (Mwatana and GRC, 2021). First, why does a country with 70% of its population living in rural areas need to import 90% of its basic staples? This makes it extremely dependent on international markets and price fluctuations. Partial explanations are addressed in Chapter 3: in particular, Yemen's population has almost trebled since unification in 1990, from 11 to 30 million in 2022, and it continues to increase at a rapid rate. This means that agricultural holding sizes are decreasing; climate change and the water crisis are also reducing cultivable land and yields. The neo-liberal development policies implemented by the Yemeni government and encouraged by the international community failed to address food security as a priority. Instead of investing in rain-fed improved staple crops and new high value crops, support was given to wealthier farmers to cultivate bananas and mangoes for export, both of which are very thirsty crops. Moreover, they are mostly grown using deep well irrigation and thus further contribute to the exhaustion of the country's limited

DOI: 10.4324/9780429059315-1

fossil aquifers. These shifts have reduced Yemeni self-sufficiency in staple crops to insignificance.

Dependence on imports for basic staples has been a problem for Yemen since the beginning of this century, but the war has worsened the situation dramatically as a result of the complete blockade imposed intermittently by the Saudi-led coalition since 2015. This affects Hodeida and other smaller ports on the Red Sea which have direct access to the parts of the country where the majority of the population live, including those in remote mountain settlements. These areas are under Huthi control. Therefore, for imports to reach these isolated communities, fuel, food and other necessities must travel on difficult tracks and roads. An essential ingredient is, of course, money, whether from earnings, remittances or humanitarian assistance. Most of the attention given to the activities of the Saudi-led coalition has focused on air strikes on civilian facilities and events, but its actions in preventing and controlling the flow of remittances, food and fuel has played a far bigger role in the country's death toll, estimated at 377 000 by the end of 2021. For example, in March 2021, the World Food Programme (WFP) deplored that not a single fuel ship had been allowed to dock in Hodeida for a full two months and 350 000 metric tons of fuel were held off the coast. Monthly fuel requirement is 544 000 tons. Restricting fuel imports to Hodeida has a number of outcomes, including far higher prices for all commodities and increased profits for traders involved, as well, of course, as worsening living conditions for the people (ACAPS, 2021).

The actions of the Central Bank in Yemen (CBY), based in Aden and under the control of President Hadi's internationally recognised government (IRG) is another important element contributing to the current humanitarian crisis (see Chapter 3). Having run out of hard currency, in 2018 Saudi Arabia provided it with USD 2 billion to provide guarantees for Yemeni traders to purchase food on international markets. As of early 2021, these funds were exhausted and importers experienced complex problems. Renewal of this facility is highly unlikely for two main reasons: the financial constraints suffered by the Kingdom of Saudi Arabia (KSA) due to increased need of financing for internal development projects and the Covid-19 pandemic on the one hand, and on the other hand the fact that the dissident Southern Transitional Council (STC) is preventing the CBY in Aden from operating effectively under the authority of the IRG.

Yemen's unique social structure

Among Yemen's unique characteristics in the Arab world is its social structure (Lackner, 2019a, pp. 190–209). There are indeed some similarities with the south Asian caste system, including that of being far more flexible than formal principles allow. The vast majority of Yemenis are tribal people, either members of tribes structured into broader and larger confederations, or members of small tribal groups which have limited, if any, affiliation to broader entities. No accurate data are available, but it is estimated that approximately 70% of the country's population are tribespeople. There are two main tribal confederations north of Sana'a, the Hashed and the Bakeel; in the centre of the country, the Madhaj is a looser confederation; the Yafi' are further south; and the Awlaqi are in the south-east. In the areas without major confederations, tribes are smaller and have lower levels of social cohesion. In the Taiz area, many people claim that there are no tribes, regardless of reality. Denial of tribal affiliation, a characteristic of 'modern' educated elites, usually only lasts until the need for community solidarity emerges, either to deal with personal crisis or to address conflict.

Anti-tribal prejudice is widely shared not only among urbanised and educated Yemenis but also by the wider international community, where discussion often focuses on the debate about the relationship between tribe and state (Peterson, 2021). As the most numerous and traditional arms bearing group, tribespeople are the dominant group in Yemen, though they do not always control politics. In the past the *sada* (sg *sayyed*) group was politically dominant in Sana'a. Officially direct descendants of the prophet, the imams in Sana'a were all *sada*, and the main ideological belief of the Huthi movement is that this group has an innate right to rule. They are widely accused of working to bring back the imamate and rule by *sada.* Indeed, in the areas which they govern, *sada* are widely privileged, including taking the majority of senior positions, though Huthi leaders deny planning the return to an imamate.

Traditionally ascribed status provided the country's social hierarchy, with the *sada* holding the top positions as religious and judicial authority. In most parts of the country the *sada* have traditionally needed the protection of arms-bearing tribesmen; however, nowadays some have taken up arms. *Quda* (sg *qadi*) are the main learned group working as judges and administrators; their status has become inherited over the ages though it was not originally ascribed. The merchant class were below tribes, *sada*, and *quda*, but the last half century has brought about a complete change as they became the main holders of wealth and also industrialists, thus improving their position in practice and allowing them to reach the higher levels of the hierarchy. There are low status groups defined as weak: they include artisans whose position varied according to their occupation. The lowest ranking was given to two groups who share the characteristic of being darker skinned: they included both former slaves who ranked above those who now prefer to be called 'marginalised' or *muhamasheen* and are still widely known in Yemen as *akhdam*.

These traditional inherited statuses remain important and are indeed reviving in the areas under Huthi control, given their determination to re-assert *sada* dominance. Over the course of the past half century, considerable changes have taken place in practice. A new social structure is emerging based on wealth and access to resources, rather than circumstances of birth. Those who have monopolised wealth and power through the privileges given by the Saleh regime to his cronies have become dominant, and include military security personnel from Saleh's area, as well as the big traders and industrialists. There is a significant overlap between the formal hierarchy and the new one. Most people's current status depends more on their differing levels of control over resources and political power, and a class structure is emerging (Lackner, 2016b, pp. 6–13).

Sects and sectarianism

Some discussions of Yemen wrongly attribute its problems to sectarianism. As a general rule, what is presented as religiously based political conflict is in fact based on political differences, using interpretations of religion to support different political interests (Alwaday and Shuja Al-Deen, 2021). Yemen is no different. Yemenis are Muslims: the country has two major sects which, until very recently, lived in harmony – the Fiver Zaydi Shi'a (discussed in greater detail in Chapter 1) whose theological differences with the Sunni Shafi'i group are minimal. Followers of both schools pray together, and their differences are not a significant social marker. Zaydis live in the northern highlands, from the Saudi border to approximately Yarim (excluding the Tihama Red Sea coast and the more desert-like areas in the east). The rest of the country is populated by Shafi'is, with a small minority of Ismailis west of Sana'a in Jabal Haraz area and a few dispersed elsewhere. People in the former YAR certainly noted that all the presidents in Sana'a were also Zaydi (but of course leaders in Aden were Shafi'i), so in the Shafi'i areas ruled by Sana'a, there was a perception of anti-Shafi'i discrimination at the political level; but, given that most leaders were from the majority tribal group, this did not become a fundamental issue.

However, as Chapter 2 discusses, sectarianism is gradually developing as a result of Ansar Allah (the official name of the Huthi movement) introducing and strengthening 'Twelver' Shi'a practices. This process is designed to strengthen political control by differentiating its movement from others through the establishment of religiously based collective identities and allegiances. Given enough time, this may well create a sectarianism which was previously absent in Yemen. Although these practices help bring together their followers to build their movement and increase support, they are also likely to worsen divisions and cause further fragmentation among Yemenis.

Organisation of the book

As others in the series, this volume focuses on developments in the last century, with the first chapter addressing the country's history and state formation. It outlines the main political characteristics of the two states which united in 1990 to form the Republic of Yemen (RoY), both republics, the Yemen Arab Republic (YAR) aligned with the West during the Cold War and the People's Democratic Republic of Yemen (PDRY) which was the only Arab state with close relations to the Soviet Union during the Cold War. In the quarter century of the RoY's existence prior to the war, the state developed formal institutions and held elections. The chapter also outlines some of the features that led to the war.

Chapter 2 discusses the various factions and parties which have been the main political institutions since the RoY was established and their relevance to the origins of the war. It also examines the role of Ali Abdullah Saleh as the main personality affecting Yemen's contemporary history and politics, as well as the rise of the Huthis and southern separatism in the decade preceding the outbreak of the war. It concludes with analysis of the main internal forces active in the war, as well as the importance of the leading international members of the coalition, Saudi Arabia and the UAE, and the reasons for the lack of achievements of UN mediation.

Chapter 3 presents the natural constraints on economic development with particular attention to the current and future impact of climate change, focusing in particular on water scarcity, an issue of greater long-term relevance to Yemenis than the current politico-military one. Analysis of economic development policies points out the convergence of the internationally supported neo-liberal agenda with the political priorities of the Saleh regime and contributes to explaining why poverty is such a fundamental feature of Yemen's development. The changes in international migration patterns and possibilities also explains the people's widespread poverty. The war economy is a continuation of the earlier neo-liberal policies with new participants but basically worsening social differentiation between a small minority of Yemeni and other profiteers at the expense of the majority.

Chapter 4 covers Yemen's relations with the outside world, giving priority attention to relations with its main neighbours, whose lasting role in Yemeni politics and society is unavoidable, and moving outwards to include its relations with the world's most powerful states. The book concludes with the prospects for a post-war Yemen and an assessment of the main economic, political and social factors which will influence the future nature of the country, both internal and international.

1 Modern state formation

Yemen has a very long history, including famous episodes and characters in the pre-Islamic period, such as Queen Saba (Sheba) of King Solomon fame (let alone modern cat food branding). However, of the many Yemeni states which have existed in the past two millennia, none covered the entire geographical area of the Republic of Yemen. In recent decades there has been notable debate as to whether Yemen can be described as a state, particularly since the two previous entities, the YAR and the PDRY, had very different regimes. The civil war which broke out after the Huthi movement took Sana'a in September 2014, worsened by the military intervention of the Saudi-led coalition, has caused further fragmentation, giving this debate even greater relevance.

Pre-Islamic Yemen

Prior to the current war, Yemen was famous since the earliest days of antiquity, with a few names, events and locations known well beyond its borders. The first signs of human habitation in Hadhramaut date to about 7000 BC, marked by significant archaeological data about the same time, such as rock paintings in Sa'ada, traces of domestication of animals in Khawlan and megaliths in Hadhramaut. During the Bronze Age (3300–1200 BC), walled villages were established in the highlands and irrigated agriculture was initiated.

The ancient south Arabian language and the first monumental inscriptions in ancient Saba date from about 1000 BC. Between 689 and 681 BC a number of states emerged: the Sabean empire with its capital in Marib, the Qa'taban state with its capital in Timna (near Bayhan in Shabwa Governorate today), Hadhramaut with its capital in Shabwa (the ancient site now in the desert) and Ma'in with Baraqish and later Qarnaw (both in Jawf) as its capitals. The states of Ma'in, Saba, Qa'taban, Awsan, Himyar and Hadhramaut all controlled, at different times the major trade routes bringing frankincense, silk and spices from the East and various other items from Africa such as ostrich feathers and ivory. All these were transported to the coasts across the Arabian Sea thanks to the monsoons, but then forced to use overland routes and camel

DOI: 10.4324/9780429059315-2

caravans to reach their markets around the Mediterranean Sea and beyond, as the Red Sea was far more difficult to navigate.

Ma'in and Saba 'developed a prosperous agricultural base and built numerous irrigation works' (Stookey, 1978, p. 11) including the famous Marib dam, built around 1700 BC which lasted many centuries. It is said to have finally collapsed in the 'year of the elephant' 570 AD following decades of neglect due to the weakening of the Himyarite state which then ruled that area. These various states overlapped both in terms of their mutual alliances and with respect to their duration and timing. Yemen was not isolated, with struggles against northern Arab tribes, and also Abyssinians coming from across the Red Sea who had a greater and deeper influence, hence the myth of the relationship between Queen Saba of Yemen and King Solomon of Abyssinia.

After centuries of complex religious beliefs in which a number of deities were honoured, monotheism emerged. Competition between Christianity and Judaism was a later development, but the first ruler who converted to Christianity was the Sabean chief at Zafar. Although Judaism had been present earlier, the first Himyarite rulers converted to Judaism in about 380 AD, leading to the neglect and destruction of many temples. This period of decline largely resulted from a change in international trade which had started by-passing the desert caravan routes. The new trade routes both included marine transport in the Red Sea itself and direct overland treks from Persia to Byzantium via the Gulf and the Euphrates, east of the Arabian Peninsula. South Arabian leaders were distracted from these fundamental economic issues by their concern with religion. Among the ensuing religious conflicts, the Jewish king of Saba Yusuf Ashaar Dhu Nuwas attacked the Christians of Najran, causing a massacre. After further conflict the Christian king Abraha took power in 535 AD in Saba and successfully prevented further attempts at direct Ethiopian rule, but he was the last Christian king, as in 575 AD the area came under Sassanian (Persian) rule.

From the arrival of Islam to the nineteenth century

In the decades prior to the arrival of Islam, Yemen was a zone of conflict between a number of tribal confederations, conflicts focused on access to the increasingly limited natural resources as, on the one hand, desert trade routes became subject to competition and on the other, desertification made settled agricultural and semi-nomadic livestock husbandry increasingly precarious. The Prophet Mohammed's interest in Yemen was due to two factors: first the Yemeni origins of his supporters in Medina and second the need to take control of the international trade from India, which came along the margins of the desert, and to by-pass the major trading centre of Mecca from which he was excluded (Chelhod, 1984, p. 18).Islam reached Yemen within the lifetime of the Prophet.Until the twentieth century, the country was divided into three main regions: first, Janad, based in the Taiz/Ibb area, including the Tihama and extending occasionally as far as Aden and Lahej; second, Sana'a covering the highlands from Sa'ada and Najran and reaching Janad in the south; and third, the Hadhramaut region covering the area of the same name today. Depending on the different dynasties in charge and changes in the balance of power, the borders between them moved over the following centuries.

For about a century from 1038 to 1138, Yemen was ruled by the Ismaili Shi'i Sulayhid dynasty who were loosely subordinate to the Fatimid caliphate in Cairo. They were based in Zabid, a city which was taken and liberated by Sulayhid and Abyssinian leaders in turn for decades. For a while, their authority reached as far as Sana'a. Its most famous personality was Queen Arwa who ruled in her husband's name for over half a century from their base in south-west Yemen, in Jibla near Ibb. Some of her income derived from the tribute paid annually by her agents in Aden and along the southern coast. She remains an extremely popular historical figure centuries later.

Sulayhid rule, focused on the Tihama and highland Yemen from Sana'a southwards, did not seriously threaten the rise of the Zaydi imamate which had emerged at the end of the ninth century AD and remained the main authority in the far north of Yemen, including Najran, while its southern limits varied. The Zaydi sect originated in the south of the Caspian Sea, and its followers, regardless of multiple religious and political divisions, shared basic beliefs in the right of descendants of Ali and Fatima to rule. As has been demonstrated through the generations in Yemen, the sect can be 'described as "pragmatic Shi'ism": minor ritual prescriptions aside, it differs from Sunni Islam chiefly in its insistence on the institution of the imamate' (Stookey, 1978, p. 83). The imam must have certain qualifications: 'he must be adult; male; free (ie not a slave); adept in the interpretation of the sources of law (*mujtahid)*; of proved descent from 'Ali and Fatima; just, generous, and God-fearing; of sound mind; courageous in war; sound of body and limb; able as politician and administrator; and a distinguished warrior' (ibid., pp. 84–85). In his interesting analysis of the Zaydi movement, remarkably still valid in the 2020s, Stookey points out that 'strangely, a sect liberal and accommodating in theology and jurisprudence became intransigent and aggressive on the level of politics' (ibid., p. 85). In Yemen, the descendants of the prophet are known as *sada* (sg *sayyed*) by contrast with terminology used in other Muslim countries where they are called *Hashemite* or *ashraf*.

Rivalry between the Fatimid Ismailis and the Zaydis was the main political theme during the two centuries when the country was divided between them in various ways and according to different areas of influence. Thus, until the rise of the Rasulids, the main religious factions in Yemen were Shi'a, with Ismaili Fatimids in the southern and western parts of the country and Zaydis in the northern highlands.

Zaydism was first introduced to Yemen by Yahya ibn al Husayn al Rassi al Hadi ila al Haqq al Mubin, known as al Hadi, born in Medina in 854 and arriving in Yemen in 893 AD. Invited by members of the Khawlan confederation he took over Sa'ada in 897 and extended his rule as far as Najran, but failed to take Sana'a. He brought his version of Zaydism to Yemen (Chelhod, 1984, p. 35) and tried to impose a very austere rule in Sa'ada, demanding restraint and honesty from his agents and his own family. This did not increase his popularity among the tribes and his philosophy was one of the reasons leading to his involvement in a series of wars against the local squabbling factions which alternately rejected his rule and appealed to him to solve their disputes. His forces reached Sana'a but he failed to dislodge the Ismaili rulers. His main legacy throughout the following millennium, has been the establishment of a system in which the main Hamdan tribes, the Hashed and the Bakeel, who are still known today as the wings of the imamate, recognise as ruler an imam from among the descendants of the Prophet's family through the Alid branch. In addition, the relationship he established with the tribes forced them to rely on the *sada* to mediate and solve their differences.

After yet another interlude of multiple conflicts, mostly within ruling families and factions themselves, the Egyptian-based Kurdish Ayyubids ruled Yemen from about 1174 to 1229. The half century of their rule was characterised by their domination over almost the entire country with the exception of two groups who successfully resisted them: the tribes of Hadhramaut and the Zaydi loyalist areas in the far north. The Rasulids then dominated Yemen for two whole centuries from 1229 to 1454; they are mainly remembered for the fact that their rule was not threatened by external powers as the main states then dominating the Muslim world were busy elsewhere. The remaining Ayyubids and Mameluks were focused on the crusades, the Baghdad caliphate had been destroyed by the Mongols, and the rising Ottoman empire was busy in Anatolia.

Internally, Rasulid leaders' claim of south Arabian origins helped them gain acceptance from the population. Although they occasionally ruled as far as Najran in the north and Aden in the south, they avoided conflicts with the highland tribes, and ruled from two capitals, Zabid in winter and Taiz in summer. They were responsible for the majority of Yemenis changing religious affiliation, from Ismaili Shi'ism to Shafi'i Sunnism.[1] On that basis they continued to compete with the Zaydis who retained their main base in Sa'ada, and whose influence fluctuated southwards according to circumstances and even included both the coast and interior of Hadhramaut. The Rasulid period is remembered as a time of wealth and prosperity for Yemen, and it left many monuments and other architectural and artistic treasures, including the Ashrafiya mosque in Taiz. In their competition with Zaydism, they turned Zabid into a world-famous centre of Sunni study, leaving architecture which led to Zabid being selected as a UNESCO world heritage site in 1993. Despite this and considerable efforts by many to preserve the city and save it, its deterioration continues.

The Rasulid regime was also characterised by heavy taxation, sometimes beyond the capacity of the landowners and farmers to reasonably satisfy. This was particularly blatant in the Tihama around Zabid. There, taxation rates varied, and the number of date palms in Wadi Zabid changed according to the extent to which excessive taxation simply persuaded farmers to destroy their trees. At the end of the Rasulid period, 120 000 date palms were taxed and Ibn Battuta recorded the exodus from the city to the palm groves for an annual party for leaders and citizens alike (Chelhod, 1984, p. 44).

Regardless of its prosperity, the Rasulid period was not one of peace and quiet: in addition to systematic challenges from the Zaydis in Sa'ada, the Tihama tribes were constantly rebelling and there were, as is often the case among ruling families, intermittent power struggles within the family itself. There were also rebellions in the mountainous areas of Ibb and Hujariya, populated by smaller farmers without the tribal weight and organisation to be involved in long challenges to central authority.

As brilliantly characterised by Stookey,

> for two centuries the two regions [Upper and Lower Yemen] coexisted in a state of mutual hostility, under sharply contrasting styles of leadership … In the south, religious sectarianism waned as a political issue … Prosperity depends upon orderly, centralized administration, and by providing such a service, the Rasulids, in their best days, fostered among the people some notion of the role of their political system in the satisfaction of their needs. In the north [under Zaydi rule], … most people became attached to a rather simplified set of Zaidi principles: the legitimacy of an imam's authority transcended that of local leaders in matters of religion; the imam had the right to threaten or to use force in collecting the canonical tithes; and the people were willing to fight, as members of their tribes, under an imam's command against non-Zaidis. The imamate was nevertheless irrelevant … to the principles of tribal solidarity and entrenched custom.
>
> (Stookey, 1978, p. 124–125)

The Rasulid dynasty was followed by that of the Tahirids (1454–1517), lasting less than a century. A Madhaj tribe,[2] they based their capital in Rada' in the centre of the country and were responsible for the building and opening of the 'Amariya *madrasa* and mosque in Rada', another amazing monument.

While external intervention in Yemen was a political characteristic from Yemen's very earliest days, in previous centuries this had come from the main dynasties dominating the Middle East as a whole. The following four centuries also involved the dominant Muslim power, the Ottomans, who first arrived in 1539 along the Red Sea coast. The first Europeans, the Portuguese, arrived in the region in the early years of the sixteenth century: they landed in Socotra in 1507, failed to occupy Shihr on two occasions (1523 and 1535) and Aden during the following decades. Unable to dominate the entire country, the Ottomans came and went, often controlling the coasts, particularly Zabid on the Red Sea and Aden and Shihr on the Arabian Sea. The Ottomans sometimes managed to govern parts of the interior as far as Sana'a, but never kept these for any length of time. On the south coast, foreign incursions persuaded the then dominant Kathiri rulers to move their capital to Seiyun in the interior of Hadhramaut in the sixteenth century.

During the following centuries, the Zaydi Qasimi dynasty (1598–1852) and others largely ruled the country, particularly the inaccessible highlands. They competed with each other, with the Ottomans and eventually with the forces of the viceroy of Egypt Mohammed Ali, who reneged on his formal allegiance to Ottoman rule when he was strong enough. Like all previous dynasties, the area under Qasimi control grew and shrank according to a range of circumstances, depending on each individual imam's ability to tax and find revenue to finance his military operations.

Zaydi rule depended throughout on two elements: 'the moral suasion of the ulama and the military power of the tribes' (Stookey, 1978, p. 150). Imams needed the tribes despite also having at their service both mercenaries and slaves. At its largest, the dynasty extended as far as Dhofar (in today's Oman) in the east and Asir (in today's Saudi Arabia) in the north. As pointed out by Stookey, the situation in Yemen made it impossible for imams to establish a centralised government as 'although the imamate was dependent upon the brute strength of the tribes, it was unable either to make them the instrument of a strong central government, or to prevent them from pursuing aims irrelevant, or hostile, to those of the Zaidi regime. The frequent primacy of tribal tradition and values over the public order the imams sought to enforce is emphasized by the fact that punishment by the imam for disobedience was taken by the tribes as calling for revenge' (ibid., p. 151).

The end of Qasimi rule was brought about by the loss of revenue from the coffee trade once Mohammed Ali's forces took over control of Mokha port in the late 1830s, while income from the highlands dropped as a result of constant challenges from local tribes. Britain's take-over of the port of Aden in 1839 made it a more profitable location from which to export coffee away from taxation. Moreover 'efforts by authorities in Yemen to prevent this diversion [of the coffee trade] simply encouraged producers to abandon coffee and plant instead the narcotic shrub *qat* which had been introduced into Yemen from Ethiopia in the year 1543, simultaneously with the coffee plant' (ibid., p. 158).[3]

Chaos and a multiplicity of clashes between local rulers led to the return of the Ottomans to Sana'a in 1872 at the invitation of local notables. During their next and last occupation of Yemen until 1918 the Ottomans ruled with improved administrative standards and the regime took some modest steps towards introducing modern education, improving communications and creating conditions in which the people could pursue their livelihoods. Abuse of power was restricted to lower Yemen as the strong tribes of the highlands were able to resist and, in particular, oppose any form of foreign rule. The Hamid al Din, a new line of Qasimi imams started a 40-year bloody struggle against the Ottomans in 1879 with the selection of Mohammed Hamid al Din, known as al Mansour, to the Zaydi leadership in 1890.

Yahia bin Mansour succeeded his father as Imam in 1904 and was initially engaged in further struggles against the Ottomans. Although weakened, the Ottomans were keen to reach an agreement with the Imam, but his demands were considered unacceptable and conflict continued until 1911. That year, the Treaty of Da'an was agreed between the Imam and the Ottomans, applicable to parts of the highlands, excluding the area under exclusive imamate control and the Tihama where Ottoman control was uncontested. The Imam recognised Ottoman suzerainty by agreeing to pay 10% of his revenues to Istanbul.

The Mutawakkilite Imamate (1918–62)

This second Ottoman period left a legacy which became extremely important during the period when the Imamate controlled the entire area after the Ottoman defeat in the First World War. It was characterised by the establishment of a standing professional army under a professional corps of officers and the opening of a number of modern schools and hospitals. Most importantly the creation of a telegraph network throughout the country enabled Imam Yahya and his son Ahmad to rule most of the country, despite the distances and difficulties of physical travel. As we have seen, until then, Yemen was almost always ruled by at least two different dynasties simultaneously: one based in the northern area mostly under Zaydi rule and the other encompassing the southern part (limited by the border with the British Protectorates from 1905 onwards) based in Taiz, Zabid or elsewhere, dominated by Sunni Shafi'is after the conversion of the people in these areas at the time of the Rasulids.

One of the main achievements of the Hamid al Din dynasty, short-lived as it was, with only two Imams, Yahya and his son Ahmad, was the establishment of a single state structure which was respected, or at least obeyed, throughout the area. However, the distinction of rule and power between the Zaydi and Shafi'i areas was consolidated under their rule. As Stookey puts it, Zaydis,

> as co-sectarians of the imam enjoyed a preferred status … [T]here were many tribes of substantial size … [L]arger coalitions … could be organized for representations to the central government. Communication was facilitated by the fact that this area furnished both civilian and military personnel to the imam's administration, and these men preserved their tribal identity undiluted.
>
> (ibid., p. 172)

By contract, the Sunnis of the southern areas were largely excluded from many of these privileges,

> a pattern was instituted in which authority over Shafi'is was exercised by Zaidis. The latter came to regard their higher status as normal and right.

> Ascriptive inferiority was understandably a source of resentment for the Shafi'is, although it took nearly two decades for them to place blame for their grievances on the political institution of the imamate and to decide that it was within their power to effect a change.
>
> (ibid., p. 173)

The imam conquered the Tihama in a war of two phases: first his forces defeated Idrisi rule in northern Tihama and Hodeida in 1925. Yahya then turned his attention to a far more formidable enemy, the Zaraniq, who were defeated in 1929 despite assistance from both the British in Aden and the emerging Saudi state. By contrast, the imam's struggle against the Idrisi in the northern part of the Tihama allowed Yemen to retain part of the area previously under Idrisi rule, but eventually the newly created Kingdom of Saudi Arabia won the renewed conflict within weeks. The imamate was compelled to sign the 1934 Treaty of Taif, initially giving Saudi Arabia suzerainty over Najran, Jizan and Asir for 40 years, in exchange for the withdrawal of Saudi troops to what is still today the border between the two countries, north of Haradh and Midi on the coast.[4]

Throughout the Mutawakkilite kingdom, Imams Yahya and Ahmad enforced their rule in a brutal and authoritarian manner, leading to numerous revolts and uprisings. The most remembered was the emergence of the Free Yemeni movement and its severe repression after the assassination of Imam Yahya in 1948 which led Imam Ahmad to settle in Taiz as his capital. Stookey explains the rationale of the imamate as

> the salient aspirations which seem to have moved the two imams were the preservation of a Yemeni society in which behaviour was governed by the principles of the faith; the continued primacy of their own dynasty; and the maintenance of control over the material resources of the society sufficient to attain the first two objectives.
>
> (ibid., p. 185)

The Free Yemeni movement, which rose in the 1940s and 1950s, was primarily reformist, seeking rule based on more modern principles and possibly greater equity in the relationship between ruler and ruled, whose ambition could be described as a constitutional monarchy. In the days prior to the establishment of any republic in the Arab world, it would have been unrealistic to expect more from any movement. The assassination of Yahya in 1948 and the establishment of the rival imamate under Abdullah al Wazir, a denizen from a leading *sayyed* family with a 'suitable' Zaidi pedigree, lasted merely a month and led to severe repression and the sacking of Sana'a. The next attempt at overthrowing the Imam seven years later was defeated even more rapidly by an even stronger Imam Ahmad. In both cases the ventures were not intended to fundamentally transform the regime but to replace one imam by another who claimed to be more just. It is notable that neither of these attempts involved the newly emerging group of foreign-trained officer class but were both led by *sada* who considered that the rule of the Hamid al Din family was unjustified in Zaydi terms, as the selection of the imam had not been carried out according to the rules of Zaydism; in the second case, it even involved brothers of the current imam. The first episode also confirmed the importance of the relationship between the imams and the northern tribes: the execution of the senior Hashed Shaykh Husayn al Ahmar by Imam Ahmad in 1948 was the fundamental reason why the Hashed tribe later supported the republican movement.

The imamate was widely described as being retrograde, preventing the modernisation of the country, ensuring its isolation from the outside world, restricting trade and all forms of modern communications, often compared to the rule of Sultan Saeed bin Taymur in neighbouring Oman. Isolationism did not prevent the imams from purchasing modern weaponry and sending Yemenis to study military skills in Baghdad, something which backfired when it was these very officers who overthrew the imamate in September 1962. By 1948 there were a number of diplomatic missions abroad. At the international level it is worth noting that the imamate recognised the Soviet Union in 1928 and established friendly relations with the Italians occupying Ethiopia in the 1920s and 1930s, the latter move primarily designed in response to the challenges coming from Britain in Aden and the continuing disagreements over that border. Trade agreements were signed with different states, including Italy (1926), the Soviet Union (1928), Iraq (1931) and others.

In 1958, Imam Ahmad even joined the short-lived United Arab Republic formed through the union of Nasser's Egypt and Syria, though this is widely rumoured to have been an error based on linguistic misunderstanding. However, the imamate played no part in this union which collapsed a year before the ending of the imamate itself.

Contrary to Zaydi tradition, both Imams Yahya and Ahmad were nominated by their fathers as successor, something which led to considerable opposition, particularly among rival leading *sada* families who considered they had candidates better qualified to hold the imamate position according to Zaydi principles. Other complaints against their rule focused, as is so often the case, on excessive taxation and economic and financial demands from the population, particularly trade and agriculture. In addition to the lack of investment in infrastructure, medical services or education, these decades were marked by increasing frustration and anger among the population at large, traders and intellectuals. as well as elite *sada* families. In addition to high taxation, corruption was a major source of frustration.

Emigration was one of the population's main responses to this situation. This greatly influenced the country's future – as many as one fifth of the population are estimated to have emigrated. As Stookey put it,

> the exodus was not only from the land. Considerable numbers left to study abroad, with or without government blessing. Others became political

refugees, at first in Aden, later principally in Egypt. The business community contributed to the exodus: they left to escape Ahmad's attempts, before and after he became Imam, either to monopolize the country's trade (as he did in pharmaceuticals) or to make sure of a cut as sleeping partner in large commercial transactions.

(Stookey, p. 195)

With respect to the state's borders, the Mutawakkilite period was marked by the border agreements in 1934 with Saudi Arabia in the north and the British in the south. This basically settled the borders which remained until unification in 1990. Already at that time, the relationship with Saudi Arabia was important, as both the imams and their opponents sought to ensure the agreement of King Abdul Aziz al Saud for their activities.

The British period in Aden and the Protectorates (1839–1967)

When the British took Aden in 1839, it was no more than a small fishing village of less than 2000 people in deep decline. For centuries, its excellent port facilities were by-passed as they were less accessible from the main exporting areas of Yemen (coffee travelled from Mokha) and the international incense routes (which travelled through the interior along the borders of the desert), while Aden's immediate hinterland did not contain any major wealth of interest to outsiders (Gavin, 1975).

Britain's interest in Aden was as a coaling station to supply ships on their way from Britain to India, its main possession in the East. Its role became all the more important after the opening of the Suez Canal in 1869, when the number of steam vessels visiting Aden grew exponentially, thus also increasing demand for coaling and supplies of food and other commodities. While Britain was primarily interested in Aden and its potential (and later actual) port facilities, it slowly increased its involvement in the interior, for two main reasons: first to prevent incursions and involvement of its rivals, primarily France and the Ottoman Empire, and second to ensure supplies of fresh produce and prevent the emergence and strengthening of local rulers. This resulted in a series of protectorate agreements with hinterland potentates imposing varying degrees of British authority, initially in areas immediately inland from Aden towards the Ottoman-controlled part of the country, i.e. Lahej, then ruled by the Abdali Sultans. This international rivalry, increasing opposition to the Ottomans combined with internecine struggles between the different local authorities gradually intensified British involvement in support of local rulers who opposed the Ottomans. Formal protectorate agreements started being signed in 1872. The immediate impact was limited but these agreements fossilised what had been more fluid, changing power relations within and between the protectorates, leading to longer term instability.

Further east, Britain also got involved in the power struggles between local rulers, preventing other European states from controlling or influencing them through a series of protectorate agreements in Hadhramaut with the Kathiri and Qu'ayti states (1888) and al-Mahra (1886). In the course of the first half of the twentieth century, they were replaced by advisory treaties deepening British influence and involvement in the internal affairs of the various states, four in the Eastern Aden Protectorate and nine in the Western, though the total number of 'state' entities in both areas was higher (six in the east and fifteen in the west, excluding some sub-entities which supposedly answered to some of the others). However, all were administered through the indirect rule system Britain implemented throughout its empire, designed to minimise cost and maximise impact.

From the 1930s onwards, British presence was restricted to a small office for each of the Eastern and Western Protectorates, staffed by a senior advisor, sometimes assisted by one or two juniors. They had access to British air power to attack and control 'rebellions' which occurred for different reasons, often connected with British attempts to restrict the right of local rulers to collect taxes. Resistance to British presence was widespread in numerous locations at different times, often with the support of the then imam ruling in Sana'a after the 1918 departure of the Ottomans.

Rebellions took an increasingly nationalist tone as anti-colonialism and Arab nationalism grew in the following decades. Northern Yemenis opposed to the imam were given refuge in Aden and both benefitted from the educational system and the greater media openness of the city. At the same time, Aden was increasingly populated by workers who had come from the hinterland (Western Protectorate as well as border areas of the imamate). This contributed to the emergence of a militant trade union movement in the port which, by the 1950s, was the second most important in the world, and in the refinery whose construction was completed in 1954. The 1950s saw a rapid and dramatic expansion in Aden's role as a trading, administrative and productive city, leading to a rapid increase in demand for labour, including openings for unqualified workers. In 1961 there were close to 50 000 workers but only 3500 were in clerical work and 6400 craftsmen and artisans (Gavin, 1975, p. 324).

Labour and political militancy started in the 1940s with demands by students who went on strike in 1946 protesting because the authorities refused to make the date of the creation of the Arab League a national holiday. In 1948 and 1956 there were major strikes and labour unrest in the port and throughout the economy. In the intervening period, the Adeni labour movement expanded with eight trades unions established by early 1956 when the strikes started and 24 by the end of the same year, moblising 4000 men. By 1962 more than a third of Aden's 22 000 working population were unionised. In 1956 they had formed the Aden Trades Union Congress which openly supported political demands alongside their trade union ones.

Constitutionally, Britain established an advisory Legislative Council in Aden in 1947 which was partly elected from 1955 onwards, though the electoral register was restricted to Aden-born and British subjects, according to a system 'which included Indians and Somalis but excluded immigrant

Yemenis' (ibid., p. 330). This council was opposed to trade union membership and Yemeni militancy, and it restricted the right to strike by the end of 1960. The trade union movement gradually morphed into the People's Socialist Party (PSP), calling for independence.

Militancy also developed in the Protectorates, particularly around the Abyan newly irrigated agricultural cotton scheme set up by the British to provide cotton for British mills. The British staffed it with low status agricultural workers who were brought from different parts of Yemen as well as local areas. To this day, many farmers in Abyan and Tuban deltas are known as *zubud*, i.e. people from Zabid in the Tihama. Others worked as sharecroppers on the lands of the local rulers.

In response to the unrest, rising labour militancy and increasing pressure from the strengthening nationalist movement throughout the region, Britain tried to create a federation in 1954 bringing together the numerous entities in the protectorates. This materialised in 1959 as the Federation of Arab Amirates of the South, including only six members of the Western Aden Protectorate, joined by a few others in the following years. Efforts to include Aden into this federation met with considerable resistance from the Legislative Council, but Britain finally succeeded with a vote on 26 September 1962. This would certainly have failed had members of the council been aware of the overthrow of the imamate in Sana'a on that very day. In January 1963 the Federation of South Arabia was officially formed: it lasted less than five years.

The rise of opposition political parties in Aden, supported by a number of hinterland organisations, led to the armed struggle which eventually overthrew the British and the Federation of South Arabia in 1967. Thus, the state which came into existence under the leadership of the National Liberation Front in 1967 was composed of entities which hardly deserved the description as states: the Federation was composed of Aden and a number of statelets, sharing a foreign policy and a set of immature administrations primarily managed by Adenis who were reluctant to cooperate with colleagues from the rural statelets whom they largely despised. Its military was more effective as almost all its personnel came from the Awlaqi tribe in today's Shabwa. As a result, it was partly perceived as a threat by people from other areas, whether rural or urban. Large parts of the former Protectorates had remained out of these various institutions, however limited they might have been.

The People's Democratic Republic of Yemen (PDRY)

Following four years of armed struggle against Britain, the People's Republic of South Yemen emerged from brief negotiations with Britain as an independent state on 30 November 1967. It is worth noting that representatives of the Federation of South Arabia simply did not feature in the negotiations, nor did anyone represent the Front for the Liberation of Occupied South Yemen (FLOSY), the successor movement to the People's Socialist Party which had played a major role in the radicalisation of the population of Aden.

Britain negotiated independence with the National Liberation Front (NLF), an organisation whose very existence it had only discovered in the months preceding independence. The NLF had taken over most of the hinterland statelets in the first half of 1967 and militarily defeated FLOSY, its rival, in Aden in August. For the first time in modern history, the very different entities of the south Arabian region were brought together under the authority of a single centralised state.

The People's Democratic Republic of Yemen (PDRY), as it was renamed in 1970, was the only socialist state in the Arab world and was closely aligned with the Soviet Union (Lackner, 1985). In 1979, it became an observer member of the Soviet-founded Comecon, which coordinated the economies of member states of the socialist world. PDRY internal politics were marked by a series of internecine conflicts, the worst of which took place in January 1986 when the leadership of the party tore itself apart, largely as a result of factional differences based on competing individual ambitions, rather than on fundamental differences in policies, whether internal or concerning international relations. Fighting started in the premises of the Yemeni Socialist Party's (YSP) Political Bureau, as the NLF had become by late 1978, and many of the organisation's remaining historic leadership were killed within a few minutes. This was followed by a short civil war in the streets of Aden and in the neighbouring governorates. Fighting took on a regionalist basis, as individuals were singled out for arrest or assassination on the basis of their area of origin, rather than on any political alignment, leading many to call it a tribal struggle, a description open to discussion.

The socialist regime implemented progressive social policies with a particular focus on enabling women to participate fully in the country's social and economic life, mainly through the 1974 Family Law which, alongside those of Tunisia and Iraq were by far the most pro-women legislations in the Arab world. Although this law did not make it impossible for men to take second wives, it made it very difficult. Significantly, it gave husbands and wives equal responsibility in household financing and management. Although by itself unable to change customs and behaviour, the law certainly contributed to reducing the gender gap, as determined women could use it (with the help of the Yemeni Women's Union) to challenge attempts at forced marriages. Its impact was far greater in urban than in rural areas. Formal equality, alongside the massive involvement of women in education, contributed to changing society significantly, even though few women reached high political or even administrative positions (Lackner, 1985, ch. 6; Ismael and Ismael, 1986, ch. 5).

Other important social policies were the attempts to end tribal and social status allegiances and settle nomads, both policies widespread not only in the socialist world but generally in 'modern' regimes. The first was implemented by the suppression of expressions of tribal affiliation in people's names, thus preventing easy identification of social status, whether tribal, *sayyed* or lower status.[5] Residential schools for nomads were established in various locations which were expected to persuade their families to settle nearby, as water, medical services and shops were also created. A further form of Western liberalism was the regime's freedom of religion policy: although leaders publicly attended mosques on major religious official holidays and Islam was decreed the state's religion in the constitution, religion played a small part in school curricula and state infrastructure investments focused on schools, medical services and roads, rather than on mosques (Lackner, 1985, ch. 5).

Internationally, the PDRY had a difficult life, surrounded by enemies – with the monarchies of the Peninsula aligned with the US in the Cold War and most of the Sana'a regimes hostile. In addition, remaining FLOSY supporters, alongside the leaders of the former statelets and the wealthier elements from the British period were all politically and militarily active at undermining the regime, with active assistance from the Saudi regime which was incensed at the establishment of an 'atheist communist' regime on its borders. Again, while the situation eased somewhat in the 1980s, the PDRY mostly survived thanks to its security and military apparatus. In this Cold War environment and with such external hostility, it is relatively easy to understand the widespread internal suspicion which prevailed within the regime, though there is little doubt that it might have fared better if it had been able to solve its internal political differences in a more democratic way via negotiations, rather than in the many armed clashes, each of which undermined the regime's credibility and increased the number of exiled opponents.

The country's constitution was promulgated in 1970 and marked by the name change of the state. It also coincided with the ascendancy of the more radical revolutionary elements. It was amended in 1978 to acknowledge the change of name of the leading political organisation to the Yemeni Socialist Party (YSP) as well as adding ten members to the Supreme People's Council (SPC), the parliament. The constitution claims allegiance to a 'national democratic revolution following a non-capitalist course' (Ismail and Ismail, p. 42). Popular participation took the form of elections to the Supreme People's Council. Politics were implemented through a single party composed by the merger of the NLF with the Baathists and People's Democratic Union (communists). The SPC also included a significant number of independents in each of the elections held, 40 out of 111 in the first elections in 1978. However, the constitution clearly stated that the Party was the leading decision-making body through the Political Bureau of the YSP, leaving the formal government institutions with lesser power (Ismael and Ismael, 1986, pp. 42–54; Brehony, 2011, p. 55).

Administratively the country was divided into six governorates, each of which had a local people's council, initially nominated but elected from 1977 onwards. However, local government was also dominated by the YSP in terms of decision making. At the community level, People's Defence Committees set up on the Cuban model acted both as community support organisations and surveillance mechanisms, preventing dissenting voices from threatening the regime. The first was established in 1973 in Aden and later they spread throughout the country, with a mix of responsibilities, including solving local social problems, managing the subsidised price allocations for basic foods, organising voluntary work in the community and education system, alongside their role as security elements preventing counter-revolutionary activities, which is what they remained most famous for.

Economic strategy focused on the construction of a socialist economy, giving priority to the public sector and the establishment of nationalised industries, as well as nationalising existing industries. The industrial sector remained small throughout the existence of the PDRY, with only nine enterprises with more than 250 workers in 1979 out of a total of 45 000. Regardless of policy, the majority were in the private sector in 1980. In rural areas, state farms were introduced on newly developed lands and on the estates of the former rulers. Elsewhere cooperatives were the norm, initiated in the early years of the state under an agrarian reform law which severely restricted private ownership of land to small holdings which produced about half of agricultural value added, largely thanks to the high price of *qat*. The Agrarian Reform, implemented through NLF-sponsored uprisings against landlords in the early 1970s, was one of the more revolutionary and radical strategies of the regime. In the 1980s, economic policy gradually shifted away from the socialist model and allowed private and cooperative sectors to develop (Lackner, 1985, chapters 6–9).

The 1986 internecine struggle within the YSP caused a civil war which killed about 5000 people and discredited the regime among the population. This lack of confidence persisted despite the fact that the regime then engaged in democratic reforms which should have increased its popularity. These years coincided with liberalisation in the USSR and the gradual weakening of the international socialist regime as well as new tensions with the YAR due to the discovery of oil in commercial quantities alongside their common border. These added up to a perfect storm of circumstances which led the new post-1986 regime in Aden to be particularly receptive to the suggestion of uniting with the YAR, the most popular of its political slogans for the past decade or longer.

The Yemen Arab Republic (YAR)

The Yemen Arab Republic also had a highly turbulent history, at least for the first 15 years of its existence. The 'Revolution' of 26 September 1962 overthrew Imam Badr who had inherited the position a mere ten days earlier after the death by natural causes of his father Ahmad. With a history of supporting more modernist and open government, he had hoped for support from the educated men and officers who had actively opposed his father in the previous decades, particularly supporters of the failed uprisings of 1948 and 1955. Instead, a group of officers sent for military training in Cairo and Baghdad by the imam overthrew him on the night of 26 September. He survived and escaped to gather troops in the mountains to regain power. The officers, many of whom looked forward to furthering the rising secular revolutionary movements of the Arab world, particularly Egypt, Syria and Iraq, were supported by Nasser who immediately sent troops to defend the revolution and civilian advisers to set up a modern administration.

The ensuing civil war lasted from 1962 to 1970 and involved up to 70 000 Egyptian troops at its peak; however, being unfamiliar with the Yemeni terrain, they were at a complete loss (Holden, 1966). It was a particularly barbaric war, not that any war qualifies to the description of 'civilised'. The Egyptians frequently used chemical weapons against villages. Most of the fighting took place in the northern highlands, where tribal structures were the main form of social and political structures. Tribal loyalties were divided between the republican movement and the royalists, not specifically on ideological grounds but rather on the basis of previous historical conflicts; for example, although very conservative, the al Ahmar family who led the Hashed tribal confederation supported the republicans as Imam Ahmad had executed their senior shaykh.

The Saudi regime provided direct assistance to the royalists, defending a monarchical regime against a republican one. This fitted into the regional ideological struggle against Nasserism in an age when republicanism, including forms of 'socialist' nationalism were on the ascendant throughout the developing world. The royalists were also secretly supported by the UK which provided mercenaries and assisted with supplies across the borders from the Protectorates (Hart-Davis, 2011, p. 382). After Egypt's 1967 defeat in the Six-Day War against Israel, a weakened Nasser was forced to reach agreement with the Saudis, including complete Egyptian military withdrawal from Yemen. Contrary to expectation, this did not immediately lead to the defeat of the Republicans, who withstood further attacks, including the notorious 70-day Siege of Sana'a in 1967–68. The war ended in 1970 with a reconciliation agreement which retained the republican regime and established the first constitution leading to the establishment of a Consultative Council in 1971. The new government was very conservative as the left of the republican movement had been defeated internally in the previous year, and it included senior royalists, who took up major positions in government. Only the imam's family were excluded and prevented from returning to Yemen.

This initial period of the republic also experienced a series of upheavals. The leader of the 1962 uprising, Abdullah al Sallal was overthrown and forced into exile in 1967, to be replaced by Qadi Abdul Rahman al Iryani who tried to balance the mutually conflicting influences of, on the one hand Saudi Arabia which provided funding and support for conservative policies and, on the other, the left-wing republican forces supported by the new socialist regime in the PDRY. This difficult act ended in June 1974 when he was overthrown in a bloodless coup by Colonel Ibrahim al Hamdi who suspended the Consultative Council in 1975.

Hamdi's regime lasted less than four years, though many Yemenis, to this day, remember it as a semi-mythological 'ideal' regime. Clearly such a short period of rule was insufficient to make a lasting mark on the direction of politics or development, but Hamdi attempted to balance relations with Saudi Arabia and the South. He tried to undermine Saudi influence by marginalising senior tribal leaders who were on Saudi payrolls and partly shared Saudi conservatism. He developed good relations with then-President Salmine in Aden, sharing populist tendencies. Internally he is remembered for the development of the Local Development Associations and their consolidation into a national structure controlled by Sana'a, as well as his efforts to weaken tribal control over the state. His balancing act failed when he was assassinated in October 1977, on the eve of a proposed visit to Aden where he and Salmine were widely believed to be planning to sign an agreement for Yemeni unity. After a brief interlude of nine months under President Ahmad al Ghashmi (himself assassinated, supposedly by an envoy of Salmine, in revenge for the killing of al Hamdi), Colonel Ali Abdullah Saleh (hereafter Saleh in this text) became president of the YAR.

This series of brief presidencies was expected to continue under Saleh, a largely unknown colonel from a minor tribe affiliated to the Hashed confederation, who achieved the presidency thanks to manoeuvring by military allies, mostly from his own area. It is widely believed that deals agreed at that time concerning the distribution of responsibilities remained relevant to internal power struggles in the following decades. Defying all predictions, Saleh remained in power for 33 years, retaining significant popular support, despite becoming an autocrat who ensured that his patronage system primarily benefitted close military and security colleagues from his home area or nearby. However, he also established the bases of the contemporary state and political institutions, whose survival to the war remain to be demonstrated.

Parliamentary institutions in the YAR have a complex history. The 1970 Constitution created a body named the Consultative Council, whose members were initially nominated, though they were supposed to be elected. This institution was suspended by Hamdi and revived by Saleh in 1978. Its task was to prepare national elections; these were finally held in 1988 and the Council then elected the president and approved the government. The 1970 Constitution was updated in 1987 and soon overtaken by the Constitution of the Republic of Yemen at unification.

Politically, Saleh continued the process of transforming the Local Development Associations from civil society community-based organisations into a centrally controlled national institution. He eventually turned them into local government councils. Nationally, Saleh sponsored the drafting of a National Pact in 1980 which was approved at a conference in 1982 bringing together influential individuals from all over the country and from different social strata. The conference adopted the pact and set up its members as a permanent institution, the General People's Congress (GPC), which has remained a major political organisation in the country, the only one permitted until the introduction of a multi-party system at unification. Expanding into the entire country after 1990, the GPC was the leading political organisation until 2015. Given its nature and limited political programme one hesitates to call it a party; though it had most of the institutional trappings of parties, it lacked clear ideological position beyond support to Saleh as ruler. Starting with 1000 initial members at the conference, it later grew to being a mass organisation. Soon it was led between its bi-annual sessions by a 75-member standing committee.

The main features of the Saleh regime in the YAR were the establishment of the GPC, ending the armed struggle between regime forces and those of the revolutionary National Democratic Front (NDF) in 1982 and integrating many of the latter's leading members into the GPC. The NDF had been militarily active since the late 1970s against his regime in the 'central region', effectively the current governorates of Taiz, Ibb, al Baydha and parts of Dhamar, and the establishment of local government institutions under central control.

The discovery of oil near Marib in 1984 led to its exploitation and soon this fundamentally transformed the relationship between the state and the population: in the previous decade the main source of foreign currency had been remittances going directly to families and communities mostly in rural areas, who used it to finance small development investments, limiting the role of the central state. Oil exploitation reversed the relationship, as the State now had the funds which enabled it to finance and support development and other investments at a time when migrant workers' incomes and remittances dropped because of the reduction in oil revenues elsewhere in the peninsula. Financial constraints at the household level, combined with the widespread belief that the state was responsible for providing collective social services, meant that communities were willing to hand over to the state responsibility for health, education and infrastructure. This represented a fundamental shift in the balance of power between civil society and the state.

The roots of Yemeni Unity

Going back to the 1970s, it is worth recalling Stookey: asserting the absence of interest in Arab unity, he adds that in Yemeni society 'there is a general sense of national identity and of sharing a common past and future destiny, although myths and symbols to which the whole population can relate remain somewhat implicit' (Stookey, 1978, p. 285). While focused on the then YAR, these comments and the following ones concerning the potential for disintegration seem remarkably prescient of developments since the 1990s.

Undoubtedly, Saleh's main achievement, certainly in his own view, was the unification of the YAR and the PDRY in 1990. While the ambitions of Nasser and other Arab leaders to achieve Arab unity always seemed an unlikely chimera, the concept of Yemeni unity made more sense. Despite significant cultural differences between Yemenis from Sa'ada and those from al-Mahra, for example, Yemenis share cultural and other characteristics which justify the use of the term nation to describe their collective characteristics. Without going to the extremities of the country, the similarities between Yemenis from

Dhamar and Abyan, for example, are very considerable, in traditions, social structures, economic livelihoods or, indeed, diet.

Historically, rulers in the various capitals of the country clearly believed that they should rule larger areas. After 1918, the imams claimed that all of Yemen should be part of their state, including the then British-occupied Aden and Protectorates. This claim was also endorsed by the FLOSY which, by its very name, indicated its allegiance to a Yemeni state. During the civil/liberation wars of the 1960s, southerners joined in the defence of Sana'a during the siege, while many northerners, including future leaders of the PDRY, were politically active in the south. Indeed, the early NLF congresses took place in the YAR (in Taiz, Jibla and Khamr). Earlier, in the 1940s, Free Yemeni movement members opposing the imam took refuge in Aden, benefitting from its more liberal approach and British willingness to allow them to operate against a regime it also opposed, rather than as a demonstration of its own liberal attitude to free political expression.

In the late 1960s (particularly after the Siege of Sana'a from 9 November 1967 to February 1968), Yemenis were looking forward to the creation of a single state, something which was endorsed by the NLF who named their state the People's Republic of South Yemen. The name-change in 1970, took place alongside an increased alignment with the left in Aden just when the YAR took a turn to the right with the integration of senior royalists in the republican government and thus deepened stress between the two regimes. In addition, members of the FLOSY and other 'bourgeois' exiles from Aden in both the YAR and Saudi Arabia fought the PDRY regime.

The tension exploded into a two-week war in September 1972 (Lackner, 1985, p. 70). Arab mediation ended the indecisive fighting, leading to the first unity agreement signed in Cairo on 28 October 1972. This was followed by another agreement a month later in Tripoli when the two presidents agreed to unify the country within a year, under pressure from Libyan leader Muammar al Qaddhafi, a firm believer in Arab unity, who saw this as a first step towards the overall aim of Arab unity. This agreement remained unenforced and relations between the 'two parts of the homeland' eased somewhat during the brief Hamdi regime.

In 1976, the northern National Democratic Front (NDF) was established, composed of YAR left wingers who had been defeated in the 1969-70 internal power struggle. Supported by the PDRY leadership, the NDF engaged in armed opposition to the Sana'a regime, particularly after the assassination of Hamdi. This led to a second war in February 1979. Contrary to the indecisive fighting of 1972, southern forces, operating with the local NDF, made considerable progress, took border towns and penetrated deep into YAR territory. Again, Arab mediation (from Syria, Iraq, Jordan) intervened to achieve a cease-fire. A meeting of the two presidents in Kuwait at the end of March yet again announced a unity agreement between the two states.

Although tension persisted, it diminished after Abdul Fattah Ismail was replaced by Ali Nasser Mohammed as the top leader in Aden in 1980. The former, originally from the north, was determined to push military advantage to achieve unity through force, while the latter was more willing to negotiate with the Sana'a leadership. Official PDRY forces withdrew but fighting between the NDF and the Saleh regime continued, punctuated by meetings between the two presidents, Saleh and Ali Nasser Mohammed. By the summer of 1982, NDF strength had diminished facilitating political dialogue and the integration of some of its leaders into the GPC when it was formed.

Further tensions arose in the mid-1980s as in the YAR citizens called for democracy and fair distribution of oil wealth. The PDRY regime was encouraged by Gorbachev to take a more flexible ideological position, which turned into pressure through reduced financial support. In 1986 more factors were added: the defeat of the Ali Nasser faction in the 1986 PDRY internecine conflict and the discovery of oil on a border area. Together they encouraged either renewed military action or the deepening of dialogue. For once Yemeni leaders took the second option and discussions on unification intensified, building on the work of the series of committees which had been established after 1979. A draft constitution was more or less ready, committees to unify the education system and the economy had also developed operational procedures. They could build on joint PDRY-YAR companies and ventures which had been established earlier in the decade, for tourism, land and marine transport, and minerals exploitation.

Regardless of political and military tensions between the regimes, Yemeni unity was an extremely popular slogan throughout the country. There had been considerable cross border migration throughout history, not to mention the fact that the existing borders were only formally established in 1934. Previous decades had seen migration due to both political upheavals and economic necessity; there were plenty of mixed families. As mentioned above, northerners opposing the imamate and later the right turn of the YAR regime, had migrated to the south, while southerners aligned with the defeated factions during various political struggles (FLOSY, statelet leaders, wealthy business people, supporters of Salmine after 1978 and supporters of Ali Nasser after 1986) and their followers moved North. Ordinary people also crossed the officially closed borders throughout the 1970s and 1980s, mostly to obtain travel documents and travel on to work in Saudi Arabia where Yemenis from the YAR benefitted from privileged migration status until the 1990 crisis. Moreover, the greater availability of consumer goods in the YAR gave the impression that life there was easier for the people in general, despite the fact that much apparent 'wealth' there among the people was derived from migration income, something which southerners working abroad also achieved.

All these factors explain the popularity of the Yemeni unity slogan. Thus, when the unification agreement was announced on 13 November 1989 by Secretary General Ali Salem al Beedh of the YSP and President Ali Abdullah Saleh of the YAR, it was universally welcomed, regardless of what appeared to be squabbles between the two leaderships.

The process of unification and its contradictions: the 1994 civil war

Proclaimed in a hurry on 22 May 1990, a mere six months after its announcement, rather than the planned year, the Republic of Yemen (ROY) had a difficult start. One reason for the rush was that both leaders were concerned about opposition to unity from various forces: in the YAR, conservative tribal leaders in the far north and the Saudi regime; in the PDRY, southerners who objected to the form taken by unity as they had agreed to a federation.

Internationally, the timing of unity was hardly propitious: a few months later, Iraq invaded Kuwait. Yemen held a seat at the UNSC and made what the US described as 'the world's most expensive vote' against US-sponsored resolution 678 authorising military action to expel Iraqi forces from Kuwait. In addition to the vast cuts in development aid from international financial institutions (IFIs), Western and Arab states, this vote also ensured hostility from the Gulf oil exporting states where most Yemeni migrants worked, and 800 000 of them were expelled from Saudi Arabia and other Gulf Cooperation Council (GCC) states, simultaneously adding these people to the unemployed in Yemen and depriving the country and their families from their remittances.

Tensions between the leaderships in Sana'a and Aden started almost immediately after unification. Fundamental differences on Yemeni politics were added to the fact that the PDRY had previously had abysmal relations with Baathist Iraq and its leaders were certainly unhappy about the UNSC vote. Saleh supported it thanks to his own excellent relations with Saddam Hussein's regime, so southerners blamed Saleh for the consequences of the UNSC vote. Shortly after unification, a series of attempted and actual assassinations of YSP leaders started: more than 150 people were killed in the three years after 1990. Widespread popular unrest was also a major feature of the period, with riots against price rises in December 1992 causing at least 13 deaths, as the economic crisis bit deeply into people's living conditions after the UNSC vote issue. The economic hopes and dreams associated with unification were promptly dashed for the population throughout the country.

By contrast this period was also one in which freedom of expression flourished with dozens of political parties being formed (of the more than 50 registered, 21 participated in the 1993 parliamentary elections), and newspapers and magazines were established representing a wide range of views (Phillips, 2008, p. 21). Political and cultural discussions flourished in social meetings such as *qat* sessions as well as in these publications. There was a succession of political dialogues and conferences bringing together members of different parties and tendencies, as well as independent intellectuals and activists from all sectors of society and professions.

The immediate issue concerned the nature and mechanisms of unification that had been agreed between Saleh and his GPC on the one hand, and al Beedh and the YSP on the other. To address the problem, the 'National

Dialogue Committee of Political Forces' was formed, including respected political figures. They prepared the Document of Pledge and Accord which was signed in Amman by Saleh and al Beedh on 20 February 1994. It was intended to solve all the problems which had arisen since unification and strengthen democratic processes in the unified state. As pointed out by political scientist Carapico, 'the national dialogue amounted to a pro-democracy movement ... [in which] the wide range of political opinion within Yemen revealed itself openly for the first time' (Carapico, 1998b, p. 244).

Its failure was apparent as military clashes started immediately following the signature of the document. Further conferences and meetings were held throughout the country in the hope of forcing the implementation of the agreement and preventing the outbreak of war. These involved intellectuals, professionals, tribesmen and all sectors of society. They held street protests,

> under the slogan 'No to War, No to Separation, Yes to the Document.' These protests were unprecedented not only because of the involvement of children, the coordinated use of simple symbols like white flags and armbands, and simultaneous action in cities and towns throughout the country, but also in the extent to which the GPC, the YSP, and other parties and organizations each tried to associate themselves with a movement that clearly represented majority public sentiment.
>
> (Carapico, 1998b, p. 257)

This short period combining extreme political tension and deep involvement of civil society and politicians in attempting to control their leaderships was probably the main period prior to 2011 when public opinion openly responded to the regime's authoritarianism with problem solving initiatives. These efforts, however widespread and significant, failed in the face of armed force.

Full-scale fighting started in April 1994, and in early May al Beedh declared the restoration of the 'Democratic Republic of Yemen' as a separate state with its capital Aden. The short civil war was decisively won by Saleh's forces, largely thanks to the support he got from a number of southern groups ranging from Ali Nasser's military (including future president Hadi) who had been defeated in 1986, and Islamist factions such as the 'Afghans' (Yemenis who had returned from fighting in Afghanistan against the 'communist atheist' regime there). Celebrating their victory, Salafi Islamists engaged in serious looting and destruction throughout the South, primarily in Aden, attacking not only the brewery and other civil society assets, but also the religious shrines associated with the Sufi tradition. This contributed to the emergence of deep bitterness and resentment over the following decade and led to the rise of the southern separatist movement from 2007 onwards.

After 1994, the whole country was ruled with the characteristics of the regime of the previous decade in the YAR, in brief Saleh autocracy and nepotism. This functioned with the connivance of its main beneficiaries, Saleh's close military and security associates and a range of individuals, tribal and other, benefiting from the patronage system. However, it is a mistake to equate regime beneficiaries with northerners, as they also included many southerners. This was the daily reality which the many constitutional and other legislative aspects failed to prevent.

The Republic of Yemen (RoY)

The long years of joint committees and negotiations during the 1980s had produced numerous draft legal documents and agreements. The main one was a draft constitution which was approved by the parliaments of both parts of Yemen literally on the eve of unification, on 21 May 1990. Drafted about ten years earlier, it shared more similarities with the 1971 Constitution of the Yemen Arab Republic than with the 1978 one of the PDRY. Its main features are discussed below.

The first three years of the RoY operated according to this constitution which was approved by a national referendum in May 1991. Formally, although it gave a majority to northerners, and specifically to conservative ones in the five-man Presidential Council, this was balanced by measures which favoured southerners: al-Beedh was appointed vice president, a position which did not exist according to the constitution, Haydar Abu Bakr al Attas (former president of the PDRY after 1986) as prime minister and Yassin Saeed Nu'man (former PDRY prime minister) as speaker of the parliament. Thus, southerners had a significant presence at the top level. The 39 ministries were evenly divided between northerners and southerners: each minister having a deputy from the other part of the country, and the parliament was composed of all the members of the two previous separate parliaments. Altogether these measures formally gave the former PDRY far more influence in the new state than its demographic weight suggested. In practice, things turned out rather differently.

Apart from the constitution, there was the 1990 Press Law, the 1991 Political Parties Law and the 1992 Elections Law. Anyone who was in Yemen at the time remembers the period as one of widespread enthusiasm and hope, despite the economic constraints and difficulties, initially perceiving repressive events (e.g. the riots in December 1992 and the assassinations of socialist leaders) as incidents which would not change the course of history. As Carapico points out,

> inscribing rights and freedoms heretofore unknown these documents also left large loopholes. The failure of the unity accords and the constitution to resolve many issues of executive, military and local power was their ultimate undoing. The press, parties, elections and security laws together created a legal framework for a relatively free and open public space, but also contained clauses restricting those freedoms.
>
> (1998a, p. 137)

This system was designed to last for a 30-month transitional period until new elections for parliament. The transition was delayed by the power struggle within the leadership, and the first parliamentary elections took place in April 1993 still within the context of both flourishing of political views and organisations on the one hand and increasing tensions between the two leaders and their institutions which had established unity on the other.

The constitution and its changes

The constitution unsurprisingly proclaimed the unity and territorial integrity of the country. By far the most discussed and controversial clause at the time concerned the role of Islam in legislation, an issue which has remained topical throughout the decades and also associated with that of 'secularism' a concept which is misinterpreted and misrepresented by its Islamist opponents. The constitution was opposed by the more conservative elements and the Islamists for being insufficiently Islamic, and by more secular groups for giving too much attention to religion. The compromise was to declare Islam as the religion of the state and Islamic law the principal source of legislation (clause 3), rather than the 'sole' source of legislation.

The constitution included a five-member Presidential Council elected by parliament for five years whose members were not allowed to engage in business activities and had to elect a chairman, who effectively was the head of state. The council could not dissolve the parliament, though it had the power to suspend the prime minister or any other minister. Its chairman represented the country abroad, called elections, nominated the prime minister and had the usual prerogatives of a head of state.

The RoY constitution was first modified to reflect the outcome of the 1994 civil war (Phillips, 2008, pp. 59–60). The September 1994 Constitution, issued two months after the defeat of the southern separatists included three major changes: first, responding to the demands of the conservatives and Islamists who had helped Saleh win the war, it stated that 'Islamic Shari'a is the source of all legislation' (article 3), leaving an element of ambiguity, as it could be argued that this allowed some flexibility in interpretation. The second major change was the cancellation of the Presidential Council, replaced by a president elected by the people (article 107) for a five-year term, renewable once. The third, maybe less significant, change was the establishment of a Consultative Council, the Shura Council (article 125), which was indeed established with 59 members (all male) three years later on 19 May 1997. The 1994 Constitution formally recognised political pluralism, thus making it unique in the Arabian Peninsula with a multiplicity of political parties representing a wide range of views despite the fact that the laws enacted to implement this were increasingly restrictive.

Popular election of the president was delayed through article 158, one of the general provisions of the constitution which states that 'the President of the Republic shall be elected for the first time following the approval of constitutional amendment by the House of Representatives' thus postponing elections and adding five further years to Saleh's rule.

The next change to the constitution was enacted in February 2001 (Phillips, 2008, p. 61). The main objective of this change was the extension of the presidential term from five to seven years (article 112). This time, again, a general provision was used to ensure that implementation of this decision would favour Saleh, as 'the seven-year term referred to in article (112) shall take effect from the beginning of the current term of the President of the Republic' (article 161), here giving him two additional years bonus! As an incentive to the parliament, the provision also extended its term by two years, bringing it to six years.

The only other significant change in this constitution was to provide some details about the advisory role of the Shura Council (articles 125 and 126) which by then had been formed. This increased its membership to 111 members still nominated exclusively by the president; it was widely perceived as a mechanism for the president to provide favours to those he wanted to reward without giving them any power or to kick upstairs senior officials whose loyalty he wanted to retain. It was widely known as 'the livestock enclosure' given its continued advisory role. The Shura Council also carried out studies and sometimes addressed contentious issues, but it never presented a serious challenge to the regime.

In practice, the RoY regime was a presidential one with a veneer of democratic institutions, mainly its two-chamber parliament which presented little legislative challenge to executive proposals. The processes since 1990 clearly demonstrated the Saleh regime's ability to manipulate and use formal 'democratic' structures to achieve its aims, primarily to ensure his continued authoritarian system and privileged access to the nation's resources. There is little doubt that real power did not reside in the formal institutions, but rather among the small group surrounding President Saleh though the parliamentary system was a kind of 'safety valve' allowing for limited expression of dissent.

The parliament and its limited power

The parliament, formally the Council of Representatives, includes 301 members elected by universal suffrage by Yemenis aged 18 and over. It has formal responsibility for legislation and to 'direct and monitor the activities of the executive authority' (1994 Constitution, article 61) it also had the authority to demand accounts from government, and to vote confidence to any new government submitted to it by the prime minister within 25 days of nomination. The government answers both to the parliament and the president (1994 Constitution, article 131), the prime minister choosing his ministers 'in consultation with the President of the Republic' (1994 Constitution, article 130). Local government is controlled by the cabinet and include elected local councils.

The 1993 Parliamentary elections

Despite some recorded limited clashes and cases of irregularity of different types (Detalle, 1995, pp. 81–82), this election was widely considered to have been a serious and effective expression of public opinion. With universal suffrage, including women, the outcome was also less predictable than might have been expected and clearly demonstrated both popular interest in the election and the wide range of political views held by the population at large. The GPC won 28% of the vote and 123 seats, the Islamist Islah (officially the Yemeni Congregation for Reform) 17% and 62 seats, the YSP with 18% of the vote had 56 seats. The remaining seats were won by smaller parties and independents, many of whom were informally aligned with one or another party (Carapico, 1998b, p. 254).

A short-lived new government was formed immediately after the election, with the three main parties, the GPC, YSP and Islah. After the 1994 civil war, the YSP was excluded from the government, ignoring the many leaders and members of the party who had supported unity and had not joined with al Beedh and his separatists. The new government included only Islah and the GPC, giving an overwhelming majority of positions, and in particular the most powerful ones, to senior GPC members, though it also included a significant number of southerners. In the months following the war, a series of decisions and laws were issued which restricted rights of expression, assembly and publication. In this way, while formally the freedoms of the constitution remained, in practice they were now severely eroded (Carapico, 1998a, pp. 191–194), a process which continued in the following decade. Opponents were immediately slandered with accusations of 'separatism', at a time when Yemeni unity was still very popular even in the South.

The 1997 Parliamentary elections

To retain his pluralist image and also to strengthen his position in the parliament, Saleh ensured that elections were held as planned in 1997. By that time curtailment of freedom of speech and expression meant that only four parties won seats: the GPC 187, Islah 53, independents 54 and the Baathists and Nasserites won two seats each. The new government was dominated by the GPC, with two independents (the prime minister and the minister of health from the South) and one from the al Haq Zaydi party for 'religious guidance'. Excluding the Islah was a 'slap in the face' for this party and its leaders, particularly Shaykh Abdullah bin Husayn al Ahmar the speaker of parliament, leader of Islah, and head of the Hashed tribal confederation, the overall confederation including Saleh's small tribe of Sanhan. The marginalisation of Islah, despite its significant number of parliamentary seats, was clearly a response to the party's rising popularity. Women represented 30% of participants and a few even ran for office, winning two seats, both in the South.

Following its marginalisation, the YSP boycotted the 1997 election for a number of reasons: the splits within the party, the defeat of the separatists who could hardly have presented candidates, and widespread hostility in the former YAR area resulting in a major loss of popularity. Turnout among registered voters was significantly lower, largely because of the widespread popular anger throughout the country at the leadership's failure to respond positively to the massive civil society mobilisation in groupings, conferences and meetings to prevent the outbreak of the war in 1994, mobilisations which took place throughout the country, in rural and urban areas.

The 2003 Parliamentary elections

By the time the third (and to date last) parliamentary elections took place in 2003, competition between the GPC and the Islah had increased, and the earlier informal agreement between them had been seriously damaged by the popularity of Islah, demonstrated in the results of the 2001 local elections. Moreover, in the face of the GPC, in 2003 the opposition created an alliance, called the Joint Meeting Parties (JMP) formed from Islah, the YSP, al Haq (a Zaydi party), the Union of Popular Forces (another Zaydi party), the Ba'ath and the Nasserists. This strengthened an earlier alliance established in 1999, called the Higher Coordinating Council of the Opposition, which had been designed to help oppose Saleh's candidacy to the presidency, but did not include the largest party, the Islah. The new JMP, led by the Islah, strengthened its position in the elections, despite the fact that it did not present common candidates; in some areas some parties presented no candidate to improve the chances of the one most likely to win.

The 2003 elections demonstrated that the GPC was perceived by the population as no more than a mechanism to organise support for Saleh, rather than a party with a specific political programme. Its real, rather than paper, programme could be summarised as 'a way to get jobs and benefits from the Saleh patronage system'. Although the YSP participated, the main opposition came from the Islah which was seen as the only effective opposition to Saleh's GPC. This was particularly noticeable in parts of the former PDRY where its candidates won the votes of many members of the lower social strata who had previously supported the Socialists. The YSP's weakness, divisions, and inability to protect the rights and advantages the people lost with unification, contributed to this shift of allegiance to the Islah whose claim to consider all citizens as being equal increased its appeal. In Hadhramaut, for example, Islah won four out of ten seats in the 2003 Parliamentary elections, thanks to the votes of the lower status *fellaheen*.

The result clearly demonstrated the determination of the Saleh regime to ensure its full dominance over the country's formal political system: it won 238 seats with 79% of the votes cast, an increase of 51% over the 1997 elections. Islah took only 46 seats (seven fewer than in the previous election) with 15% of the vote, leaving the YSP far behind as the third party, with only eight seats and 3% of the vote, yet again reflecting its weakness due to deep differences of opinion and ambiguity on the issue of separatism. The Nasserists (three seats) and the Baathists (two seats) returned with a combined 1.7% of the votes, while the remaining four seats were held by independents.

It is worth noting that, regardless of the weakening influence of the parliament over the years, actual turnout at elections increased from one election to the next, demonstrating popular willingness and interest in the political process: in 1993, 36% of the eligible voters participated, in 1997 this increased to 40% and in 2003 to 53%. Contrary to its constitutional importance, in practice parliament in Yemen has been little more than a recording chamber due to the fact that its rules and regulations have been ignored and flouted by both government and the powerful in the regime. Members have been well aware of their lack of power:

> there was a sense that their primary purpose was to rubber stamp decisions made by the executive and provide an outward veneer of democracy to citizens and to foreign donors. They [members and former members interviewed] pointed to the decline in the effectiveness of the parliament since its inception, generally agreeing that the parliament elected in 2003 was the worst on record.
>
> (Phillips, 2008, p. 80)

Decentralisation and local government: the 2001 and 2006 local elections

Increasing power for local administration, also discussed within the framework of decentralisation, was an outstanding issue from the moment of unification onwards, particularly given the fact that the previously negotiated federal state was cancelled unilaterally by the Saleh-al Beedh agreement on the eve of the announcement of unification. Politically aware people, southerners in particular, called increasingly vehemently for decentralisation. They perceived this as a mechanism to reduce Saleh's grip on the state's administration and to restore an element of democracy to the new state. After the 1994 civil war, this debate focused on the Local Authority Law. During the following years, increasingly bitter arguments in parliament and civil society unsuccessfully challenged the GPC's proposals.

The Local Authority Law issued in 2000, gave only marginal power to the local authorities, leaving most control at the central level, with Sana'a based ministries in charge of their local staff, something particularly relevant for health, education and security, the only three sectors present throughout the country. The law attributed considerable responsibilities to the governorate and district levels, without the financial means to implement them. The long list (Local Authority Law, 2000, article 123) of sources of income focused on a few local resources such as shop and market rents, vehicle and transport taxes, local taxation, trading permits, for example in *qat* markets and the like. The list included largely laughable items which were of zero relevance to most of the country, such as hotel taxes and parking fees! Governorates remained dependent on central government funding, and therefore on the good will of the regime.

The 2001 local elections at governorate and district levels were the first opportunity for the population to challenge the Saleh regime's policies after the promulgation of the Local Authority Law. These challenges were stronger at local than at parliamentary elections. The extent of violence around local elections was higher than for the parliamentary ones, indicating both the increased importance attributed to them by the population and the strength of feeling against Saleh's GPC: in 2001 there were 47 deaths, but in the parliamentary elections of 2003 there were 'only' seven (NDI, 2006, p. 6). Although the usual irregularities were observed and took place probably on a larger scale than observed, the outcome gives an indication of public opinion, provided that one adjusts one's interpretation of the results to reflect the fact that most irregularities were in favour of the GPC.

Overall comparison of the results in 2001 and 2006 local elections shows a marked increase in success for the GPC, reflecting the Saleh regime's improved 'management' of the elections. In 2006, the GPC won 85% of the governorate level and 76% of the district level votes by contrast with 58.5% and 58.6% in 2001 respectively. By contrast, Islah won 7% of the governorate and 12% of district level votes in 2006 by comparison with 20.4% and 23.3% in 2001, while the YSP's returns hardly changed dropping roughly from 4% to 3% between the two elections. It was clear that, without 'management' of the electoral process, results might have given a majority to the opposition. The regime learnt that lesson as, indeed, these were the last elections held prior to the downfall of the Saleh regime.

In response to increasing opposition and popular frustration at all levels as demonstrated during the electoral process, the Local Authority law was amended in 2008 (Law 18 of 2008) to give greater power to the local authorities. The main change concerned the mechanism for the selection of governors: while according to the 2000 law they were appointed by the Minister of Local Government after approval of the Council of Ministers, the amendment allowed for their election by the governorate and district council members. This resulted in a significant change: from unification onwards, the overwhelming majority of governors had been senior military/security officials with little previous connection to the governorate they ruled, and their role had been to prevent dissent. By contrast, most of the governors elected in 2008 were from the governorate concerned and only a few had military/security positions. However, reflecting the 'management' of the 2006 elections, only three were independents, all the others were members of the GPC. This system did not survive the 2011 crisis and its consequences. A decade later, once again, the overwhelming majority of governors, whether Huthi of Hadi appointed, are military/security cadres.

In all these elections, women's involvement was insignificant: in the 2006 local elections, only 27 women were candidates from a total of more than

1600 and 7 won at the governorate level, with an even worse record at the district level where there were 122 women out of a total of 19 000 candidates, with 28 winning. This despite the fact that women voters registered in large numbers, forming 42% of the total of 9 247 370 registered voters.

Members of the local councils whether at the governorate or district level were from the locality itself, many of them community leaders, whether tribal or other, such as medical and education cadres. However military and security personnel were also often elected, as they were perceived to have greater influence than others demonstrating popular perception that elections were mechanism to obtain community infrastructures and services. However, appointed officials also included men from other locations, who were generally supporters of the regime. The Local Authority Law also set selection criteria for positions which were highly exclusive, in particular the holding of university degrees.

Presidential elections

Saleh remained president from 1978 to 2012 under a wide range of mechanisms; in the RoY, he was first elected by the (unelected and later elected) parliament. In 1999 for the first time he was elected by popular vote, ensuring his success by making sure that the 'competing' candidate was little more than a farce. The electoral commission having rejected all the serious candidates, it retained that of a junior member of the GPC who had two claims to fame and justification for standing: first, he was a southerner; and, second, he was the son of the first ever president of the PRSY after independence. He did not in any way campaign against Saleh, even suggesting at public meetings that he did not ask voters to vote for him! The result hardly came as a surprise, with Saleh winning with 96.3% of the votes, despite claiming on more than one occasion that he did not want 99% success. The official turn-out of 66.6%, despite the suspicious figure, may be reasonably realistic insofar as considerable direct and indirect pressure was put on citizens to participate.

This situation can be put in stark contrast with what happened seven years later, in the 2006 elections. In the face of popular discontent due to inflation, increasing poverty of the majority of the population, and disappointment at the quality of the 2003 elections, Saleh engaged in a theatrical farce, claiming that he would not stand for re-election to make place for a younger generation (Phillips, 2008, p. 16). This was promptly followed by mass street demonstrations by his supporters demanding that he stands. The opposition, grouped into the JMP, succeeded in agreeing on a single candidate, a genuinely independent southerner, former oil minister Faisal bin Shamlan, who had an excellent reputation throughout the country. Despite less than enthusiastic support from the main opposition party, the Islah, he won 23% of the votes, and Saleh only 77%, despite the presence of other candidates. This was achieved, most importantly, despite considerable pressure on the electorate to vote for Saleh through a process including a multiplicity of 'encouragements' as well as 'discouragements'.

The terminal decline of the regime

Parliamentary elections scheduled for 2007 were first postponed to 2009 and then again delayed due to acrimonious arguments within parliament, and between parliament and the presidency, about proposed changes to the electoral register and, yet again, the constitution. The JMP, although a minority within parliament, firmly opposed Saleh and the GPC's attempts to further strengthen their position, something they needed to do as support in the country had dropped considerably as demonstrated by the 2006 presidential elections. Popular frustration had become a significant factor due to worsening poverty, lack of job opportunities and the blatant display of the wealth of the small super wealthy and their families.

The JMP demanded a full review of the electoral register carried out by a renewed Supreme Council for Electoral Registration where it would be adequately represented. Saleh tried to organise yet another change to the constitution, which would enable him to stand again in 2013, thus reaching a time when his son Ahmad would be 40 and be allowed to stand in the next presidential election, following the succession model of other authoritarian 'republics' (Syria by Hafez al Assad, Egypt by Husni Mubarak, Libya by Qaddhafi and Iraq by Saddam Hussein). These parliamentary struggles between the regime and parliament were taking place against a background of worsening social and economic problems throughout the country, as discussed in the next chapter. they ended with the uprising of 2011 and the eventual ouster of Saleh.

Conclusion: the Yemeni state

There has been considerable debate as to whether Yemen is a 'state' worthy of the title. As Carapico reminds readers, the generally agreed criteria for a state include 'defined borders, a monopoly over violence, a constitutional order' (Carapico, 1998a, p. 199). A mere eight years after the establishment of the Republic of Yemen, she pointed out that it may develop 'a state capable of either democracy or full-fledged dictatorship'. Two decades later it can be said that it has done neither. Until 2015, the country teetered on the edge of dictatorship without actually ever becoming the fully autocratic and dictatorial state found elsewhere, whether in the Middle East or beyond. Although no parliamentary election took place after 2003, the presidential election of 2006 were serious and presented a real challenge to Saleh, though he certainly made sure he would not lose.

The Yemeni regime throughout that period included a range of mutually contradictory elements of state formation, some associated with autocracy while others demonstrated a level of continued freedom of expression and representation of different social and economic interests significantly higher than found elsewhere in the Arab world.

There is at least one level where the definition of a state applies, and that is the borders: the Saleh regime achieved agreed borders both with Saudi Arabia (2000) and Oman (1992). Constitutionally, as we have seen, a number of modifications were made, primarily to remove the 'power sharing' elements which had been agreed prior to unification and which gave much space to the southerners, and simultaneously ensured greater presidential authority. The feature of statehood which was least achieved concerns the monopoly of violence though, until the current war, it could be said that the ultimate control over violence resided with the Saleh regime, despite a series of challenges to the central state's authority:

- persistent localised tribal and other clashes throughout the country, including politically/socially/economically motivated kidnappings
- increasing tensions between different military factions focused on the succession to the presidency
- regional tensions manifested by a rise of sectarian politics, mostly the Huthi movement in the far north
- regional tensions resulting from the flawed unification process, demonstrated by the emergence of southern separatism.

In the 1970s it was widely said that the YAR did not have a state or control the country beyond the triangle of the Sana'a-Hodeida-Taiz-Sana'a asphalted road network linking these cities. At the time the socialist regime in the PDRY exercised centralised control over the population throughout its territory. Neither of these assertions fully reflects reality, certainly not in the 1980s when Saleh took control of most of the people and territory of the YAR; he transformed the community-led Local Development Associations into formal local government councils and established the GPC. Ongoing local military clashes were, as often as not, encouraged or sponsored by his military/security staff to influence or take over control over 'rebellious' community leaders. During the same period, the control existing in the PDRY was not quite as strict as the regime might have wished, partly as a result of the high level of labour migration out of the country.

Discussion of the nature of the Yemeni regime has focused on the dictatorship versus democracy debate and the role of civil society and the population at large in politics. In Yemen, as Phillips (2008) points out, the

> state is not necessarily weak because of the relative strength of society. Thus, while the state is unable to successfully penetrate society and its recourse to the politics of survival undercuts its own legitimacy, the fragmentation enacted on society by the state ultimately leaves both state and

society weak and poorly equipped to adapt to changes in the political environment.

(Phillips, 2008, p. 6)

After unification, in the 1990s in particular, while many deplored inadequate internal governance under the Saleh regime, the reality was that the regime controlled state institutions and interventions, including political, social and economic developments. Descriptions of Yemen as a 'weak' or 'failed' state, point out that formal state institutions had little control over decision making. This fails to recognise the gap which existed under Saleh, between the regime and formal government. Saleh's regime by-passed the formal state institutions, whether elected such as the parliament or appointed such as the government and ministries. These were effectively little more than transmission belts for decisions made by the regime itself, namely Saleh and his closest associates, a small group of kleptocrats, who benefitted materially and politically from his regime's policies.

The regime and the influential international financial institutions and bilateral financiers all shared the same interests and belief in neo-liberal economic policies even if they diverged in rhetoric and politics. Ordinary Yemenis and their communities depended on Saleh's patronage system for their limited access to development investments and state services as well as employment opportunities in administration and industry. This partly explains his lasting popularity throughout the country where there were constant calls for his visits. On these occasions literally bags of cash were distributed and social and economic community level projects decided which were frequently implemented with far greater speed than anything that went through the formal processes.

In a long-term perspective, it is clear that the area currently within the borders of the RoY has never had lasting stability under a single ruling group. The cultural and political divisions between the Zaydi highlands, the Shafi'i lowlands and the eastern Hadhramaut meant that, more often than not, they were ruled by rival rulers. Centuries, if not millennia of history, clearly have contributed to the problems and fragmentation which are affecting the Republic of Yemen which has only existed for less than a generation.

Notes

1 Shafi'i Sunnism is the version of Islam practiced throughout most of Yemen; it is one of the four main jurisprudence schools of Islam and is prevalent mainly around the Indian Ocean.

2 For a basic introduction to the tribal confederations and structure, see the introduction above pp. 2–4.

3 *Qat* (Catha edulis) is a mild stimulant drug, widely used in Yemen and the Horn of Africa, which must be consumed fresh. In Yemen its complete value chain

provides an income for thousands of producers, pickers, packers, transporters and distributors throughout the country.

4 The YAR later claimed these territories, and this caused significant tension in the 1970s and following decades, finally 'definitively' solved with the border agreement of 2000. The issue may re-emerge with Huthi dominance in the 2020s.

5 For a brief summary of the ascribed social strata in Yemen, see Lackner (2017a); for PDRY social policies, see Lackner (2021a).

2 Politics and the disintegration of a nation

The previous chapter outlined how the Yemeni state changed over the centuries, administered by a number of different entities – first, dynasties of one sort or another and, in the last half century, republican regimes, again on different models. Although the YAR and the PDRY were republics, they were also authoritarian single party states. They did, however, assert conflicting allegiances during the Cold War, the first to a Western capitalist model and the second to the east European socialist one. The Republic of Yemen's first constitution followed the modern Western model, including multi-party democracy and a neoliberal economic strategy promoting the private sector and downgrading state intervention. In the quarter century during which it was operational, the constitution was modified to increase autocracy and the concentration of power within a small group of acolytes of President Ali Abdullah Saleh. This was done both formally and informally through a combination of practices supported where necessary by formal constitutional changes.

The area included in the centralised Republic of Yemen succeeds two states from the previous decades, and numerous earlier ones, including a collection of statelets in the case of the Western Aden Protectorate. The question which arises in the 2020s concerns Yemen's future; elements of an answer can be found by addressing the issue of whether Yemen is a nation in the usual meaning of the term. There is little doubt that between the late 1950s and the early 1990s, most Yemenis considered themselves to be members of the Yemeni nation, and even today, if met outside of the country, most Yemenis would describe themselves as Yemenis before delving into their more localised identities.

However, the changes which have taken place since the mid-1990s, vastly exacerbated since the full-scale civil war started in 2014,[1] raise fundamental questions as to whether Yemen can continue to exist both as a state and a nation. The latter aspect will be discussed further in this chapter, while the future of the country as a state, already raised in Chapter 1 will be revisited in the conclusion. Yemeni politics in recent decades can only with great difficulty and effort of the imagination be discussed separately from the multiplicity of challenges to state authority, whether through peaceful means or military struggles.

DOI: 10.4324/9780429059315-3

Political parties and developments in the first decades of unification

Until unification, both the YAR and the PDRY were one-party states, with the General People's Congress (GPC) in the YAR and the Yemeni Socialist Party (YSP) in the PDRY. Unification and the first constitution of the Republic of Yemen (RoY) allowed political pluralism. The first three years of the RoY saw the creation of more than 50 political parties, many new but others emerging publicly from earlier underground operations. Some were revivals of organisations which had existed in the 1950s, particularly in the then Aden and Protectorates, demonstrating the longevity of certain groups (or possibly just of their leaders!). The number of parties shrank rapidly and most of them have not been significant, though it is worth noting that resurgence of old ones demonstrated the absence of new political thinking outside the Islamist sphere.

The General People's Congress (GPC)

The General People's Congress (GPC) was created in 1982 by Ali Abdullah Saleh as an organisation whose main objective was to support his policies and his personal position as president. As pointed out by Phillips in the mid-2000s,

> to be a member of the GPC … requires no necessary ideological leanings. … Islamists, former socialists, merchants, tribal leaders, moderates, hard-line religious conservatives, and some genuinely progressive reformers all exist side by side under the GPC umbrella. As a party, the GPC is driven by the desire to maintain power, perceiving its biggest threats to come from the tribes, potential renewed efforts from the South (particularly the historically autonomous Hadhramaut region) to secede from the unified republic and, more recently the Islah party. It works to incorporate the powerful elites from each group into the president's patronage network. … For its lower-level members, belonging to the GPC brings benefits and an element of protection. It is made clear to people in many professions, particularly teaching and academia, that finding a job or career progression is not likely without a GPC card … Political decision-making does not begin and end with the party caucus but rather with a shifting set of alliances between notables and traditional (generally tribal and religious) and military leaders – not all of whom are even necessarily GPC members – at the top of whom is the president. The ruling party itself is far less important than the individuals who are its leading members.
>
> (Phillips, 2008, pp. 50, 52)

Despite, or maybe thanks to, its lack of clear policies and political positions, and certainly thanks to the benefits it could provide for its members, the GPC developed a strong presence throughout the country down to the district level. As mentioned in the previous chapter, it dominated parliamentary elections without too much effort though it had to deal with far more challenges at local elections.

Its composition was always heterogeneous, all the more so as a result of the many political upheavals in the country's history. For example, many of the leaders of the YSP defeated in the 1986 struggle in the PDRY joined the GPC, among them current President Hadi and some of his ministers. Members of the 2003 GPC parliamentary group (still current as no elections have taken place since then) are now split into a number of factions: some remained with Hadi and are mostly in exile in Riyadh, Cairo or elsewhere; others, including those 'aligned' with Saleh's son, Ahmad Ali Saleh, have remained 'independent' and are found in various locations out of Yemen, and have formed rival groups to those operating with President Hadi. While those who remained in Sana'a have come under Huthi control and, despite retaining the name GPC, have no authority and are unable to assert positions challenging those of Ansar Allah, the official name of the Huthi movement.

Within Yemen itself, the GPC's importance for ordinary people, has probably diminished considerably for two main reasons: first, that it is not currently in a position to assist people with jobs or any other practical support in their daily lives; and second, that it lacks a coherent political programme or strategy which could mobilise people to strive for a post-war regime. Whether the GPC will be able to re-establish itself as a significant force is difficult to assess, but it is worth noting that, given its continued presence throughout the country on the ground, however partial, it is the one existing organisation which could compete with the part-Islamist Islah party at the national level. If appropriately managed and able to develop a political programme attractive to the majority of Yemenis, it has the potential of becoming a party which could roughly be described as social-democratic, or possibly Muslim-democratic on the model of European Christian-democratic parties. This is the kind of party which some of its leading members, such as Dr Abdul Karim al Iryani, tried to create in earlier decades, but were largely prevented from doing so by Saleh whose primary focus was to ensure it remained a personal support institution.

The Yemeni Congregation for Reform, known as the Islah

In the 1980s, despite the official illegality of political pluralism, but with the Saleh regime's complicity, various Islamist groups existed in the YAR. They had different levels of commitment to Muslim Brotherhood ideology, operated underground, and formed the Islamic Front which helped the Saleh regime defeat the leftist National Democratic Front in the 'central region' of the YAR in the early 1980s. Some of their leaders were then included in the GPC at its creation in 1982. Throughout that decade, the Islamic Front had considerable support throughout the country through the 'scientific institutes' which created a social base for Islamist ideology in the following decades. They were extremely important as many people sent their children to study there in the absence of state schools (Lackner, 2019b, p. 130–131).

As Schwedler put it, shortly after unification 'the core members of the Islamic Front joined with others who shared highly conservative and sometimes radical social visions to collectively form the Islah party' (Schwedler, 2006, p. 71). The Islah, officially the Congregation for Reform, was established in September 1990 under the leadership of Shaykh Abdullah bin Husayn al Ahmar, the leading shaykh of the Hashed federation. It was initially composed of the Islamist Front and senior tribal members of the GPC particularly from the Hashed and Bakeel confederations. Saleh supported its creation with two aims: first to strengthen his democratic pluralist credentials by encouraging the existence of an Islamist oriented party; second, to rival the YSP ideologically and culturally.

Although it is not as diverse in views as the GPC, Islah does include a range of positions, largely derived from the different organisations from which it emerged, but all share conservative Islamism as a fundamental belief. At the simplest level, the Islah has two main components: Islamists throughout the country and tribal people from the far north of the country who, although religiously conservative, are not necessarily Islamists; they ensured that the leadership of the party remained under the control of its founder Shaykh Abdullah bin Husayn al Ahmar (deceased in 2007). The link between the two components is complex and 'the labels "tribal" and "religious" wrongly suggest a level of cohesiveness among the various branches that obscures complex relationships and does not reflect the group's internal dynamics. In practice, tribal leaders are also religious, and many Islamists have tribal ties' (Schwedler, p. 71). Since the death of Shaykh Abdullah, despite the continuing presence and importance of northern tribesmen in the party, its leadership has passed to the Islamist tendency.

Frequently described as the 'Muslim Brotherhood' party in Yemen, particularly by the UAE leadership which has a phobia against anything remotely connected with political Islam, this description is only partly accurate. The Islah's Islamist ideological branch

> may be more accurately described as a collection of somewhat diverse actors: members of the Muslim Brotherhood, followers of al-Zindani and his radical (now Salafi) teachings, and Salafi Wahhabis who do not follow al-Zindani, to name only the most prominent. Islah also includes Zaydis among its ranks, though many complain of a 'glass ceiling' that prevents Shi'a from holding prominent or influential positions in the party.
>
> (Schwedler, p. 72)

Here she clearly refers to the ideological followers of Islah, who are Shafi'i (the branch of Sunni Islam prevailing in most of Yemen) as there are large numbers of Zaydis in the party, specifically all the Hashed tribespeople and other followers from that part of the country who are often described as having 'sunnised' (Alwaday and Shuja Al-Deen, 2022).

The Islamist element of the party is nowadays dominant both ideologically and numerically. It is not formally associated with a non-existent international Muslim Brotherhood umbrella, and includes the full spectrum of Islamists, from moderate to extremist elements, barely stopping short of militant jihadism. Over time it has developed its own policies in response to its analysis of political conditions in Yemen, independently of what has happened in other countries. This faction has a large number of supporters throughout the country, including members of most ascribed social groups, as well as the different emerging classes. There are no statistics either on the number of members or on the social status and origins of its members. However, its electoral results are indicative of the support it has, particularly as the various frauds implemented at different elections to ensure GPC success have clearly reduced its official following: in 1993, Islah obtained 380 000 votes; in 1997, it was 650 000; and in the most significant 2001 local elections, the figure reached 980 000, though its best score was 1.3 million at the 2003 parliamentary elections (Phillips, 2008, p. 146).

It is estimated that, in a situation similar to that found elsewhere, support from the wealthier and higher social strata such as the *sada* is more limited whereas the party has far more support among other social groups. In particular, there is clear evidence that thousands of poor people, whether from low ascribed status or tribal origin, as well as leading members of the tribal majority are Islah supporters. Interestingly, as is the case in many other countries, despite the party's retrograde position on the role of women in politics and society, Islah has considerable female support.

Like the GPC it has a formal structure, including an executive committee and a consultative council, composed of elected members. Much of its leadership, not only Shaykh Abdullah, had close relations with the Saleh regime. Economically, its leaders benefitted from the patronage system and gained considerable wealth, the prime example being Hamid al Ahmar, son of Shaykh Abdullah, but there are plenty of others. The party also opened offices throughout the country, down to the district level, ensuring a national presence comparable to and competing with the GPC. The fact that many of these offices in the southern governorates were formerly those of the YSP and were handed to Islah by the regime after the 1994 civil war both gave it a popular base and marked the defeat and weakness of the YSP.

The Islah party programme issued in 1991 is vague at best, and has not been significantly updated thirty years later. It represents the lowest common denominator which could be agreed. It asserts that Islam should be the fundament for all decisions, that justice and personal freedoms are to be defined by Shari'a, that there is equality between all citizens and that consultation must be the basis of political decision-making. Such a broad set of 'policies' reflects fundamental disagreements between the factions primarily on the place of democracy and the role of women. These differences divide the party between the more 'moderate' Muslim Brother element and the extremist Salafi leaders such as al-Zindani and al-Daylami who have made numerous statements which contradict party policy; Zindani in particular has, for example, made explicit anti-democracy statements.

In earlier decades these divergences were smoothed over by the universal respect accorded to Shaykh Abdullah, whose main objective was to remain close to the Saleh regime:

> the tribal power within Islah took up the positions of authority necessary to tie the party as closely as possible to President Salih and his ruling GPC party while the younger, integrativist [sic] Muslim Brotherhood ideologues assumed responsibility for formulating official party policies across a wide range of issues. As a result, Islah publications, political and electoral programs, and official states over-represented Muslim Brotherhood perspectives and downplayed the more radical visions of al-Zindani as well as the political outlook of Shayk 'abd Allah, who held conservative Islamist views but never prioritized Islamist objectives over maintenance of his bases of tribal power … The party saw a division of labor in which Shaykh 'Abdallah represented ties to the highest levels of power, the Muslim Brotherhood leaders ran the party bureaucracy, and al-Zindani continued to control the Islamic institutes that taught a radical reading of Islam and provided local military training and recruits that joined the *mujahidun* in Afghanistan. Although undesirable to many of the more progressive Islamist voices within Islah, al-Zindani was seen as a key personality for the solidification of a strong Islamist bloc that could challenge the power and programs of the YSP.
>
> (Schwedler, p. 178)

The results of the 2003 elections reveal the party's attraction for numerous disenfranchised groups in the country: for example, it has considerable support in Aden where, before a 'deal' to exchange seats with the GPC elsewhere, it won four of the ten seats, to the single seat of the YSP. In Hadhramaut, despite the political and social dominance of *sada* and tribes, five Islah candidates won seats thanks to the fact that thousands of lower social status agricultural community members voted for them. These had previously been the core supporters of the YSP as they had benefitted both from the socialist land reform and the egalitarian ideology of the PDRY regime. While Islah did not promise a return to their previous economic status, its main ideological belief that all are equal before Allah and that there are no social differences based on colour or birth origin was very attractive to this group. Islah also won many seats in the areas of high population density and poverty with higher educational standards and greater political awareness: the capital, Taiz and Ibb governorates as well as areas close to the capital such as Amran and Sana'a governorate, the latter more signs of allegiance to the Hashed leadership than to Islamist ideology.

Over the decades of the Saleh regime, the Islah party increased its popularity and importance but its inability to provide the extent of material support in the form of jobs and access to privileges from the state reduced its opportunist attraction and limited its expansion to genuine supporters of an Islamist political agenda. This is not to say that it didn't provide anything: its wealthiest leaders, in particular Hamid al Ahmar controlled some of Yemen's largest and most powerful companies and was therefore in a position to provide jobs and privileges to its supporters. Part of the party's considerable wealth was derived from the vast fuel smuggling operations, run by its leaders.

The Islah party's wealth enabled it to establish its charitable organisation, the Charitable Society for Social Welfare (CSSW), which maintained an active presence throughout the country and distributed both basic necessities and cash to poor supporters, mainly in Ramadan. It also financed small-scale development projects including women's centres throughout the country. This strategy has been used by Islamists in many countries and, in Yemen as elsewhere, has been successful in persuading thousands that Islamist approaches can provide solutions to people's problems. However, its economic policies did not challenge the capitalist neo-liberal agenda.

During the 2012–14 transition phase, Islah dominated the Hadi government, and its competition with the GPC was at the forefront of struggle within the formal government structure, marginalising other participating parties and groups. Since the war started in 2015, it only features in official discourse to the extent that it remains the main cohesive force within the Hadi government, due to the disintegration and fragmentation of the GPC. Most significantly the army aligned with the Hadi IRG is led by either members or close allies of the Islah party. The UAE's assimilation of the Islah with the Muslim Brotherhood is at the core of the problems between the UAE leadership and the Hadi government, and therefore is also relevant to the problems which have emerged between the UAE and Saudi Arabia, as the latter perceives Islah more as a tribal group and is less focused on its Islamist agenda. Given these pressures and the strange alliances which have emerged in Yemen in the past, possible future cooperation between Islah and the Huthis, though unlikely, is not inconceivable, as are other equally unlikely alliances.

The smaller parties

The attraction of the Islah and Islamist politics has been all the greater in the past decades as their ideology and politics were basically in competition with no one. More traditional 'secular' parties such as the GPC lack ideology, while both Ba'athism and Nasserism are outdated and discredited: in the first case, by the feuds between Iraq and Syria as well as the visible absence of any 'socialism' in the states under their control; and in the second case, by the collapse of Nasserism following the death of Nasser and the adoption of neo-liberalism by his successors. In the states where these had prevailed, the word 'socialism' had lost all meaning, at a time when the concept of socialism was under attack worldwide by both neo-liberalism and religiously conservative organisations whose ideologies are similar but whose rhetoric is based on religious discourse, whether Christian or Muslim or indeed anything else, e.g. Hinduism in India.

The Yemeni Socialist Party (YSP)[2] had a special and slightly different place and fate. Emerging from the nationalist movement of the 1950s and in particular from its left wing which considered Nasserism 'petty bourgeois' and insufficiently radical, it is the successor to the NLF and took that name in 1978 when it was the ruling party in the PDRY. It then followed policies closely aligned with those of east European communist parties, promoting the public sector and policies which provided basic social services to all. The three major internal conflicts within the PDRY were only partly based on ideological differences between the factions: the first in 1969 marked the victory of the left over the less radical nationalist elements, the second in 1978 marked the end of the most radical form of 'ultra-leftist' socialism, associated with 'Maoism' and President Salem Rubaya Ali (known as Salmine), with a more 'traditional' pro-Soviet group taking over. The third and most murderous of these conflicts in 1986 was little more than a simple power struggle, despite attempts to give it the appearance of some ideological differences between the two rival groups.[3]

The last four years of the PDRY witnessed fundamental changes for the YSP for a number of reasons: first, it had lost credibility with the population as a result of its internal faction fights; second, the ideological struggle waged against socialism and communism continued and was strengthened by the widespread perception of wealth and comfort in neighbouring states; and thirdly, these elements coincided internationally with the end of the socialist system in eastern Europe. These factors led the YSP to undergo significant transformations through internal debate, which turned it into a social democratic party and member of the Socialist International. Under its new form at the time of unification, it could be described as similar to comparable parties in Europe, such as the Labour Party in the UK, the Social Democrat Party of Germany or the Socialist Party in France.

This transformation could have helped it become a leading party post-unification, with great potential to achieve support from millions of Yemenis whose main hope is to have better living conditions through reasonable income and adequate social services with a transparent and democratic government. Its new political positions could have made it attractive by comparison with the competition, were it not for two fundamental developments: its divisions over the unification process and the 1994 civil war on the one hand and the ongoing successful hostile campaigns waged throughout recent decades by Islamists of all hues. The latter fitted in neatly with the dominant worldwide neo-liberal agenda.

Unfortunately, the YSP effectively destroyed itself in the course of the conflicts over unification. As it was perceived by the population at large as the party of the South, this initially limited support north of the pre-1990 border. Within the former PDRY, it lost support because of its internal divisions over the issue of southern separatism. After the series of attempted and actual assassinations of YSP leaders between 1991 and 1993, in 1994 parts of the YSP leadership initiated and led the short-lived separatist Democratic Republic of Yemen during the civil war, while others stayed in Sana'a and declared their loyalty to the unified state. This did not prevent Saleh from confiscating YSP properties and offices throughout the country and handing them over either to the GPC or to Islah. Weakened institutionally, the party eventually decided to boycott the 1997 elections.

The YSP was not only considered to be the southern party, it was also the party defending the poor and calling for social justice, an end to privileges, nepotism and corruption. These messages failed to impress a population whose experience of the reality of unification was largely negative and who heard similar claims from other parties. By the time the YSP re-entered electoral politics, its position had been undermined by the increasing strength of Islah throughout the country including in YSP strongholds. Based both on Yemenis' strong attachment to Islam and the successful media attacks presenting it as atheist and communist, both words associated with evil, the Islah benefitted from the infrastructure of the YSP which it had obtained after 1994. However, more importantly, it benefitted by its claim of supporting all citizens' equality, regardless of ascribed status, at a time when the former leading social groups in the South were aggressively re-asserting their dominance and openly discriminating against the lower status groups and the poor in general.

In addition to the YSP, Yemen has a number of smaller parties, some new and others revived after unification, which achieved minimal representation in the parliament: among them the Nasserists and the Baathists, as well as two parties representing the *sada* social group, the Union of Popular Forces and the al Haq party. Each of these either had members in the parliament or ministers in government at different times. In the face of increasing monopoly of power by Saleh's GPC, in 2003 prior to the election they all got together to form the Joint Meeting Parties (JMP), an informal grouping of opposition parties initially designed as an electoral pact according to which they would not present competing candidates where one of them might win. Given their relative influence, the Islah was by far the dominant element in the JMP. Although it later developed something more closely resembling collective action; even by 2010, Phillips's description of it a few years earlier remained accurate:

> it also mirrors one the GPC's main characteristics – an ideologically bereft umbrella group for elites that exists to protect their group interests … its members' historical backgrounds thus range from the extreme left to the

> extreme right ... its members have therefore had to settle on a lowest-common-denominator basis of agreement in order to stay together. In avoiding some of the more loaded political arenas, the basis of agreement has been set around calls for political and economic reform. These short-term goals represent the JMP's endeavour to create a new inclusive ideological banner for itself in the absence of other value positions.
>
> (Phillips, 2008, p. 124)

By 2005, the JMP had developed sufficient coherence to produce a 'Document on National and Political Reform' which formed the basis of its programme for the 2006 presidential and local elections. This 'called for the peaceful rotation of power, respect for the law and the constitution, an end to corruption, the clear separation of powers, stronger limitations on the role of the military and security apparatus, civil service reforms, greater popular empowerment and a functioning parliamentary system' (ibid., p. 157). While these presented a fairly clear set of principles, the two major issues on which its component parties were unable to reach any kind of agreement are noticeable by their absence or ambiguity in this document: the role of Islam and Shari'a in political life, and the position of women.

Within the parliament, in 2008–10, the JMP maintained a united front in demanding reform of the electoral register which had been heavily manipulated to favour the GPC. It also objected to yet another proposed change to the constitution which would have enabled Saleh to stay in power for even longer. This ability to agree was simply due to their sharing the same objections to the GPC/Saleh strategies and the hope that a new electoral register would allow them to gain more seats and more influence in a future parliament. The other issue arising in 2009 was the postponement of the parliamentary elections, which the JMP called for to enable the preparation of a new electoral register. Given its dominance, the Islah only gave way to other parties on issues where it considered that this would not impinge on its own power and control.

Jihadism

Yemen is often mentioned as a hotbed of terrorism and the ancestral homeland of the most notorious jihadi, Usama bin Laden. This largely obscures reality, particularly as it is presented as the most significant feature of the country and only with respect to the 'threat' this poses to the West. In particular it is worth noting that this phenomenon is a far greater threat to Yemenis than it is to the West, and even so, it is far from ranking among the top priorities for Yemenis who have so many other crises and problems to deal with.

Jihadism became relevant in Yemen as it did in other countries in the region with the return of jihadi volunteers from Afghanistan after the defeat of the communist regime there in 1989. Yemeni 'Afghans'[4] were involved in attacks on two hotels in Aden in 1992, and were among the main elements which helped Saleh win the 1994 civil war. They put their ideology in practice in Aden and elsewhere in the south by sacking establishments which they associated with 'communism', including such 'threats' as health centres, schools, local administration offices alongside more obvious targets like the beer factory and Sufi shrines (Cook, 2022, p. 79). In 1998, a kidnapping of tourists in Abyan went very wrong when a clash with counter-attacking government forces led to the death of four tourists. Their most spectacular action was the attack on the USS Cole in Aden port in September 2000, killing 17 US naval staff. More recently the 'underpants' bomber in 2009 and other attempts at sending explosives around the world (e.g., the cartridge explosives in 2010) have attracted world attention, but it is worth noting that they have not carried out any noticeable actions outside of Yemen since that time.

Despite occasional spectacular actions, the movement has always been weak in Yemen and is not tribally based as is so often claimed. The Saleh regime's actions against the movement were halfhearted at best. Indeed, they were a mix of instrumentalization, cooperation and repression, depending on the specific political objectives of the regime at various times. For example, after a period of repression and suppression between 1999 and 2005, when the Saleh regime was primarily concerned with cooperating with the US and obtaining training, weapons and political support from the US, the situation changed after Yemen was rejected from the US-funded Millennium Challenge Fund in 2005. Within a few months, a group of senior al Qaeda leaders 'escaped' from prison in Sana'a and resumed active service throughout the country.

In 2009, after al Qaeda in Saudi Arabia had suffered serious setbacks at home, many of its members and leaders moved to Yemen, and the two groups joined to form al Qaeda in the Arabian Peninsula (AQAP), which has been active ever since, primarily in Yemen, though it has claimed responsibility for a few actions in Saudi Arabia. Since the war started in 2015, AQAP was said to have taken control of Mukalla and coastal Hadhramaut in the summer of 2015. Contrary to claims by the Saudi-led coalition, its members left a year later by negotiating with the coalition, taking heavy weapons as well as plenty of the cash acquired through port fees, taxation and bank raids during that time. Since then, AQAP has carried out occasional attacks mostly in remote locations and against official government or separatist forces in the southern part of Yemen. There are strong indications of some cooperation between AQAP and both coalition and separatist forces, each accusing the other of working with jihadis. In the 2020s, AQAP's presence on the ground is the justification claimed by the UAE for the continued presence of its forces in Hadhramaut and Shabwa, as well as for that of a small number of US special forces alongside (Kendall, 2021).

Other than the southern governorates, there are also groups of jihadis in two areas in al Baydha governorate, which occasionally engage in military encounters against Huthi forces or those of the government if and when attacked. There is one particular location and family which is deeply divided between all the Yemeni political and military factions, the Dhahab family.

Military action in their village is systematically described as targeting AQAP, without taking into consideration the fact that most of what happens locally is between different factions within the same extended family, where ideology plays a minor part. But that is where the Trump administration's first and most disastrous action took place in January 2017 when, in addition to killing 25 Yemenis, including children, the US lost one marine and a helicopter.

Daesh (also known as ISIS or ISIL) has been unable to put down any roots in Yemen, where AQAP is by far the most significant jihadi movement. Most Daesh associates are basically AQAP dissidents.

Roots of the war

While the first decade of unification was one of hope, a time when many believed that either the Saleh regime might change or might be replaced through the democratic process, the second decade saw the rise of tensions on various fronts which led to the uprisings of 2011 and the eventual collapse of the Republic of Yemen as created in 1990. Economic problems (primarily reduced income from oil exports and the worsening water crisis, alongside the absence of alternative economic development policies) played a major role and are discussed in the next chapter; here we focus on the political challenges emerging against the Saleh regime.

By the third parliamentary elections in 2003, popular hopes of effecting significant political change through formal mechanisms had lowered. Despite Saleh's reduced political support and increasingly widespread criticism of his economic and social policies from members of the national elite and from international financial institutions, let alone the population at large, his control over the formal, democratic, political process was increasingly authoritarian and unresponsive to Yemenis' needs. There was widespread recognition that the formal democratic processes were systematically manipulated. In addition to economic decline, three main elements combined to build the crisis which erupted in the next decade. First, Saleh's 'divide and rule' policy ensured a series of mainly small but meaningful local conflicts, whether tribal or other, throughout the country on a regular basis. The other two elements developed into the major crises which now dominate Yemen: the rise of the Huthi movement and the emergence of southern separatism, the first in the far north of the country and the other at its extreme south.

The rise of the Huthi movement and the six Huthi wars

The far north of Yemen, and in particular the city of Sa'ada, has been the heartland of Zaydism since the ninth century (see Chapter 1), and all the imams who ruled larger or smaller areas of Yemen until 1962 were Zaydis. Without going into theological discussions, Zaydism is a form of Shi'ism, known as Fivers, i.e. they consider the rightful succession to Mohammed as being only the first five caliphs, by contrast with Iranian Shi'ism, known as the Twelvers, who consider the first 12 Caliphs as legitimate. In terms of daily observance there is little to differentiate Zaydism from Shafi'ism.

Politically, the dominance of Sa'ada-based Zaydism ended with the birth of the republic in 1962, although, until 2012, all presidents of the YAR and the RoY were Zaydi. Saleh facilitated the opening, in 1980, and the later rise, of a Salafi school and community, the Dar al Hadith, in Dammaj (a village near Sa'ada, now effectively a suburb of the city), established by Muqbil Al-Wadi'i, a Salafi convert from Zaydism who had spent many years in Saudi Arabia. His school flourished and over time became a large community of locals, other Yemenis and foreign followers (Bonnefoy, 2011).

The presence of a Salafi movement was perceived as a provocation by the local Zaydi leaders who responded with the creation of a Zaydi revivalist movement in 1992. The 'Believing Youth movement' was led by Husayn al-Huthi, a member of parliament (1993–97), whose relationship with the Saleh regime deteriorated as the Salafi movement in Dammaj grew. It eventually broke down in 2004 with the first war between the Huthi movement and the Saleh regime, followed by a further five conflicts between the two sides. Each of these wars was worse than the previous one in levels of violence and destruction, duration and geographical expansion beyond the Sa'ada core area, and each increasingly demonstrated the Huthis' growing strength. Following internal debates and differences within the movement, it adopted the name Ansar Allah (the Partisans of God) in 2011, which gave it a clearer political identity in the popular uprisings (Brandt, 2017).

A number of aspects of the six Huthi wars remain relevant (Brandt, 2017). First the important role of General Ali Mohsen. He was Saleh's front man in the Huthi wars and was clearly inadequately supported by Saleh. Many Yemenis believed that Ali Mohsen had been sent to fight to Huthis as part of Saleh's strategy to undermine him personally in their rivalry over the succession to the presidency. Since 2016 he has been vice president of the Hadi regime and its main military leader, using tribal troops from his home area, facing the Huthis and their tribal supporters on the northern front of the war. The second element relates to the nature of the relationship between the *sayyed* supremacist Huthi movement and the northern tribes since the full-scale war started in 2015. In the course of the wars, increasing mismanagement by Saleh gradually turned many of the tribes of the region against him, and they joined the Huthis, not because of ideological agreement but simply as they shared a common enemy, namely Saleh and his associates, explaining why they did not come to Saleh's rescue when the Huthis turned against him in December 2017 (Brandt and Weissenburger, 2022).

The February 2010 cease-fire held, not because the problem and differences had been solved but because the uprisings of 2011 and the changes in fortune of the regime meant that resumption of fighting on the northern front ceased to be a priority. The 2011 uprisings also saw a reversal of alliances (neither the first nor the last) as the Huthi movement joined the popular uprising against the Saleh regime in the cities thus, within a couple of months, finding itself alongside Ali Mohsen and his military forces in opposition to Saleh. Within two years, the Huthis were allied with Saleh against the transitional government in which Ali Mohsen had a major role, long before he became vice president.

Despite internal differences which remain important, the Huthi movement, is primarily characterised by a belief that *sada*, (descendants of the Prophet through his son-in-law Ali) have the innate right to rule (Alwaday and Shuja Al-Deen, 2022, p. 60). Ansar Allah claims that it is not planning to re-establish an imamate based on this belief, but evidence from the area it has now ruled for close to a decade, demonstrates inordinate and systematic privileging of *sada* for senior appointments whether political or military. Non-*sada* appointees to senior positions are widely believed to be mere fronts. Moreover, the most powerful positions are kept within the Huthi family. According to Zaydi belief, a leader needs to demonstrate his competence, in addition to being born in the right social stratum, hence the widespread belief that the Huthi family leaders are planning to become the formal rulers of the country is not far-fetched, as they could provide theological justification for their claims, even if they do not use the word imam. A theocracy modelled on that prevailing in Iran is a more likely model of Ansar Allah ambitions. Huthi indoctrination of youth through the education system reinforces their retrograde ideology (Haykel in Hamidaddin, 2022; Shuja al Deen, 2021).

Locally, the Huthi movement's popular support in its early days came from the widespread perception that the far north of the country was neglected with respect to development investments. This perception was widely shared throughout the country, demonstrating the extent to which the vast majority of Yemenis considered that others were doing better than themselves, also reflecting the reality that economic and social investments were well below popular expectation, particularly given oil exports and the ostentatious wealth displayed by the leadership's cronies.

In the current war, the Huthi–tribal alliance is based on two elements: first the common enemy, specifically the Saudi-led 'aggressors', and most importantly, yet again, Ali Mohsen and his forces. The shared Zaydi creed is an additional factor. However, looking ahead, it would be a mistake to assume that this alliance is stable, as the tribes will give priority to their own concerns once the external enemy has been dealt with. There is little doubt that the tribes, and in particular the larger northern tribes, will not look favourably on the establishment of a theocratic regime.

The southern separatist movement

The first decade of this century saw the rise of another major movement in fundamental opposition to the Saleh regime, which remains at the forefront of the political crisis two decades later. As discussed above, the unification process between the YAR and the PDRY turned into bitter rivalry within months. The 1994 civil war in which the separatist forces were defeated, followed by discrimination against southerners, led to growing anger and resentment as the Saleh regime made no effort to appease them with concessions which would have restored confidence in the dream of Yemeni unity.

Among the actions which embittered the population was the privatisation process which, rather than being implemented in a professional manner, was turned into a mechanism to hand over urban properties to Saleh associates whether from the north or the south. In rural areas, the agrarian reform was reversed and lands were supposedly returned to their previous owners. However, in many cases, both old farms and land which had been made arable under the socialist regime went to Saleh associates, whether civil or military (Lackner, 2017b). Beneficiaries of this bonanza included returned southern exiles who had opposed the socialist regime and taken refuge in neighbouring countries, including Saudi Arabia and the UAE. With respect to employment, southern professionals were unable to get the types and levels of employment to which they considered themselves entitled, particularly given their comparatively higher educational qualifications. Overall, in the former PDRY area, living standards dropped with high rates of inflation, low salaries and high unemployment.

The payments of pensions and salaries to the 86 000 or so military and security personnel who had been forcibly 'retired' after the 1994 civil war was the trigger which initiated the southern separatist movement. Frustrated at the non-payment or long delays in the payment of their pensions, let alone their complete inadequacy to finance basic needs, in late 2006, they formed the Association of Retired Military, Security and Civilian Personnel. As most of these men came from the governorates of Lahej and the southern part of Dhala‘ which had been the main recruiting grounds for the military/security sector in the PDRY, their movement and the subsequent rise of the separatist movement, were primarily based in these areas and in nearby Aden, the official 'economic' capital of the RoY. Their approach was initially peaceful, calling on all southerners to support demands for adequate incomes and/or restoration of their employment. The regime responded to their demonstrations with violence, expanding the movement to most areas of the former PDRY. Most significantly one of the outcomes was the emergence of an increasingly separatist agenda and calls for the return to the pre-unification borders.

In the following years, due to the complete lack of compromise from the Saleh regime, the violent repression, and the continuing frustration of people in the South with respect to social and economic issues, the movement grew beyond its original group, to encompass significant numbers of people, mostly in the main cities of Aden and Mukalla, but also in smaller towns and the rural areas. It is in this context that the national uprisings of 2011 intervened.

The 2011 uprisings and the transitional regime

The uprisings and the Gulf Cooperation Council Agreement

For millions of Yemenis, the many months of popular uprisings in 2011 were interludes of optimism and hope reminiscent of the early days of unification.

People throughout the country were involved, of all ages and all areas, most social statuses, poor and less poor, urban and rural, tribal and other, men and women. Beyond the simple slogan demanding the departure of Saleh, discussions in the 'Change Squares'[5] focused on social and political changes, demands for democracy and equity in economic opportunities, better social services, and an end to corruption and nepotism. There were 'change squares' in all the governorate capitals, whether major cities like Taiz, Hodeida and Aden, or smaller towns like Mahweet and al Ghayda, and they were active far beyond 2011.

In 2011, there were basically two major confrontations, the first was the popular uprisings in the 'change squares'. They were the site for the emergence of political debate between people of different geographic origins, ages and social strata. Debate focused on the types of state and government structures that people were striving for, but all shared a vision of real democracy in which the needs and ambitions of the majority of the population would be addressed. There were local differences in focus and duration, as well as participation. In Aden and other southern governorates, there was more emphasis on the failure of unification but, overall, it was a movement which can be described as united in its diversity and openness.

This element was marginalised after the 18 March 'Friday of Dignity' massacre which led to the emergence of the other element of the 2011 events, the intra-elite struggle which undermined the democratic movement. The defection of Ali Mohsen and his elite troops, as well as that of a number of Saleh government members, all of whom announced their alignment with the revolution, fundamentally transformed the movement and introduced a military struggle between armed factions supporting and opposing Saleh.

The involvement of the international community started early on but took a more active role in April, when its representatives on the ground came to the conclusion that Saleh would be unable to control the situation. The group of ambassadors representing the 'Friends of Yemen' semi-formal international grouping established in 2010 to 'help bolster international political support for Yemen, and to assist Yemeni-led efforts to tackle the underlying causes of instability' (UK Gov, 2013). This group included the GCC states who took the lead at this point, and included the future UN Special Envoy appointed (initially as advisor) that month. It is likely that foreign intervention would have been less prominent in the absence of armed confrontations and a split in the ruling group. This split was the trigger which persuaded the diplomats that the Saleh regime was no longer sustainable. They therefore supported a transition to a regime which would be acceptable both in their capitals, by not making too many concessions to popular demands, and on the ground, by responding to some of the political and economic demands of the street movement.

With these objectives in mind, they took a draft under discussion among Yemeni personalities, and turned it into the 'Gulf Cooperation Council Initiative'. This was signed and approved by all Yemeni political leaders in April 2011 with the exception of President Saleh, who dithered and successfully delayed signing through a range of tricks, some of them more entertaining than others. Throughout the year Yemeni personalities and representatives of the international community made numerous attempts to persuade Saleh to resign. Eventually, in the face of the military stalemate, under pressure from his medical condition (he had been severely wounded in a bomb attack on his palace mosque on 3 June, and had been treated in Saudi Arabia), and additional pressure from UNSC Resolution 2014, on 23 November 2011 he signed the Gulf Cooperation Council Agreement in a formal ceremony in Riyadh, the capital of Saudi Arabia, leading to his resignation as president in February 2012.

In addition to the rather vague April document, the GCC Implementation Mechanism, was also signed on that occasion, detailing the procedures and steps of the planned two-year transition period. Saleh still retained considerable popular support, which explains why it was impossible to force him out of the country or even to exclude him from active politics within Yemen. So, although he was compelled to abandon the presidency, he remained head of the GPC, the largest and most influential political organisation in the country. The two-year transition period defined in the GCC agreement formally started on 21 February 2012 with the election of Saleh's former vice president Abdu Rabbu Mansour Hadi as president in an uncontested election.

The transition (2012–14)

The transitional regime, under the GCC Agreement, had a number of features and characteristics which almost certainly ensured its failure. Determining which weakness in the agreement bears most responsibility is difficult, but between them, they left little likelihood of success. The GCC Agreement stated that the transition to democracy had to be completed within two years, an unrealistic timetable under the best of circumstances, which did not prevail in Yemen. Another constraint was the continued presence and influence of by then former President Saleh, enabling him to sabotage much of the programme, in particular the security sector reform. The Hadi government's attempts to replace Saleh-appointed senior military/security commanders were either successfully delayed or entirely prevented, partly because the foreign state appointed by the GCC Agreement to support it, namely the US, was less than enthusiastic, having spent decades supporting and training these very forces.

The 'government of national unity' was designed for failure: according to the GCC agreement, it was to include 50% GPC ministers, i.e. Saleh supporters, with the other 50% members of the opposition, i.e. the JMP, led by Islah with the addition of the 'new forces' emerging from the popular movement, defined as 'youth, women and civil society'. With the history of corruption which had dominated administrations for decades, this resulted in a government whose priorities were factional and self-serving rather than promoting good governance or addressing the social, economic and political problems faced by the nation. Paralysis ensued, services continued to deteriorate, and nothing was done to alleviate the worsening living conditions of the population. The 8.2 billion USD pledged for economic development by the international community in September 2012 failed to materialise, so there were no funds for investment in infrastructure or economic development.

Finally, the National Dialogue Conference (NDC) lasted ten months and ended in January 2014. It had been promoted as the main mechanism for the transformation of Yemen's institutions to respond to the demands and needs of Yemenis. Its task was to translate agreed popular demands into a series of decisions on all aspects of social, political and economic life in a document which would form the base for the constitution of a 'new' Yemen. It suffered many problems, but two stood out at the time and remain valid a decade later: the selection process for its 565 members included a majority of members of different factions from the existing elite. UN support was seriously defective, though it is important to remember that its intervention ensured good representation of women (28%, rather than the planned 30%), of youth (20%) and of 'civil society' (7%) (Lackner, 2016b, p. 43). The presence of women certainly influenced some of the NDC's outcomes, in particular that all state institutions should include 30% women under the new constitution. Its nine working groups produced more than 1800 'outcomes' as its recommendations were called, published in a document which is still referred to a decade later as the basis for a solution to the country's problems, even though some of these were mutually incompatible.

Most significantly the NDC failed to propose solutions to the country's major issues, the role of the Huthi movement (in NDC terms, 'the Sa'ada question') and the conflicting demands of southerners. After the NDC was completed and had been unable to agree on the details of a future federal state, these were rapidly and formally dealt with by the decision of a Hadi-appointed committee to turn the country into a federal state with six regions. This was immediately rejected by the Huthi movement and the southern separatists.

On the delayed completion of the NDC and when it was obvious that all the tasks of the transition period could not possibly be completed within weeks, the UN Special Envoy unilaterally extended the term of President Hadi's presidency without either formal specification of its new duration, or reference to any constitution or other legally valid document, or indeed without the authority to do so. The year 2014 saw the unravelling of the transitional process. First the commission established to draft a new constitution was riven with internal conflict and only completed its work in early January 2015. Admittedly its task was not easy: its responsibility was to take up the 1800 'outcomes' of the NDC and use them to draft the new constitution. The Constitution Drafting Committee was also the site for further disagreements between the Huthis, the southern separatists, and the members who were focused on the concerns of Yemen as a united entity.

Outside of the confines of the formal process, developments on the ground undermined what remained of the transition. Between 2012 and 2014, while participating in the NDC and other discussions with the transitional regime, the Huthi movement had been busy consolidating its control over Sa‘ada governorate and expanding it in the neighbouring governorates of Hajja, Amran and al Jawf. As already mentioned, throughout the country living conditions continued to deteriorate, thus depriving the transitional regime of the popular support which might have saved it from the assaults of its opponents. Saleh and the Huthis shared rejection of the formal transitional process and their informal cooperation became an effective operational alliance in 2014, as the Huthi movement expanded its territorial control southwards, initially to Amran city and by September taking over the capital Sana‘a. They achieved this almost bloodlessly, as the military/security commanders and institutions, still mostly aligned with Saleh, made no move to halt their advance, rather the contrary. Popular demonstrations against the fuel price increases decreed by the Hadi government in rushed compliance with demands of the International Monetary Fund and the World Bank, helped the Huthis gain popularity at the expense of the already discredited transitional government.

After the Huthi take-over of Sana‘a, final, desperate efforts by the UN Special Envoy led to the signature of the Peace and National Partnership Agreement (PNPA) supposed to form the basis of a new government including Ansar Allah. This remained a dead letter. The new government formed by Hadi in November lasted barely three months. By January 2015, Hadi and his government resigned in the face of Huthi demands which would have reduced them to clerks. Put under house arrest, Hadi escaped a month later, was followed by the Huthi–Saleh forces to Aden which he then had to abandon in the face of their military assaults. He ended up in Riyadh, having, while in transit, called for GCC military intervention to restore himself and his ‘legitimate regime’ to power.

While the transitional regime in Sana‘a persisted in focusing energies on other issues, southern separatism strengthened as the popular social, political and economic demands of the 2011 uprisings were overtaken by events and the more intra-elite struggles around the transition period came to dominate discourse. By 2013 many southerners were no longer mobilised by national calls for social and economic reform despite the fact that more than half of the members of the National Dialogue Conference (2013–14) were southerners, not all of them separatists. Some separatist groups had self-excluded from the NDC on the grounds that the only form of debate possible was one between the two former states, these included leaders of earlier regimes such as al Beedh. In February 2015, Hadi’s declaration of Aden as Yemen’s temporary capital was the prelude to five months of extremely heavy fighting in the city, which was defended by a wide range of groups, most of them separatists and including Jihadi Islamists. By end July the city was eventually ‘liberated’ thanks to the active military intervention of United Arab Emirates (UAE) forces who were part of the coalition (Day, 2022, pp. 37–49).

The war

Internal military clashes within Yemen are hardly unusual and have taken place throughout history. Although the outbreak of the current conflict was little surprise to many in Yemen, few expected it to be lengthy and bring about the disasters which have effectively destroyed the country through years of war. It was a predictable escalation of the tensions which had been building up over the past decade, but this war is substantially different from all previous conflicts. There are three main reasons for this: first, the direct international involvement in the fighting; second, its contribution to the social and political fragmentation of the country; and third, its duration. Two important issues are covered elsewhere in this book: Western arms sales to the coalition in Chapter 4 and the rise and importance of the war economy discussed in Chapter 3.

The Saleh–Huthi alliance

With the collapse of the transitional regime established by the Gulf Cooperation Council Agreement, the balance of forces within Yemen clearly favoured what was then the Saleh–Huthi alliance, as the Hadi regime had failed to earn the loyalty of most of the military/security units. Even when it succeeded in appointing new commanders at the helm of institutions, most middle and lower ranking officers remained loyal to Saleh. This was particularly true in the most effective, well-trained and well-equipped units. In the course of the six conflicts between the Huthis and the Saleh regime, the Huthis had developed impressive military skills, which is one of the reasons they were never defeated (another reason was that Saleh did not provide the necessary technical and material support for his fighters led on the ground by his rival, Ali Mohsen). The Hadi regime thus lacked military clout as, in addition to the above, it had alienated its main supporter Ali Mohsen's Islah-backed First Armoured Brigade which his regime had failed to assist when they were attacked by the Huthi–Saleh alliance in 2014.

While the Saleh–Huthi alliance was largely one of equals in 2014–15, the balance of forces gradually shifted in favour of the Huthis in the following three years. Both relied on fighters from tribal groups from the northern Zaydi region, whose leaders decided on their political alignments according to various factors: the comparative strength of the leaderships, the benefits that reached their members, political alignment, previous historical commitments, including the fact that for centuries the Zaydi tribes had been ruled by *sada* and many of them retained elements of fear and respect for *sada.* It is essential to remember that tribal leaders operate thanks to the support of their members, which itself depends on their ability to respond to their needs, whether social or economic. Recent decades have created a widespread belief in Yemen as elsewhere, that leaders, whether national, regional or tribal, are duty bound to provide jobs and incomes for their citizens/followers.

Community leaders therefore tend to prioritise their own and their group's immediate interests and concerns when deciding their allegiances. As Saleh's strength and influence waned from 2012 onwards, tribal leaders, particularly those of the tribes surrounding Sana'a, found he was increasingly unable to respond to their demands, hence their allegiance transferred to the new rising power, the Huthis.

Militarily, once the fighting started in 2015, the Huthis actively worked to increase their strength to the detriment of Saleh's: they did this by ensuring that new appointments to senior posts went to their own supporters. As Saleh-appointed commanders were killed by coalition airstrikes and ground fighting, the Huthis replaced them with their own appointees, primarily among the *sada*. One Saudi airstrike was particularly important in this respect, the attack on a funeral ceremony in Sana'a's Great Hall on 8 October 2016, had a major impact on the balance of forces between Saleh and the Huthis. It killed at least 37 senior commanders close to Saleh, including the head of Republican Guards; replacing him was at the heart of conflict between the two factions and a new appointment was only made after Saleh's killing. By late 2017, with the balance of power effectively transferred to the Huthis, Saleh made the desperate move of trying to reverse his alliances and join the coalition to fight the Huthis. This came too late as, by then, he was effectively a Huthi hostage. In the absence of the support he had previously relied upon from the tribal leaders around Sana'a, the confrontation between his forces and those of the Huthis ended within two days with his death.

The Saudi-led coalition

In February 2015, with the transitional government under house arrest, the UN Security Council passed resolution 2201. While acknowledging the inability of the government to function, it still called for the implementation of the GCC Agreement and did not put Yemen under Chapter 7 of the UN Charter, which would have authorised military intervention, thus leading to frustration and criticism from the GCC states. In March, having fled Aden which was being bombed and attacked by Saleh–Huthi forces, and before he even reached Riyadh, President Hadi appealed to the Gulf Cooperation Council for direct military assistance. Earlier discussions had been held between the Saudi ambassador and the transitional government in anticipation of the need for open intervention, so technical preparations had been made enabling the coalition to launch military strikes within hours. On 26 March 2015, the Saudi-led coalition launched the 'Decisive Storm' offensive with airstrikes, renaming it 'Restoring Hope' within a month. However, this optimistic name change was disavowed by subsequent events. Within four months, airstrikes were supplemented by the arrival of Emirati ground forces in Aden which enabled local resistance to liberate the city from the Saleh-Huthi military.

Since the war started, fighting on the ground has been by Yemeni and Sudanese troops, with a lesser involvement of the Emiratis and very limited presence of Saudis on major fronts. Air strikes by the coalition, mostly Saudi and Emirati have remained unchallenged as the Yemeni air force under Huthi/Saleh control was destroyed in the first hours of the fighting in 2015. Though in the course of the years, the Huthis have developed and expanded an increasingly strong and competent collection of UAVs (commonly described as drones) both for surveillance and attack. The missiles they have used have mostly been old Scud missiles bought by Saleh. Thanks to Iranian technical support, Huthi drones and missiles are increasingly being upgraded to extend their range and accuracy.

Officially named the Coalition to Restore Legitimacy in Yemen it is commonly described as the Saudi-led coalition, an accurate description. Other than Saudi Arabia, the only decision-making state is the United Arab Emirates (UAE). Originally including all the Gulf Cooperation Council states except Oman, Qatar was expelled from the coalition alongside other measures in the June 2017 internal GCC crisis initiated by the KSA and UAE; it successfully stayed out of it since the January 2021 al Ula agreement which formally ended this crisis. Other states officially participating included originally Egypt, Jordan, Morocco, Senegal and Sudan. Since then, Morocco has withdrawn (February 2019) and some other states, Jordan and Egypt in particular, had little effective involvement on the ground. Sudan has been particularly active with thousands of troops on the ground, and Eritrea has provided a base for the UAE on its soil. Yet others on whom the Saudis were relying, Pakistan in particular, declined to participate.

The Emiratis have mainly fielded commanders; after the September 2015 Saleh/Huthi attack in Marib which killed 50 Emiratis, few of their ground troops remained. They also deployed Colombian and other mercenaries under UAE command in 2015 and 2016, in addition to small groups of counter terrorist mercenaries (including US citizens) to kill off their enemies in the country, primarily Islahis (Roston, 2018). The Emiratis and Saudis deployed thousands of Sudanese troops on various fronts, though after the 'withdrawal' of the UAE in the summer of 2019, and following the 2019 revolution in Sudan, fewer Sudanese remain on the ground. Saudi ground military presence in Yemen has been mainly active in separating UAE supported southern separatist elements from those of Hadi's internationally recognised government and is discussed below in the context of the southern problem.

Following the Stockholm Agreement of December 2018, discussed further below, and in the absence of any military strategy likely to defeat the Huthis, in mid-2019 the UAE announced its formal withdrawal from military involvement in Yemen, effectively leaving Saudi Arabia in full charge of the Yemen war. By mid-2021 it still retained a small but significant military presence in strategic locations: in particular, Mukalla's airport in Riyan, the gas exporting port of Balhaf, a base in the interior of Shabwa, and on Perim

Island (known as Mayun in Yemen) which controls the Bab al Mandab where new air facilities were built in 2021. They also have a significant military, political and social presence in the Socotra archipelago.

The main military tool of the coalition has been aerial bombing, and the number of attacks has varied over the years according to both military and political priorities and international pressure to avoid civilian casualties. Completing three years of decreased airstrikes, 2019 saw a total of 1181 airstrikes. In 2020 there was an increase of 82% in bombings to 2155, more than half of which were in Jawf and Marib governorates, which are the main sites of the Huthi offensive starting in early 2020 and Marib remained the main battle ground throughout 2021. Between March 2015 and the end of 2021, thc Saudi-led coalition carried out 24 276 air raids, with up to 72 362 air strikes (Yemen Data Project, various dates).

Seven years of Huthi-Coalition fighting

Following Huthi gains north of Sana'a in Amran in 2014, culminating with the bloodless takeover of the capital in September 2014, military action extended in 2015 with the internationalisation of the war. Coalition forces, including mainly Yemeni ground troops liberated Aden by end of July. The coalition ground and air forces were active in the corridor north of Aden and west towards the Bab al Mandab, and also liberated much of the north east, particularly Marib governorate and thus controlled the main land border post with Saudi Arabia in the desert, at al Wadi'a. The coalition managed to recover a small area on the north-west of the country, thus cutting off the Huthis from the minor port of Midi, near the Saudi border in May 2017.

Elsewhere many fronts remained static from late 2015 in particular the Nehm front (a mere 60 km east of Sana'a city) which the Huthis took in early 2020 during their renewed offensive in the north-east, threatening the city of Marib, the last remaining stronghold of the IRG in the north-east of the former YAR's territory. In addition, Taiz city and governorate have been active frontlines, with little change, largely due to serious and frequent confrontations within the anti-Huthi forces. Al Baydha Governorate remains under Huthi control but has also been the site of ongoing fighting throughout the period.

The western Tihama coast remained under Huthi control throughout 2015 and 2016. After the failure of the Kuwait negotiations in 2016, coalition strategy was to take Hodeida city and its port, the main entry point for the vast majority of imports to Yemen and also the logistics hub both for commercial imports and for international humanitarian interventions despite the ongoing 'blockade'. It is essential to remember that since the beginning of the century Yemen has depended on imports for about 90% of its basic staples. In 2017, the UAE, with considerable help from Sudanese troops and local resistance forces, re-took the southern part of the Tihama including the port of Mokha. In 2018, thanks to the forces of Tareq Saleh (nephew of the former president) who worked with the coalition, progress was made and, despite international opposition, they attacked Hodeida starting what promised to be a long and bloody battle. After months of heavy fighting, the offensive was interrupted by the Stockholm Agreement, which brought about a shaky cease-fire in Hodeida city and governorate, significantly reducing the level of fighting until mid-2020 when it intensified again. As of late 2021, the Huthis hold most of Tihama including Hodeida city and are challenging the coalition forces along the southern part of the Red Sea coast, having rapidly progressed south following unilateral withdrawal of coalition forces. The latter are unlikely to abandon Mokha or the Bab al Mandab Strait which controls entrance to the Red Sea and the Suez Canal.

Breaking the longest lasting stalemate in the north east, in January 2020 the Huthis launched an offensive on the main fronts of Nehm and Marib. They took Jawf and parts of Marib governorate, reaching a new stalemate by the end of 2021 around its capital, Marib city, where the Saudi forces have demonstrated stronger commitment to supporting the Hadi government forces. It has been clear throughout 2021 that, despite considerable resistance from local and IRG forces, Saudi airstrikes are the main reason Marib city has not fallen, as the remaining distance separating Huthi positions from the city is open territory where these strikes are effective and there is no protection for the attacking forces.

Why are the Huthis successful despite the overwhelmingly stronger coalition forces?

Regardless of the details, Huthi technological capacity has significantly improved in the course of the war, most likely with some help from either Hezbollah or directly from Iran. Initially the Saleh–Huthi alliance used some of the large stocks of Scud missiles bought by Saleh in the previous two decades and launched dozens of attacks on Saudi territory, mostly in the southwestern neighbouring former Yemeni provinces of Jizan, Najran and Asir. By late 2017, they targeted more distant sites in Saudi Arabia and hit Riyadh airport for the first time in October 2017. This was followed by further strikes with the increased range of their missiles demonstrating access to advanced technology.

The Huthis also build drones: the first record of a Huthi drone strike was in February 2017 when they attacked a government-controlled site in Marib. Since then, their UAV capacity has improved and they hold almost yearly (2017, 2018, 2019, 2021) 'exhibitions' of their new 'home-grown' sophisticated weapons. They publicly display new, more sophisticated drones and missiles, using these occasions as propaganda tools. According to the Huthis' claims on the fifth anniversary of the beginning of the coalition offensive they fired 1067 missiles, 410 into Saudi Arabia and 630 against the internal enemy (Al-Manar, 2020). They launched 4116 drones, 669 of them carrying weapons, while 3490 were equipped with cameras for surveillance operations. Huthi anti-aircraft capacity has also improved. While some of their claims seem excessive, there is evidence that they downed four Apache helicopters, and one Saudi fighter aircraft, in addition to the Moroccan and Bahraini planes, which were downed early in the war. The Huthis themselves claim to having carried out 29 attacks on ships in the red Sea by 2021.

A very significant element explaining Huthi success is, of course, the disarray of their enemies. The Huthis who, regardless of internal differences, act as a well-organised and managed military unit, are facing a multiplicity of opponents, who cannot be simply described as Hadi's IRG supported by its international allies. Official IRG forces include those on the Marib front, manned by units associated with the military leader and Vice President Ali Mohsen al Ahmar, fighting alongside local tribes people. Elsewhere, IRG forces are aligned with the same leader as well as with President Hadi near his own home area in the Abyan midlands and Shabwa. In these governorates, the threats they face come as much from the STC and other southern separatists as from the Huthis. On the Tihama coast the forces of Tareq Saleh who does not recognise the IRG government but cooperates with it, fight in coordination with some southern troops. These, and the southern separatist STC forces closely follow orders from the UAE authorities. In the anti-Huthi units, divisions and rivalries play a major role in preventing them from facing the Huthis effectively; for example, UAE-supported forces consider Islahi-connected units to be greater enemies than the Huthis, and this includes the main military forces aligned with the IRG, particularly those under the command of Ali Mohsen. In addition, KSA support with military equipment and ammunition is limited by concern for corruption and the sale of materiel to the Huthis, leaving front line troops inadequately equipped.

The war in the South: the importance of southern separatism

International attention has primarily focused on developments in the original conflict between the IRG and the Huthis, but Yemenis in non Huthi-controlled areas have also suffered from the worsening tension between the government and southern separatists. As we saw in Chapter 1, the process of Yemeni unification in the early 1990s led to rapid disenchantment in the former PDRY, now known as the southern governorates. This simmered and grew over the decade following the defeat of the separatists in the 1994 civil war. Although no new southern political parties emerged in the following decade and southerners joined the national anti-Saleh and pro-reform uprisings of 2011, southern militants' commitment to a new governance at the national level was limited.

With the transitional regime introduced by the GCC Agreement in 2012, the importance of southerners in the new regime should have contributed towards reconciliation, as both the president and the prime minister were southerners. Despite the disproportionate representation of southerners in the NDC (56% by comparison with their being about 30% of the nation's population), the rejection of participation by some of the more extreme southern factions and the divisions among southern participants meant that this issue, alongside that of the Huthis, remained unsolved by the NDC.

As mentioned earlier, the first months of the internationalised war involved heavy fighting in Aden, appointed the temporary capital by Hadi in February 2015. The Hadi government never really settled into Aden: most ministries had left their civil service staff behind in Sana'a where they continued to operate the administration, first under Huthi–Saleh and from 2018 onwards under exclusively Huthi control. Many IRG ministers were rarely present in Aden, in rented accommodation and with minimal staff. The main sovereign ministries, except for the Interior, mostly operated out of Riyadh.

Throughout the liberated areas, local authorities of one kind or another ran whatever administrations there were, as funding was primarily provided by outsiders, particularly after the 'transfer' of the Central Bank to Aden in September 2016 (discussed in the next chapter). Aden remains a city suffering insecurity and terrorist attacks to a greater extent than elsewhere. Mukalla, the capital of Hadhramaut governorate, was 'occupied' and managed by the jihadi al Qaeda in the Arabian Peninsula (AQAP) for about a year starting in mid-2015 but was 'liberated' by agreement.

A quick look at a historical political map helps in understanding some of the issues relevant to the South and needs to be recalled here: the South was highly fragmented under British rule and earlier (see Chapter 1), and only united as a centralised state under the PDRY. Since unification and particularly since the war started, regional differences within that area have increased, socially, administratively, and militarily. War-related fighting has been concentrated on Aden and other locales contested for one or another reason. Hadhramaut, although having significant social and economic divergences between the coastal and the interior areas, retains a certain unity as a cultural entity, while Shabwa has been largely divided between its western part, more fragmented and socially similar to its neighbouring areas and its less populated and more desert-like east, closer to Hadhramaut. Both these governorates have significant natural resources which the rival political factions want to control.

The tribes and leaders of Abyan and Lahej are very fragmented and have been involved in major conflicts opposing each other during the British and PDRY periods which are reflected in post-2015 struggles. The southern part of Dhala' Governorate was part of Lahej until that governorate was formed in 1998 and separatist demands only focus on that part of the governorate. The remote governorate of al-Mahra, with a very small population, has only recently been linked by asphalted roads to the rest of the country. It has its own culture and its people are more closely connected to Socotra, Oman, the UAE and Saudi Arabia, than to Sana'a or Aden. Their relationships are cultural, economic, and political; for example, Saudi Arabia has issued passports to many leading tribesmen for many decades, while others had access to UAE passports. Issues of social strata and class formation (discussed in the introduction) also play a role.

In the absence of any administration, let alone a competent one, frustration has grown in the South in the past decade. Since 2015 the coalition was initially represented by a strong UAE military presence. After 2018 both the

UAE and Saudi Arabia have been involved in financing the government and a range of attempted efforts at restoring the physical infrastructure of the city of Aden and beyond.

When, on 27 April 2017, President Hadi dismissed two leading separatists, Minister without Portfolio Hani bin Breik, a well-known Salafi leader, and Governor of Aden Aydaroos al Zubaydi, they promptly, on 4 May, set up the Southern Transitional Council (STC).[6] Other than stating its objective to struggle to 'reinstate the southern state', the announcement was remarkably lacking in a specific programme. It merely blamed the IRG for all ills and claimed allegiance to the regional coalition states, calling for Saudi Arabia and the UAE to support its demand for southern independence. Two other points of interest: first al Zubaydi's claim to leadership is based on his own self-appointment and his position is legitimised by himself alone. Second it admits the existence of other southern movements, calling on Hirak (the generic name for southern separatist movements) to work with it, though its behaviour since then clearly negates this recognition.

The STC is only one of many separatist groups in southern Yemen. Since its creation in 2017, it has achieved prominence thanks to financial and diplomatic support from the UAE. Its offices in Europe and beyond have given it an international public presence which explain a recognition unrelated to its actual presence on the ground. In addition to financing the STC's diplomatic efforts and hosting its leaders' families and associates, the UAE has recruited, trained, deployed and financed the STC's military forces. They are 'Security Belts' in the western governorates and 'Elite forces' in the east, mostly under Salafi leadership; their allegiance to the UAE is largely opportunistic.

From day one, the STC's main enemy has been President Hadi's internationally recognised government. The roots of their mutual hostility are found in earlier internal southern conflicts, in particular the January 1986 'events'. At that time the 'winning' faction involved people from Dhala'/Lahej, including the father of one of its main leaders, and the losing faction included current President Hadi and others from Abyan/Shabwa. Two major confrontations have taken place in Aden and surroundings between the STC and the Hadi government, the first in January 2018 in Aden and the second, decisive one, in August 2019. The August 2019 confrontation resulted in the expulsion of government forces and officials from Aden. Taking place at a time when the UAE had 'withdrawn' from Yemen (while officially continuing as members of the Saudi-led coalition), this forced the Saudi authorities to take full responsibility for addressing this crisis. The Saudi government immediately started mediation efforts aimed at bringing about a reconciliation between the two fighting groups. After months of negotiations, the Riyadh agreement was signed on 5 November 2019, in the presence of the crown princes of both the UAE and Saudi Arabia. This is significant insofar as it is the only evidence of UAE support to the Saudi efforts.

Just as the Stockholm agreement was intended to be a first step towards ending the conflict with the Huthis, the Riyadh agreement was designed to restore reasonable relations and cooperation between the Yemeni members of the coalition and to be implemented within two months of signature. Its main clauses included the return of the government to Aden, the redeployment of most military forces away from Aden under the supervision of Saudi Arabia, with a few government forces returning to guard the presidential compound, i.e. primarily removing STC forces from the city and enabling the government to operate there. A new slimmed down government was to be formed, with half its ministers from the South (at a time when the existing government already had more than 50% southern membership). Throughout 2020, there was no progress in implementation, but a new government was finally announced in December 2020. The number and importance of ministers' presence in Aden depends on the vagaries of the complex relationship between the KSA, the UAE, the IRG and STC as well as the level of dissatisfaction of the population with the lack of services and difficult living conditions in the city. Overall, IRG presence in Aden is on sufferance from the STC which effectively controls the city as of 2021.

The intervening period had been one of frequent serious military clashes between the two sides, in which the UAE has, on occasion, openly supported the STC forces. Clashes were mostly west of Aden in Lahej, and eastwards in coastal Abyan and Shabwa governorates, with the IRG retaining control of significant areas, and leaving the STC with only the first 60 or so km of the coast east of Aden under its control. Failure to control Shabwa is a major constraint for the STC's ambitions. STC presence further east is even more tenuous end 2021.[7] The STC president's abortive declaration of 'self-rule' on 25 April 2020, following universal internal (from most governors) and international negative response, was rescinded later in the year. However, even after the formation of the government, he frequently repeats his earlier claims that southern independence is his main objective, alongside assertions of representing the whole South (South 24, 2020; Southern Transitional Council, 2019), assertions which are disproved by the situation on the ground in most of the southern governorates.

Aden remains the focus of conflict thanks to its symbolic importance as the temporary capital, which is particularly important for the coalition as, without a government there, Hadi's internationally recognised government is no more than a government in exile. For the STC, Aden is also important as a stronghold, the main city with a large population, port and significant economic infrastructure, in addition to being the historic capital of the South. Living conditions remained dire at the best of times and the population has gradually become frustrated at STC failure to provide security or basic services, regularly manifested through street demonstrations which the STC represses with force.

In the early 2020s, the rivalry between the IRG and the STC remains a very live issue which has a profound impact on the overall military situation. The UAE-backed STC forces challenge to the IRG weaken the anti-Huthi front, effectively creating a situation where, objectively, they are cooperating with the Huthis against the IRG. It is also relevant beyond Yemen, insofar as it reflects increasing tensions between Saudi Arabia and the UAE whose long-term relationship has been marked by a rivalry which was eclipsed for a few years by the myth of the great relationship between MBS and MBZ. This is discussed further in Chapter 4.

UN mediation and internationally sponsored negotiations

Ever since the uprising of 2011, the UN has had a series of Special Envoys for Yemen, who initially tried to ensure a peaceful transition, then tried to prevent the outbreak of war and, since 2015, worked to re-establish peace. Their work has been frustrating and marked by lack of success, as can be seen by the sequence of their activities.[8]

Within weeks of the coalition's initial offensive, the United Nations Security Council (UNSC) approved Resolution 2216 which, in late 2021, remained the underpinning legal authority for UN peace efforts, constraining them. Under Chapter VII of the UN Charter, it

> demands that the Houthis immediately and unconditionally a) end the use of violence, b) withdraw their forces from all areas they have seized, including the capital Sana'a, c) relinquish all additional arms seized from military and security institutions, including missiles systems, d) cease all actions that are exclusively within the authority of the legitimate government of Yemen, e) refrain from any provocation or threats to neighboring states, including through acquiring surface-surface missiles, and stockpiling weapons in any bordering territory of a neighboring State. …
>
> (UNSC, 2021, p. 3)

It also established an arms embargo against the Huthis. In plain English, it demanded Huthi complete surrender. Within months, let alone seven years later, its demands were completely unrealistic, as there is no reason to even begin to think that the Huthis, having taken and maintained control over two thirds of Yemen's population, its capital, main port and best watered areas, would agree to such terms.

Why it has not been replaced by a resolution more aligned with reality on the ground is a legitimate and important question. The main reasons are first that it explicitly states the legitimacy of President Hadi and therefore, given other aspects of the situation, is really the only legal justification for him to remain in position, despite his absence from the country and his government's extremely limited authority within Yemen. It also endorses the Saudi-led coalition's military actions, and is therefore supported by Saudi Arabia whose legitimacy to intervene might be challenged outside of this resolution. Finally, the 'pen-holder' for Yemen at the UNSC is the UK, whose international policy priorities are to ensure continued good relations with GCC states, whose financial investments are expected to help the UK economy post-Brexit.

A couple of short conferences in Switzerland were held in 2015, when the UN Special Envoy Ismail Ould al Sheikh successfully brought together the

IRG and the Huthis but nothing of substance emerged. This was followed by three months of meetings held in Kuwait between April and August 2016 which failed to achieve an agreement due to the unwillingness of the Yemeni parties to compromise, regardless of some significant concessions by Saudi Arabia.

No meetings could be organised between the two parties for the following two years; an attempt in September 2018 by the third special envoy, the Briton Martin Griffiths, simply failed to happen as he had not taken the measures necessary to ensure that the Huthis would be able to travel safely there and back, not an irrelevant issue as it had taken them three months to get home after the Kuwait talks. The deadlock was broken following a completely unexpected event, the assassination in Istanbul of Saudi journalist, Jamal Khashoqji on 2 October. International pressure from the US and the UN combined with international civil society pressure due to the threat of impending famine throughout the country forced the Saudis to actively encourage the IRG to take a more flexible attitude.

Under UN sponsorship, the meeting held in December 2018 in Sweden, produced the Stockholm Agreement. It is composed of three documents: the weakest of all concerns Taiz where the parties merely agreed to form a committee including representatives of civil society, which should meet and establish its terms of reference. Nothing had happened by late 2021.

The second concerns the exchange of prisoners. Agreed in principle prior to Stockholm, lists of 16 000 prisoners were handed over in Stockholm and the exchange was to be implemented by the ICRC, which was to be given only ten days in which to interview and arrange the releases starting on 21 January 2019, while the two sides had 40 days to verify the lists. Highly ambitious in scope given the numbers involved, no prisoners were released under its auspices by spring 2020, though a new agreement, covering 1000 prisoners was made in late April 2020. Finally, in mid-October 2020, 1080 prisoners from both sides were freed (including some Saudi and Sudanese citizens) leaving the remaining thousands awaiting further UN progress on the issue (UN Security Council, 2020). It is worth noting that hundreds of prisoners from both sides have been released, entirely outside the UN process, through a series of localised agreements negotiated by tribal and other respected community leaders in different sites at different times in recent years.

The third element of the Stockholm Agreement concerns Hodeida governorate and its ports. It is the only one which has had a limited impact. It led to the formation of the United Nations Mission to support the Hodeida Agreement (UNMHA) on 16 January 2019 through UNSC Resolution 2452, which includes the deployment of international monitors. Having got through two leaders in a few months, a third, more compliant Indian general was appointed in September 2019, Lieutenant General (retired) Abhijit Guha of India as the Chair of the Redeployment Coordination Committee (RCC) and Head of the UNMHA. Between its establishment and mid-2020, beyond a reasonably effective cease-fire in the city, it achieved little other than approving the 'unilateral withdrawal' of Huthi forces from the ports, a move which was loudly condemned by the government who correctly considered it a mere 'change of uniforms' by the Huthi authorities. A sniper attack in March 2020 wounded a government liaison officer, leading to the government withdrawing from the mission. His death a month later provoked recriminations from the IRG which blamed the UN for failure to medivac him. Problems in Hodeida city and governorate have increased again since mid-2020, with intermittent fighting and continuing stalemate.

By the time he finally quit the position in June 2021, Special Envoy Griffiths had spent more than a year trying to get the Huthis and the IRG to sign a 'joint declaration' whose substance was basically to cease fighting and resume negotiations. Initiated as part of the UN Secretary General's appeal for all fighting to stop throughout the world in order to focus on the Covid-19 pandemic, this appeal had little impact in Yemen. Griffiths' tenure of the position was even less effective than those of his predecessors, lacking any notable achievement, though the constraints imposed by UN procedures and the resolution certainly bore some share of responsibility.

In September 2021, a fourth special envoy, Hans Grundberg, took up the position, starting with a few advantages: his nationality as a Swede, coming from a neutral country; his former position as EU ambassador to Yemen, which ensured detailed knowledge of the complexities of the situation; and his ability to call upon the active support of the EU and its member states, also perceived positively by Yemenis. In addition, he started work shortly after the USA's final debacle in Afghanistan simultaneously reduced confidence in the US from coalition partners and, conversely increased the credibility and potential influence of European states in the region, and consequently in Yemen.

Despite these advantages, he has a particularly difficult task ahead, and will need all the support he can summon, both at the UN and in the region. For the UN to achieve any progress, the first step is to replace UNSC 2216 by a more realistic resolution recognising reality in Yemen: first the fact that the Huthis control two thirds of the country's population, are on the offensive and therefore will not withdraw to their pre-2014 positions and second, by contrast, that Hadi's internationally recognised government represents very few people and controls little of the territory.

Creating a delegation to face the Huthis at the negotiating table would also help. Handing over Yemen to the Huthis would be a disaster for Yemenis, but ignoring their importance is also unfeasible. Should Grundberg be able to form a credible and serious delegation to deal with the Huthis, and armed with a new resolution, success would depend first on willingness of the Huthis to negotiate (which cannot be assumed) and second on sufficient pressure from the international community at large on the KSA and UAE.

This is where the Biden administration in the US could contribute: despite being weakened by its undignified withdrawal from Afghanistan, it has taken some positive measures in Yemen: removing the Huthis from the Trump administration's last-minute declaration including the Huthis in the US's list of Foreign Terrorist Organisations was obviously welcome, although many considered that this could have been achieved in exchange for some concession, and that it wasted the opportunity. Explicit US support for a new UNSC resolution would be an important contribution complementing the appointment of its own special envoy, an experienced diplomat, who had little impact during the first months of his tenure. The decision to stop supplying offensive weapons to the KSA was also largely a symbolic statement which has not been followed by action, given the ambiguity of the term 'offensive'.

The impact of the war: starvation and human rights

The war's impact on the population has been devastating. Starting from an already high poverty level of half the population prior to the war, the percentage and absolute figures have increased exponentially in the first seven years of this war. Reliable figures are unavailable, partly due to the absence of accurate baseline information and the weak statistical structures in the country, reliance on partial localised and mostly qualitative surveys, and of course on the political objectives of the different parties involved, Yemeni belligerents, and international humanitarians, who see advantages in either increasing or decreasing any figures. Hence figures presented here must be treated as mainly indicative of the situation, rather than as statistically valid data.

While there has been notable international media and other attention to the damage caused by direct military intervention, mainly the coalition's 23 470 bombing raids, said to have caused more than 18 000 civilian casualties between March 2015 and August 2021, far more people are dying from starvation-related diseases than from direct military activity, probably close to 377 000. The UN system has not declared a famine in Yemen for three main reasons: first, the fact that evidence is lacking, second technical statistical requirements for such a declaration are impossible to obtain in the country and, in any case, people rarely die directly from hunger, but usually from various diseases caused by malnutrition. Third, it would demonstrate that the UN system and its multiple funders have all failed to prevent it: of the USD 17.5 billion provided for humanitarian support between 2015 and 2020, 28% came from the USA, 16% from the KSA, and 12% from the UK. The use of starvation as a military tool has been analysed by Mundy (2018) and more recently in a lengthy and detailed report by Mwatana and Global Rights Compliance (2021).

According to UN humanitarian agencies, in 2021, 20.7 million Yemenis are in need of humanitarian assistance of one kind or another, representing two thirds of the country's population, including 16 million who are food insecure, i.e. hungry and malnourished in plain English. The World Food Programme, which receives the highest percentage of humanitarian funds, in its best period in recent years, reached 13 million of them, but in most months between 8 and 10 million, i.e. approximately half of them. By August 2021, it assessed that 5.6 million people were in emergency situation, i.e. 'one step away from famine'. Whether famine is an appropriate word to describe the Yemeni humanitarian crisis is debatable; what is clear is that the billions spent on humanitarian assistance have failed to significantly impact the crisis which continues to worsen raising questions about the effectiveness of the strategies and approaches used to address it.

The fundamental reasons for this complete failure to effectively address the most basic human right to food and water necessary for decent living conditions are numerous and mostly war related: first and foremost, the blockade of Hodeida and other Red Sea ports, reducing the amount of food and fuel imported, both essential to providing the population with their needs; second, the collapse of the economy and the very occasional payment of (already inadequate) salaries to about 1.2 million civil service staff, mostly teachers and medical personnel, who have about 6 million dependents between them; third, increasingly high prices, due to rising purchase and transport costs, to which must be added the multiplicity of charges from the various 'authorities' encountered between landing and the ultimate beneficiaries.

The Humanitarian situation has attracted reasonable media and other attention. By contrast the constant and egregious attacks on other human rights receive less attention despite the determined efforts of Yemeni human rights defenders such as Mwatana, the Mothers of Abductees association, as well as international organisations such as Human Rights Watch and Amnesty International. In a summary of the main breaches of international humanitarian law on the sixth anniversary of the beginning of the international involvement, in March 2021, Mwatana summarised the list of these breaches, including details of those committed by the coalition, the IRG, UAE-backed separatist forces, as well as Ansar Allah (Mwatana, 2021). Other than damage by airstrikes which only involved the Saudi-led coalition, all parties are involved in a depressingly familiar and terrifying series of breaches of international human rights law, let alone failing to manifest any sign of basic human compassion. The list includes destruction of civilian infrastructure (roads, bridges, schools and medical facilities), direct restrictions to the distribution of humanitarian supplies and access to those in need, recruitment and use of children in military action, arbitrary detentions and enforced disappearances as well as torture of those held.

Conclusion

Politically, the country is now fragmented. The Huthis control about a third of the land and two thirds of the population, where they rule with an iron fist, arresting and ill-treating any dissidents, however mild their criticism, and impose social norms fitting into their retrograde interpretation of Islam. This is primarily focused on women whose movements and dress are restricted and on youth who are actively indoctrinated through changes in the educational programmes. The rest of the country is under a wide range of local authorities, with little involvement from an internationally recognised government which has very little influence and does not even ensure that civil servants receive their salaries, let alone issue new laws and regulations or attempt to enforce existing ones. As for norms, these differ according to the identity and ideology of locally powerful individuals. One thing is clear, there is little effort to strengthen civil and human rights, and the anti-Huthi forces, particularly the STC, also oppress the population. Both UAE and KSA forces have been credibly accused of ill-treatment and arbitrary detention of even mild dissenters.

What is clear from this chapter is that Yemenis have failed to develop a political system able to deal peacefully and by negotiations or elections to address political differences or promote political programmes. Most political organisations and military groups are aligned with one or another rival elite, rather than offering Yemenis socio-economic and political programmes to address their problems. None of them shows concern for the difficulties the population faces daily. The YSP comes closer than many to having a political programme responding to socio-economic constraints, but even then, it fails to propose policies which would attract substantial support and their formulations and presentation are weak. Moreover, it operates in a hostile political and media environment. Other parties are now increasingly sectarian, as is the case of the small *sada* parties, while the two largest are closely aligned with rival factions of the ruling elites on a clientelist basis, regardless of rhetoric. Their membership is usually based on the search for benefits, rather than on ideological commitment.

Yemen's political elites have shown neither commitment nor concern for the survival and living conditions of the majority of Yemenis who have been suffering worsening poverty, hunger and disease since the war started. Leaders' hollow appeals to 'the great Yemeni people' have usually preceded actions which have demonstrated an insulting thorough disregard for their citizens.

When the full-scale internationalised war started in 2015, few thought it would last so long or be so destructive. It has demonstrated a number of important facts: first, that the Saudi regime, regardless of the billions spent on purchasing advanced weaponry and training, is unable to defeat an army of ill-equipped but determined and militarily skilled men. Second, it has raised questions about the relationship between two close allies, Saudi Arabia and the UAE, whose objectives are increasingly diverging. Third and most importantly, political developments since Yemen united have led to increasingly bitter and deep fragmentation, not only between the north and the south, but also within both of these previous separate states, divisions increasingly based on creed, social origins, and economic interests. Politics have been an important element of this, but economic policies have played an equally, possibly more important, role and are discussed in the next chapter.

Peace will eventually return to Yemen. Academic research has found that civil wars rarely last more than a decade, leaving Yemenis to continue suffering for a while yet. But they also rarely end with solutions which significantly improve living conditions for the population at large, thus suggesting a difficult future for the people searching for better lives. International intervention in Yemen, whether by the states directly involved in the coalition, or other members of the international community, including the UN have certainly failed in the objective of creating the 'new' Yemen promised in 2011, assuming this meant greater equity, less corruption and the basic necessities for a decent social and economic life.

Notes

1 Yemenis argue about whether the war started in 2014 or 2015. For a brief summary of this debate see Bonnefoy (2021, p. 22).
2 Whose predecessor, the 'United Political Organisation, the National Front' (UPONF), integrated the Baath and Communist parties in October 1975, see Lackner (1985), pp. 70–73.
3 See Lackner (1985), (2017a) and Brehony (2011) for details of the politics of the PDRY period.
4 'Afghans' was the term used to describe the guerrillas who came back to Yemen after 1989, including mostly Yemenis but also some other Arabs who were not welcome in their own countries.
5 Yemen had 'change squares' where people met as the 'liberation square' in Sana'a had been occupied early on by Saleh supporters who were firmly entrenched there.
6 For further information on the STC, see https://stc-eu.org/en/sueduebergangsrat/.
7 On these, see Al-Hamdani and Lackner (2020).
8 Details of the role of the UN are discussed in Helen Lackner (2020d).

3 Constraints on economic development

Increased poverty and the worsening livelihoods for the majority of the population have, as we have seen, significantly contributed to instability and conflict in Yemen. Although there is evidence that the poorest are rarely those who initiate uprisings, the deterioration of living standards and in particular reduced hope of improvements from one generation to the next, alongside the collapse of the already small middle class in Yemen, were probably the strongest factors motivating the 2011 uprisings as well as a major cause of the war.

There is no doubt that the country's endowment in natural resources is limited, but other countries have overcome similar constraints. Yemen's entry into the world economy took place when globalisation was hostile to the emergence of national low or medium technology industrial enterprises. In the absence of protectionist measures, prevented by free trade rules imposed by Yemen's international 'partners', local manufactured products were unable to compete with cheap imports primarily from East Asia. While this international context must be taken into consideration in analysing the country's failure to develop an economy providing employment for its population, examination of its resources and potential indicates that different economic policies could have ensured a significantly better standard of living for the population as a whole. This chapter examines these different factors and the role they play in the ongoing crisis, all of them issues which will remain active and relevant once the current war ends.

The country's natural endowment and climate change

Yemen has few natural resources compared to many other states: in addition to its limited hydrocarbons there are other minerals, none of which has yet demonstrated significant economic potential, thus limiting income-generating possibilities for labour and investors alike. The country's population continues to grow at a high rate close to 3% per annum, which means that its population doubles in about 20 years, putting even more pressure on its resources. In 1990, Yemen had a population of 12 million people, in 2022 it is about 30 million. In this period, natural resources and the economic base have not

DOI: 10.4324/9780429059315-4

increased. Although urbanisation has grown, Yemen remains a country where 70% of the people live in rural areas, mostly in its 37 000 small villages and settlements dispersed in a mostly mountainous terrain. In addition to the obvious need for economic diversification due to the worsened pressure on natural resources, climate change has significant impact on the situation.

Climate change

In Yemen, climate change has now been a reality for well over a decade. 'Unprecedented', 'once in a century', 'exceptional', catastrophic climate events have been taking place routinely every few years since the beginning of the century. In 2015 two cyclones, Chapala and Megh, hit Yemen within a week and the trend has continued since, with two further cyclones, Sagar and Mekunu, in 2018 and the floods of 2020 and 2021. Drought and floods have become the norm and reduce agricultural incomes. Most importantly, the sequence of floods and violent downpours is depleting aquifers and already forcing people to leave their villages and migrate to areas which still have water (Lackner, 2020c). Although these migrations start as temporary measures with people returning once their local wells have filled, over time they become permanent and villages are abandoned, thus causing additional pressure on available resources and encouraging social tension in their locations of resettlement.

Droughts are interspersed with violent downpours causing increasingly frequent destructive floods. In the past, destructive flooding was occasional and only usually affected a single area but, in both 2020 and 2021, a series of devastating floods affected distant and agro-ecologically unrelated sites, including three of Yemen's major cities. Floods do not compensate for droughts: the sudden and violent downpours hitting parched soils do not infiltrate and replenish aquifers, instead they destroy water management structures, wash good soils away, destroy terraces, leaving barren rocks. Locust swarms have been a regular occurrence for centuries, but are worsening, and in 2019 and 2020 the plague of locusts has been particularly destructive from East Africa to South Asia; Yemen is one of their feeding and breeding grounds on the way.

Forecasts are, by definition, unproven but important nonetheless. The 2010 World Bank forecast for climate change in Yemen remains valid a decade later, and no update has been published. It has three main scenarios for Yemen, the most likely being 'hot and dry' and 'warm and wet'. Regardless of which actually materialises, 'Yemen will be getting warmer, most likely at a faster rate than the global average … there will be more variability of rainfall patterns within years [and] there will probably be an increased frequency of intense rainfall events and therefore possibly an increased risk of floods' (World Bank, 2010, p. 20). Overall, temperatures in Yemen have increased by 1.8°C in the past 50 years and there has been a decrease of 9% in total annual precipitation during this period, the latter unevenly distributed to the detriment of the areas which depend on rain-fed agriculture. With a wide range of regional variations, forecast temperature rises average 2.3°C with increased durations of heat waves. The expected increase in rainfall and temperatures in the temperate highland zone will not reduce the country's dependence on imports of basic staples.

In addition to the water issues discussed below, desertification and rising sea levels are among the most significant problems resulting from climate change. Rising sea levels will affect living conditions for millions: three of Yemen's major cities (Hodeida, Aden and Mukalla), important smaller towns (such as Shihr, Mokha, Ahwar), as well as hundreds of small fishing villages along the 1900 km of the country's coast, will have to develop adaptation strategies. In addition to the infrastructure issues involved, saline intrusion in coastal aquifers from rising sea levels and over-exploitation of the local aquifers are reducing availability of both domestic and agricultural water along both the Red and Arabian Sea coastal plains. Desertification is reducing agricultural and pasture lands by an average of about 3-5% per annum, a severe problem in a country whose agricultural land is already in such short supply (World Bank, 2012, 79; Kingdom of the Netherlands, 2019).

Water[1]

Alongside the other countries in the Arabian Peninsula, Yemen lacks permanent rivers reaching the sea. However, with the exception of south-west Saudi Arabia, it is the only country in the Arabian Peninsula where some areas receive sufficient rainfall to enable rain-fed agriculture. The country benefits from monsoon rains thanks to its mountain ranges in the west, which rise to 3000 m altitude and trap the clouds and humidity from the Red Sea. Although most of the country has less than 50 mm rainfall per annum, some highland areas have more than 250 mm, and a few receive more than 800 mm. Therefore the mountainous areas have the highest population density and enable rain-fed cultivation of staple drought-resistant crops like sorghum and millet, thanks to generations of terracing and careful management of the steep slopes. However, these are also areas where the geological structures do not facilitate long-term retention of ground water, due to the 'basement complex'.

Water scarcity is a fundamental constraint to Yemen's economy. Annual water extraction pre-war was vastly greater than its renewable supply: 3.5 billion cubic meters (bcm) with 2.1 bcm recharge, so one third of the water extracted comes from non-renewable fossil aquifers. While during the fighting there may have been some reduction in pumping due to fuel shortages and higher prices, the overall picture remains largely unchanged, particularly as solar pumps are increasingly replacing both diesel and electric ones for shallow as well as deep agricultural wells (Aklan and Lackner, 2021).

The World Bank estimated in 2010 that Yemen's groundwater reserves were likely to be depleted by about 2040, though predictions for depletion have changed over the decades. Per-capita water availability has dropped steadily in past decades as known available resources have remained static, if not diminished, while population growth has continued. In 2014, per-capita availability was as low as 81 m^3, expected to drop further to 55 m^3 by 2031. International standards call for 1000 m^3 per capita for all needs, including agriculture, while the less demanding Falkenmark indicator establishes absolute water scarcity below 500 m^3 per capita. Yemen's conditions are way below either level.

These absolute figures need to be interpreted with care: water management is by far the country's major long-term problem, threatening its very existence, but the situation varies from one area to the next and the distribution of the aquifers is the reverse of that of population density. Regional variations in water availability mean that, if most of the country is to remain habitable, water management policies have to be both firm and sophisticated to ensure that immediate human and livestock needs are prioritised. Water policies will also have to take into consideration the different availability and access conditions prevailing in each area, confirming that, like most other things, water management depends on politics. Social sensitivities must also be taken into consideration, resulting from historical groupings and allegiances, but it is likely that further internal forced population movements will be unavoidable.

In Yemen as in many other countries it is estimated that 90% of water is used in agriculture. The introduction of pump irrigation in the twentieth century enabled both a significant increase of population and agriculture in areas which were previously only suitable for pastoralism and long-distance trade. Rain-fed agriculture used to be dominant, particularly in the western highlands and other mountainous areas, supplemented by spate irrigation whenever seasonal water flowed in the wadi beds, and could be diverted to the fields through sophisticated networks of channels. Depending on the size of the flood and the fields, these could be smaller or larger traditional structures, all needing annual maintenance. In recent decades, thanks to pumping, both shallow and deep well irrigation contributed to the water crisis: the increase in well-irrigated surfaces has been impressive, from 37 000 ha in the 1970s to more than 400 000 ha in the 2000s. This has taken place at the expense of the sustainability of the aquifers and also worsened social inequality, helping to explain both the worsening water and political crises. During the same period, as irrigated areas increased by a factor of 15, rain-fed agriculture declined by 30% (Lackner, 2019b, 2021c).

Without water, no life; hence access to domestic water is the priority. A small percentage of agricultural water is actually used for domestic purposes by rural families. While some domestic rural water projects have their own sources and include storage and distribution networks, millions of households still obtain their domestic and drinking water from shallow wells, springs, cisterns, and agricultural irrigation pumps, much of which of course is polluted to varying degrees. Women and children collect and carry it for significant distances, usually up steep slopes, on their heads or by donkeys in 20 l jerry cans. In locations where the water is piped to the houses, sanitation systems are usually absent, largely because the organisation responsible for water supply, the General Authority for Water Supply and Sanitation (GARWSS) has only recently become involved in sanitation issues, mostly just on paper. By 2015, before war-related destruction, 68% of all Yemenis, but only 55% of rural Yemenis had access to 'improved' water, however this definition is very generous, and includes water from shallow wells and springs which has merely not been directly polluted by contaminants before being drawn (ESCWA, 2021; Dorte, 2012, pp. 290–291).

Urban water supplies have been problematic for decades. Sana'a has often been described as the first world capital likely to run out of water, and only 40% of its households are connected to the urban network. Since the beginning of this century, authorities decided not to connect some neighbourhoods (including wealthy residential ones such as Attan) to the network. Thus, in Sana'a and elsewhere in the country, the majority of households are dependent on private sector tanker supplies either for their entire supply or as a supplement to the official network. The Sana'a basin is both an agricultural area for high value crops such as *qat* and grapes and the source of water for the country's rapidly growing capital: extraction is estimated at five times recharge (270 million m^3 against 51 million m^3). Prospects are grim.

By comparison, the crisis has been far deeper in Taiz since the 1990s and presents the most blatant example of the type of problems likely to develop elsewhere in the country. There, the 40% or so households connected to the municipal network have been getting water once every 30 to 60 days in the past three decades, despite a series of foreign-funded projects. The projects failed both to ensure adequate supplies to the city and to acceptably manage the rural–urban transfers of water. Competition between rural and urban needs remains a fundamental issue, occasionally turning into armed conflicts (Lackner, 2019b, pp. 221–223). A further example of 'mismanagement' is the issue of fruit production in the Tihama: in 'midstream wadi Zabid, [banana cultivation] increased from 20 ha in 1980 to 3500 ha in 2000, … at the expense of sustainable use of groundwater resources as the number of drilling wells … increased by more than five times between 1987 and 2008, from about 2421 to 12,339 wells' (al-Qubatee et al., 2019, p. 811).

At the current rates of extraction, it is likely that a number of aquifers will be depleted by the end of the 2020s. In the south this concerns the most important spate-irrigated agricultural areas of Wadis Tuban (Lahej Governorate) and Bana (Abyan Governorate), while in the north, the most sensitive to this depletion are the Sana'a and Sa'ada aquifers, the latter the area where the Huthi political and military movement started.

Yemen's lasting water crisis must be addressed as a matter of urgency to ensure that people throughout the country have access to their basic human right of potable and domestic water. Without the firm implementation of policies to ensure this, forced migration of thousands, later millions, will have a dreadful social and political impact within the country, and eventually force people out of Yemen, heading for neighbours Saudi Arabia, Oman and the UAE, regardless of physical or indeed military efforts to prevent such movements.

Hydrocarbons

Yemen joined the oil-producing club in the Arabian Peninsula very late and, although the most populated state in the region, it is by far the smallest producer with the lowest known reserves of both oil and gas. After decades of unmet hopes, the first commercially viable oil discoveries were made in the YAR in Marib in 1984, promptly exploited for export by the US company Hunt, followed by Russian discoveries in nearby Shabwa in the PDRY in 1987 (which indirectly led to unification, see Chapter 1) and finally in the RoY in Hadhramaut in 1991. Quantities remained modest, with peak production reached in 2001 with 400 000 b/d (barrels/day). Since then, it declined to about 150 000 b/d by the time the current war started in 2015, and reserves are close to exhaustion, hence a revival of significant oil production and exports is highly unlikely short of major equally unlikely discoveries. The country has been surveyed in detail and the world is now turning away from hydrocarbons. After almost complete collapse of oil exports in the first years of the war, production restarted, reaching 17.5 million barrels for the whole year in 2019 (i.e. less than two days of production in Saudi Arabia), 14.2 million barrels of which were exported. Compared to 2014, a year when production was 'normal' due to declining oil reserves, the oil and gas sector suffered a contraction of 80% by end of 2019 (Republic of Yemen, Ministry of Planning and International Cooperation, 2020a, p. 2), a blow to the state's resources as hydrocarbon exports covered close to 60% of public revenues.

With diminishing oil production and small reserves, much hope rested on its replacement by gas exports. Significant separate gas reserves were found in 2000 in the Marib-Jawf field. It took time to organise production and in particular to finance and construct the necessary infrastructure. Reserves estimated at 10 trillion cubic feet are significant, but the cost of constructing the LNG terminal in Balhaf, pipeline and all other facilities, amounted to USD 4.5 billion, ensuring that state income from gas remains low. Yemen LNG is Yemen's largest economic enterprise, and primarily foreign owned. The French Total company holds a 39.62% share, the state-owned company Yemen Gas Company (16.73%), Hunt Oil Company (17.22%), SK Energy (9.55%), Korea Gas Corporation (6%), Hyundai Corporation (5.88%), and GASSP1 (5%) (Yemen LNG website). Total production capacity will reach 6.7 million tons of LNG per year (mt/y), a quantity which was not reached prior to the company closing down for *force majeure* in 2015. Restarting its operations post-conflict as well as the likely income accruing to Yemen will depend on a number of factors including stability and control of the pipeline and Balhaf terminal by the Yemeni state, as well as the cost of repair to the facilities, in addition to political agreements between the different owners of the Yemen LNG and the Yemeni administration.

The company made unfavourable sale contracts in 2005 with the main purchaser, the Korean Kogas paying USD 193 per ton for Yemeni gas compared to USD 689 for Qatari gas. One of the few achievements of the Hadi transitional regime was to review this selling price with Kogas, though it failed to renegotiate with Total. The original agreement was another example of corruption and underhand deals losing very significant income for the state, thus reducing the funds available for social services, development projects or infrastructure. In any case, given world prices, demand and supply of gas, the income expected for Yemen between 2010 and 2015 was no more than USD 300 million annually, not enough to cover the shortfall resulting from lower oil exports. What market is open to Yemen and under what conditions in the future will depend both on the outcome of the war and the demand for gas, at a time when the world is moving towards renewable energy sources.

Other potential economic resources

It is clear from the above that Yemen cannot rely on hydrocarbons to finance its development, let alone provide employment for its population, the sector being highly automated and needing very few unskilled and few skilled personnel. While other minerals exist in Yemen, including significant quantities of various stones suitable for construction and some precious metals, none of these had been developed for export and only the former used in the local economy.

A resource which is often perceived as a constraint is the country's large labour force. It grows at about 4.6% per annum and merely to maintain the current employment rate 150 000 jobs must be created annually. Only one in five young men has a job, and the skill level of young Yemenis is low: only half have completed nine years of education and less than one third finished secondary school. Future employment prospects, following previous history, are closely connected with international migration, an important element discussed separately below.

A sector with notable potential is tourism in an age when this has become a major industry internationally. Despite the country's impressive potential, in 2009, it only formed 2% of GDP (Dorte, 2012, p. 247). Worldwide, its dramatic reduction in 2020–21 due to the Covid-19 epidemic, is likely to be a temporary setback. In a post-war economy, Yemen could develop a cultural environmentally friendly tourism strategy. Not only does it have important archaeological sites, it also has many Islamic monuments, wonderful mountain sceneries for hiking and beaches for water sports. This sector could also provide significant employment at all skill levels throughout the country, in rural and urban areas, thus allowing equitably distributed opportunities. Tourism development obviously requires political stability; in earlier decades, whenever the activity started to take off, it was set back by kidnappings, and political insecurity including terrorist incidents. It will also be important for Yemeni tourism to avoid reproducing some of the negative features of tourism elsewhere, both ‘sex’ tourism and the mass tourism found in many places; to this end, a strategy distinguishing Yemen from some of its neighbours would be an advantage.

Agriculture and fisheries are both discussed below. Sustainably managed in the interests of the thousands of small-scale producers, they could contribute to improving living conditions for millions of Yemenis. There is considerable potential for fish farming and processing, again ideally managed in an environmentally sustainable way. To maximise benefits for Yemenis, prioritising small-scale artisanal fisheries would be the best way of increasing employment and providing adequate incomes for those involved. Here again, the prospects of climate change need to be addressed in any planning, including the rise in sea levels. In agriculture, focus on rain-fed, high-value subsistence and commercial crops, suitable for small-scale producers, would be an important contribution.

Economic infrastructure

Yemen has a wide range of terrains, including very steep slopes and precipitous inclines. Sudden violent downpours and flash floods need to be taken into consideration when planning roads and bridges. With 333 districts and 37 000 villages, the construction of roads and physical communications has been an expensive enterprise and still fails to reach many places. However, for military reasons among others, the Saleh regime invested considerable amounts in roads to enable it to reach remote areas in case of political disturbances. Most major roads have been financed through loans and grants from external agencies, including the major IFIs and some bilaterals, while local paved and unpaved roads have been a community responsibility.

There have also been efforts to connect remote settlements by motorable tracks as emigrants invested in vehicles and wanted to use them. Transport is necessary to reach towns to find work, to send local produce to markets, reach medical facilities, and most importantly to bring in basic necessities in a country which is dependent on imports for about 90% of its basic staples (wheat, rice, sugar, tea, etc.). These initiatives started in the 1970s by autonomous community organisations and, since the late 1990s, have been funded by international financiers through partly ‘self-help’ institutions such as the Social Fund for Development (SFD) and the Public Works Project (PWP).

Yemen has no railways, and air travel is too expensive for most people, in any case it only reaches the main towns: Sana'a, Hodeida, Taiz, Aden, Mukalla, Seiyun and al Ghayda (although a small town, it is the capital of the remote al-Mahra Governorate, otherwise difficult to reach in less than a 30-hour drive from the capital). So, road transport by collective taxis and buses is the main method of travel for most people in a society whose high level of mobility is a shared cultural characteristic.

By contrast, the country has been an early developer of an advanced telecommunications structure, once mobile telephones were introduced. Today most people's internet connections come through their telephones. There are numerous mobile phone networks mostly owned by some of the country's wealthiest individuals. Existing statistics on the prevalence of their accessibility and use are out of date, but figures from 2016 indicate that 17.5 million Yemenis had mobile phones, which probably means more or less the entire teenage and adult population (Statista, 2017). This enables people to have access to the world, by-passing the media used in the twentieth century, an important contribution to people's living standards and also opening possibilities for education, employment and a better understanding of the world, in addition to entertainment and communications with friends and relatives elsewhere. The war has affected the infrastructure, but has not completely interrupted communications, which all sides consider essential, thus they have not cut off access.

Internet and social media can potentially play a significant role in complementing the country's weak educational structure. Despite decades of investment in education, Yemeni skill levels are far below the country's need to establish a workforce adapted to a twenty-first century economy. Illiteracy is still extremely high, particularly among women, with an adult literacy rate for women of only 35% in 2004 (male 73%), and although the youth literacy rate for women was 61% (male 93%), this still perpetuates high levels of female illiteracy for generations to come (World Bank, 2020). By 2016, total primary school enrolment was 94%, with female enrolment significantly improved at 87%; but female drop-out rates, particularly towards the end of primary school, are very high. In 2015, the primary-school-age population was more than 4 million, and that of secondary school 3.7 million, so the demands and burden on the education system were very considerable for a poor country without a war. At the most basic level, even before the war, in 2014, almost half of youth were not in school or training. Although most of the figures presented above are less recent than would be desired, they are the latest available and it is also important to note that all figures relating to Yemen are largely indicative of trends and overall situations, rather than statistically correct. In the absence of up-to-date information, the following is clear, while the situation had improved by 2015, it deteriorated systematically after the war started, with up to two million children kept out of school for a range of reasons, most of them very valid, including the destruction of schools and their occupation by internally displaced persons (IDPs) or military entities.

In addition to enrolment and participation, the Yemeni education system suffers from many weaknesses, in particular the low quality and standards of teachers and the large numbers of 'ghost' teachers; syllabi and programmes that have not been adapted to deal with a modern economy; insufficient budgets, which mean that schools are not equipped with basics such as books, let alone computers and internet access, or, in many cases, even electricity or sufficient furniture. The Ministry of Education was also known as highly corrupt, explaining both ghost teachers, inadequate and unpaid salaries and the lack of equipment. While these features characterise education throughout the country, in addition in both Huthi and STC-controlled areas, a new generation of students is affected by fundamental changes in the syllabi, promoting Huthi and separatist ideology respectively.

As is the case in many countries, vocational education is undervalued. The GCC states have financed considerable investment in infrastructure for decades, partly to create a semi-skilled labour force which might find employment in those states, but also to fill gaps in Yemen itself, where many small enterprises are staffed by unskilled people who have lacked the opportunity of training and whose production is therefore of low quality. In 2015–16, there were 84 vocational training establishments, almost four per governorate, distributed throughout the country and providing training in a wide range of topics, including computing, the internet, etc. However, the total number of students was only 34 767, a ridiculously small number by comparison with the needs of the country and the overall skill shortage, let alone for those who wanted to migrate internationally. Women formed merely 15% of the total. As for university graduates in the year 2013–14, a total of 33 427 students graduated from the many public and private universities, representing barely 10% of the relevant age group.[2] Most universities suffer from the same quality deficiencies as the rest of the sector.

Thus, in addition to the low numbers of educated people, education suffers from fundamental problems with respect to its ability to answer the country's economic needs: low teacher competence and inappropriate syllabi and courses. The number of entrants into the labour market far exceeds the number of jobs available, though teaching positions could be created for thousands of them given the shortage. However structural adjustment policies, combined with a high level of corruption in the education sector, have meant that few teachers are adequately qualified or committed to their work and 'ghost' teachers form a major category, something evident on any visit to a school, particularly in rural areas.

Economic policies

Economic policies implemented since the establishment of the RoY have systematically prioritised the Washington Consensus neo-liberal philosophy which was shared by the Saleh regime and promoted by the Bretton Woods institutions. Neither the 2011 uprisings, nor the transitional regime, let alone the warring factions since 2015 have challenged these strategies. The 1990–91 crisis was an opportunity for Yemen to address its economic crisis outside of the powerful Washington Consensus framework. At the time, with the demise of the Soviet bloc, socialist strategies were largely discredited and it would have been difficult for Yemenis to promote them, despite the fact that the YSP had become a more social-democratic party and was at pains to distance itself from its political past. In addition, the tensions emerging from unification meant that politicians, whether in power or in opposition, were preoccupied by politics and may have thought that the standard formulas might solve the economic crisis resulting from the return of close to a million former workers from the GCC states. This was the first missed opportunity for a re-setting of economic policies.

When Yemen re-entered the international development aid community in 1995, its regime uncritically adopted in full the policies recommended by the World Bank and the IMF, which focused, as elsewhere, on stabilisation of the currency, structural adjustment, development of the private sector, rather than on poverty alleviation. Its promoters initially perceived success as the currency remained stable, subsidies on basic commodities were reduced, the state sector shrunk through the privatisation of services such as education and health. However, these changes, alongside complete disregard at the form taken by privatisation, contributed to a gradual serious deterioration of living standards. The IFIs gloated about the success of the mitigating measures they initiated at the time, most notably the establishment of two institutions which remain active a quarter of a century later, the Social Fund for Development (SFD) and the Public Works Project (PWP). Both were designed to compensate for the supposedly short-term drops in living standards expected by structural adjustment but, given worsened poverty, remain essential tools in the IFI arsenal.

Both are parastatals operating according to private sector procedures, providing high salaries to their senior staff and implementing most activities by consultants, in a system now described worldwide as the ‘gig’ economy. One result was the recruitment of senior staff from line ministries who abandoned their secure jobs for the high salaries, and thus depleted said ministries of their best qualified cadres. At the local level, consultants were casual workers without security of employment, medical insurance, pensions, or paid leave. Thus, according to official staffing figures, these institutions appeared lean and effective at demonstrating the advantages of the private sector.

This process gradually undermined state institutions to the point of collapse, all at the expense of the population who were compelled to pay for services at a time when their incomes were falling. Accusations of corruption of state institutions, while often accurate, were used in media campaigns to encourage people to believe, largely inaccurately, that private sector institutions were cleaner and more efficient and would provide better services to the population. A well-managed public relations campaign, emphasising the claimed advantages of privatisation, contributed to a positive perception of these policies, with few defending the public sector. The side effect of weakening state institutional capacity was not displeasing to some of the more neo-liberal among developmental decision makers.

While corruption in both institutions was initially largely absent, this situation changed over the decades and these supposedly temporary projects are, in the 2020s, among the few remaining functioning and entrenched mechanisms for foreign development funding. Thanks to their excellent international reputation as rapid disbursers and effective implementers, they continue to obtain generous support and grants from IFIs and most major bilateral funders.

Their 'independence', efficiency and performance are attractive to funders who want rapid disbursement of their grants and loans and have less concern for long-term sustainability or the deleterious effect this approach had on the country's cohesion. In addition, their projects often duplicated similar ones implemented through line ministries.

Documents such as 'Yemen's Strategic Vision 2025' and the Poverty Reduction Strategy Programme (PRSP) both issued in 2002 complemented the Second Five Year Socio-Economic Development Plan for 2001–05. Production of these documents was an essential condition for Yemen to continue receiving international financing. Close reading reveals some of the policy divergences between the Yemeni teams and their international advisors representing IFI views. Disguised through official 'development speak' both the PRSP and the Five Year Plan focus on reducing government expenditure, implementing a generalised sales tax (increasing indirect taxation which has a greater impact on the poor), reducing public expenditure while raising 'the efficiency of the civil service, retrenchment of excess public sector employees, reducing disguised unemployment, while raising salaries and wages for employees in the administrative apparatus of the State in addition to rationalization of spending on non-developmental activities' (Republic of Yemen, 2002, p. ix).

In practice the result was deteriorating living standards for the majority, as well as increased state indebtedness. It also meant worsening dependence and consequent compulsion to accept the conditionalities imposed by the IFIs, demonstrating, yet again, the power of the strings attached to financial support. National courageous efforts at resistance, within the Ministry of Planning and International Cooperation (MOPIC) (see Lackner, 2017a, pp. 241–242), were defeated and, as in earlier cases, the results of this plan were well below expectation. Under IFI pressure, the next development plan was renamed the Socio-Economic Development Plan for Poverty Reduction (2006–10) with a rhetoric of over-ambitious social improvement objectives but proposing to achieve them through the same neo-liberal strategy. Its successor for 2011–15 coincided with the 2011 uprisings, followed by the war. Throughout the decades, failures were never attributed to the policies but to extraneous factors, like the tribal system and corruption, which had little, if any, relevance to the failure of the strategies promoted. While deploring the weakness of state institutions, the role of IFI-supported policies in weakening them was ignored.

Finance

Yemen's finances have never been in particularly good shape. The war has taken a toll which is likely to have very long-term consequences. Yemen, by contrast with its neighbouring African countries, has remained largely a cash economy, with only about 10% of the population holding bank accounts and 'telephone money' was absent until the recent currency problems which have increased since 2016.

The country's situation deteriorated immediately after unification, as a result of the financial constraints imposed by its neighbours during the Gulf War: a balance of payments deficit of 12% in 1990, increased to 16% in 1994, while inflation rose from 33% in 1991 to 120% in 1994, while the riyal fell from USD 1 = YR 12 in 1991 to YR 160 in early 1995 (Awlaqi et al., 2019, p. 9). Its gradual decline meant it reached USD 1 = YR 215 by 2015, followed by a precipitous decline during the war. Improvements after 1995 took place under the implementation of IFI-induced structural adjustment plans which, while indicating progress on IFI indicators, simply hid the reality of worsening poverty on the ground.

The overall evolution of the Yemeni economy is reflected in changes in the country's GDP,[3] which reached a peak in 2010, only to drop thereafter and dramatically so after 2015. Between 2014 and 2020, it contracted by more than 50% (Republic of Yemen, Ministry of Planning and International Cooperation, 2021b, p. 1), increasing the total loss of USD 89 billion between 2014 and 2019 (Republic of Yemen, Ministry of Planning and International Cooperation, 2020a, p. 2). Short of a solution to the war, this trend is likely to continue, and Yemenis' living conditions are continuing to deteriorate. Table 3.1 gives a rough indication of GDP evolution since unification.

Although GDP data only give a rough idea of the state of the economy, there are currently no reliable alternatives to provide a better understanding of people's living conditions. However, according to studies by the UNDP (2019; Hanna et al., 2021), economic output decreased by 50%, and the war is setting back economic development by decades: should it end in 2022, development would be set back by 26 years, and should it not be solved till 2030 then the set-back would be 39 years, bringing the country back to its level of 1991. The same report estimates the number of indirect conflict deaths by 2030 to be 1.5 million on calculations prior to the emergence of the Covid-19 pandemic.

Table 3.1 Changes in Yemen's GDP since unification

Year	*Total GDP USD Billion*	*GDP growth %*	*GDP/per capita*	*GDP growth per capita*
1990	11.7	(1991) 6.3	1001.4	(1991) +1.2
1995	15.8	5.7	1060.7	+1.3
2000	20.3	6.2	1168.7	+3.2
2005	25.0	5.6	1243.4	+2.6
2010	30.9	7.7	1334.8	+4.7
2015	24	–27.9	785.3	–29.8
2016	20.8	–9.4	694.1	–11.6
2017	19.6	–5.1	643.1	–7.3
2018	18.0	0.7	632.9	–7.6
2019	18.0	2.1	631.5	–0.2

GDP in Constant USD 2010, source World Bank data base.

The major financial impact of the war results from the problems of the Central Bank of Yemen (CBY). With two centres of government in the first year of the war, and failing to make significant military progress, the IRG turned to economic warfare in its efforts to defeat the Huthis. The CBY has been the main front of this war since the Hadi government's decision to transfer its headquarters to Aden in September 2016, disregarding the advice of the IFIs and others. The mostly exiled IRG had retained some control over the CBY's activities which was running out of cash to pay civil service salaries, its major outgoing. The banking system had also run out of foreign currency to finance its large import bills due to the collapse of exports. In September 2016 reserves had dropped to USD 700 million. As put by Anthony Biswell of the Sana'a Centre for Strategic Studies, the

> move fractured the institution … and left both branches with severely reduced institutional capacity … [Aden] took with it the CBY's international recognition, and thus the right to access global financial systems and international support, and to print new currency. The Sana'a-based branch continued to operate under Houthi control, having kept the vast majority of the central bank's staff, informational archives and purview over Houthi-held areas, which include the country's largest population centers, commercial markets and business and financial hubs.
>
> (Biswell, 2020, p. 6)

The initial and most lasting impact of the CBY crisis throughout the country has been the non-payment of salaries to about 1.2 million civil servants since September 2016, for seven full years at the time of writing. The vast majority of teachers, medical workers and administrative staff have remained effectively without salaries since then. Every few months, they receive about one month's salary. Rough estimates suggest that selected staff and pensioners have received about YR 10 000 a month over that period. Aden's printing of notes led to a money supply increase of 53% by 2018 (ibid., p. 6). By end of 2019 the Aden Bank had printed YR 1.7 trillion worth of new bills (ibid., p. 35), resulting in the rapid loss of value of the riyal. The Huthis responded by banning the use of the new notes in the area under their control. This initially selective move became a blanket ban end 2019, followed by the introduction of e-riyals through three local banking systems, as well as mobile phones. The printing by the Aden CBY of trillions and the ban on their use in Huthi-controlled areas, has increased the differential in value between Aden and Sana'a, reaching more than 40% by end 2021, with YR 1700 to USD 1 in Aden, while it remained stable at YR 600 in Huthi-controlled areas.

The lack of income from petroleum exports has reduced the availability of hard currency for the Aden CBY, which, from early 2018 onwards depended on a deposit of USD 2.4 billion by Saudi Arabia to guarantee imports of basic commodities through financing letters of credit for private sector imports of basic commodities at a preferential exchange rate. The monthly need in foreign currency to cover food imports is about USD 80 million, though many traders get some of these funds from the money exchange companies. The final payment from this source was made in December 2020, leaving the IRG unable to assist traders to import basic necessities. Given the continued tension between the IRG and the separatist STC and the latter's occasional hijacking of containerloads of new cash, it is unclear who controls currency and finances in Aden, as well as the STC's resistance to implementing the November 2019 Riyadh power sharing agreement. These are all good reasons to explain the KSA's reluctance to renew its financial support to the CBY, particularly as Saudi Arabia also has other financing priorities, including the Crown Prince's highly ambitious prestige projects.

Public expenditure dropped by 47% in 2018 compared to 2014, resulting in the suspension of investments as well as worsening indebtedness. The country's financial position in 2021 is critical: its USD reserves have collapsed, renewal of the Saudi backing for imports is highly unlikely, income from oil is very low with exports having risen to 17.5 million barrels in 2019 from 12.7 in 2018, though the income was affected by the lower prices. With a currency akin to monopoly money in the areas not under Huthi control, inflation throughout the country is estimated at 145% since the beginning of the war.

The role of internal and international migration, remittances, development assistance and humanitarian flows

Emigration has been a basic feature of the Yemeni economy for centuries, partly due to a difficult natural environment which has limited economic development from local resources, as well as periodic floods and droughts. Recent development and economic policies have failed to create sufficient employment thus ensuring a continued need for Yemenis to migrate to support their households. This is particularly the case for rural areas with high population density, such as the highlands of Ibb, Dhamar, al Baydha, Taiz, Lahej and al Dhali'. In the first half of the twentieth century, men from these areas headed for Aden with different ambitions: finding work and employment locally, on ships and eventually overseas, as well as seeking education and freedoms unavailable under the imamate. In the 1950s and early 1960s, Britain recruited Yemenis from the Protectorates and beyond to work in the UK, just as it did in its colonies (the Windrush generation). This generation of migrants worked in heavy industries, such as steelworks in the UK and car manufacturing in the US, though in the US there was also a large number of Yemenis working in agriculture on the west coast.

The wave of migration changed direction in the 1960s and 1970s with the introduction of restrictive immigration laws in the UK just as new possibilities were emerging in the Arabian Peninsula. The Gulf states have remained the main destination for Yemeni labour for the past half century, even though there have been ebbs and flows according to both economic and political factors. After the 1973 oil price rises, opportunities in the region increased exponentially in construction and services, and Yemenis flocked to Saudi Arabia and beyond. Yemenis from the YAR had privileged access to Saudi

Arabia where, unlike all others, including citizens of the PDRY, they did not need sponsors. Thus, a fair number of citizens of the PDRY crossed into the YAR, obtained local identity documents, and went to the KSA as YAR citizens while others were sponsored by Saudis of Yemeni origin, particularly Hadhramis. In the late 1970s, about 1.2 million North Yemenis were in Saudi Arabia, and estimates are that up to 40% of the country's men (al-Eryani, 2020) worked in Saudi Arabia. In 1988, 10% of the PDRY's total population was abroad (PDRY, Central Statistical Organization, 1989, p. 47).

The situation changed gradually in the 1980s due to two main factors in the, by then, GCC states: first, reduced oil revenues meant a temporary fall in demand for foreign labour as a whole. Second, when the upturn came, authorities in these states decided to replace Arabic speaking labour by workers from South and South-East Asia to avoid having Arabs, whom their citizens might consider as brothers and might want to treat with less discrimination. Rulers feared that these workers, from Egypt and Yemen in particular, might bring republican and other revolutionary ideas challenging their authoritarian rule.

After the expulsion of close to a million Yemenis from the GCC states following the 1990–91 crisis over the Iraqi invasion of Kuwait, the number of Yemenis in these states gradually recovered from the mid-1990s onwards, reaching between 1 and 1.2 million in the early years of the last decade with, as previously, the overwhelming majority in Saudi Arabia: less than 5% of them have any formal vocational training and they include some professionals, but the tendency is reversed by the new restrictive Saudisation policies initiated in 2016, which increasingly encourage resident Yemenis to leave, precisely when more Yemenis than ever need to migrate to earn an income in war time.

Saudi policies, in addition to expelling thousands of irregular migrants, are stricter by the year, intended to increase employment of Saudi citizens and discourage foreign labour: foreigners officially employed must pay increasingly expensive residency permits and prohibitive fees for accompanying dependents rising to SR 400/month per dependent in 2020. In addition, with the new restrictions of the types of jobs open to Yemenis, unemployment is becoming widespread, as well as competition for the few jobs available, whether legal or otherwise. According to a study on remittances for Yemenis,

> this means that an expatriate worker living with his wife and three children will have to pay for his dependents … [which added up to] SR 16 800 at the end of 2020 … For expatriates working in sectors that have been Saudized official and unofficial fees for securing a job may reach SR 20 000.
>
> (Awlaqi, 2019, pp. 25–26)

These are annual fees, in addition to which the workers have to live and their expenses for health and education have also increased enormously. According to the same report, Yemeni wages range between SR 1500 and SR 2500, and their monthly basic expenditure was about SR 2000 when the fees were first introduced, at their lowest level. Cancellation of subsidies have increased living costs in the KSA: fuel, medicine, bread, have also become more expensive, while, since 2017, electricity and water subsidies are restricted to Saudi citizens. Unsurprisingly, the situation worsened with the Covid-19 pandemic.

There are various estimates of the number of Yemenis who have left Saudi Arabia since the introduction of these new regulations, and those who remain have almost all sent their families home despite the families returning to war zones. One frequently mentioned estimate gives a figure of 70% Yemeni workers in Saudi Arabia losing their jobs by 2020. Given the financial cost of staying, it would seem pointless to do so. While the actual number of Yemenis leaving Saudi Arabia in the past decade is unknown, the World Bank reported that 'about 3.9 million migrants were deported from Saudi Arabia between March 2011 and August 2018' (World Bank, 2019, p. 11), the majority were certainly from south Asia, but there is no doubt that Yemenis formed a significant percentage of that figure. More recently IOM records of Yemenis returning from Saudi Arabia through the northern land border point was 138 000 for the years 2018–20, though the closure of the border due to Covid-19 measures meant that the number in 2020 was far lower than earlier. This of course does not account for those crossing the borders elsewhere.

The importance of remittances to Yemen's economy cannot be overestimated and is rarely given the attention it deserves. In the YAR, remittances reached a peak of USD 1.39 billion in 1977, around 77% of GDP, equivalent figures for the PDRY are not available. After the downturn of the 1980s, they rose to USD 1.5 billion in 1990,[4] but fell by more than a third in 1991 to USD 0.99 billion, gradually recovering in the following years. Remittances only returned to the USD 1.5 billion mark in 2010. In the second decade of this century, remittances rose to more than USD 3 billion per annum, though the unchanged figures published by the World Bank for the years 2016–19 are not entirely credible as they ignore the impact of the war, ending with a total of USD 3.77 billion for 2019. It is also to be noted that these figures are not fully comprehensive as they exclude cash carried by people across the border, though the money transferred by the larger cash transfer companies is included. According to the MOPIC, in 2017 remittances represented 25% of per capita GDP, and in 2018 12% of overall GDP (World Bank, 2019, p. 20). The year 2020 saw a further worsening of the situation. Remittances since the war started have come primarily from Saudi Arabia which is still estimated to host close to two million Yemenis, despite many having been forced to leave due to the Saudisation policy. While Yemenis are likely to return to Saudi Arabia once the Covid-19 pandemic is under control, their numbers are unlikely to reach earlier heights and the amounts remitted home will drop.

Another important feature of remittances is that the actual amounts reaching households are significantly lower than in the past despite the fact that total amounts remitted have more than doubled in the second decade of the century. The number of benefitting households has increased and, as a result, each one receives less. Moreover, each riyal has a lower purchasing power due to inflation. Since the 'transfer' of the Central Bank of Yemen (CBY) to Aden, remitting cash to Huthi-controlled areas is more difficult for those not using the money transfer organisations operating in both Saudi Arabia and Sana'a, as it is impossible to use US corresponding banks, which further complicates the transfer process. In 2020, a new problem emerged from the freeze imposed by Lebanon on its banks, which had been used as corresponding banks and 'storage' for foreign currency by Yemeni banks, causing additional difficulties for Yemeni businesses and even individuals.

Despite increased international assistance, remittances remain a main source of foreign exchange for the country and also of income for thousands of families. However, to have a more accurate understanding of the figures in Table 3.2, it is important to note that the actual amount which reaches Yemenis from international aid is substantially less once overheads, personnel and transport costs of the numerous international agencies have been subtracted, leaving remittances as the most significant source of foreign currency actually reaching the country.

It is particularly noticeable that per capita development aid flows to Yemen remained extremely low prior to the explosion of the current crisis and the considerable increase in humanitarian aid: in 2010, Yemen received USD 29 per capita compared to an average of USD 52 for least developed countries and USD 37 for Middle East countries, excluding high income ones, and USD 85 for sub-Saharan states. Overseas Foreign Assistance (ODA) increased dramatically on a per capita basis after 2015 but was mostly humanitarian rather than development investments, demonstrating that the massive pledges made

Table 3.2 Comparative share of remittances and foreign aid in the Yemeni economy (USD current)

Year	*Remittances*		*Foreign aid*		
	Amount USD billions	*% GDP*	*Amount USD'000*	*%GNI*	*USD/capita*
1990	1.133	17.0	449 830	8.02	37.6
1995	1081	25.0	171 000	4.20	11.2
2000	1288	13.4	311 280	3.5	17.5
2005	1283	7.6	296 530	1.9	14.4
2010	1526	5.0	667 080	2.3	28.2
2015	3350	7.9	1 778 000	4.3	67.1
2016	3.77	14.1	2 300 000	7.4	84.7
2017	3.77	16.1	3 234 000	12.1	116.2
2018	2.70	16.7	7 985 000	34.0	280.2
2019	2.40				

Source: World Bank, in Lackner, 2017, pp. 244 and 252, updated from World Bank website 27 January 2021 remittances for 2018 and 2019 from Republic of Yemen, Ministry of Planning and International Cooperation (2020b, p. 5).

in 2012 (USD 8.4 billion) by the international community were never fulfilled with total aid (humanitarian and development) in the two years before the full-scale war started at only USD 883 million, barely more than 10% of the amount pledged for development support in September 2012!

Since 2015, per capita humanitarian aid flows increased dramatically, though again it is important to note that not all of this actually reached Yemenis. The UN Office for the Coordination of Humanitarian Affairs (OCHA) has been holding annual pledging conferences to raise funds for its Humanitarian Response Plan, which received different levels of international support over the years. In 2019, humanitarian assistance to Yemen through the UN's Humanitarian Response Plan amounted to USD 3.6 billion or 87% of the USD 4.2 billion appeal, an excellent record by comparison with other years. In 2020, the appeal, already 25% lower, was only financed at 59%. The pledging conference in 2021 raised USD 61% of the USD 3.85 billion requested (UN Secretary General, 2021a). This was described as 'disappointing' by the UN Secretary General (UN Secretary General, 2021b).

The shift from development to humanitarian assistance is one of the many tragedies faced by Yemenis. While humanitarian aid does, to some extent, address immediate urgent needs in food, fuel and medical services and supplies, it is only through development funding that individuals, households and communities can liberate themselves from dependence and gradually recover their self-sufficiency. Although the data in Table 3.3 are not fully comprehensive, they demonstrate the trends in the past decades, in addition to showing how little support reaches Yemenis. The extraordinary figures for 2015, with 99% humanitarian funding, is due to the fact that when the internationalised war started, the World Bank, the main remaining source

Table 3.3 Evolution of humanitarian and total assistance to Yemen in the last decade (USD current '000)

Year	*Humanitarian funding*	*Total ODA*	*Percentage humanitarian/total*	*Total population (millions)*	*Per capita receipts (humanitarian)*
2011	299 590	478 000	48	23.8	1.26
2012	425 385	712 000	60	24.5	1.73
2013	452 957	1 040 000	43	25.2	4.35
2014	430 086	1 163 000	37	25.9	1.66
2015	1 762 535	1 778 000	99	26.7	6.80
2016	1 791 043	2 301 000	78	27.4	6.53
2017	2 364 772	3 234 000	73	28.2	8.38
2018	5 230 847	7 985 000	65	28.5	18.35
2019	4 059 108			29.2	13.90
2020	2 157 130			29.8	7.24

Sources: UNOCHA FTS for Humanitarian, World Bank Data for Total, CSO estimates for population, population estimates from RoY CSO until 2017 and World Bank thereafter.

whose funding is described as 'development', stopped all financing to Yemen. It later resumed its funding, using the UN Development Programme (UNDP) to route its financing, thus by-passing internal administrative constraints.

The rural economy

International migration is particularly important with respect to the country's access to hard currency and the incomes of households with migrant members. However, in practice, it has been overtaken by urban labour as the main source of rural household incomes. Since the beginning of this century, most migration has been internal: although the majority of the 70% of Yemenis living in rural areas perceive themselves as agriculturalists, agriculture's share of GDP has dropped over the decades. While smallholders were able to support their households from their crops and livestock up to the end of the twentieth century, the main change in the past two decades has been the shift in comparative importance of agriculture and off-farm income; the latter has taken two main forms: the first is state employment as civil servants and military/security personnel, and the second is unskilled labour by male family members in towns and major Yemeni cities, relegating agriculture to second place.

This change was due to the following combination of factors: reduction in holding sizes over generations due to population increase, lower yields resulting from climate change, water scarcity, soil degradation and loss of land from erosion, changes in diet and expectations, and the need for additional income to finance medical, educational and other new expenses. In addition, poverty has encouraged the concentration of land ownership. The neo-liberal policies of the Saleh regime and the international development financiers disproportionately benefitted larger more powerful landowners who bought smallholdings, further impoverishing the sellers.

This shift in the main sources of income for most families has a number of implications: first it indicates worsening poverty for many households due to irregular and limited remittances from the towns. Second, sooner or later, it leads to changes in the balance of power within households, with junior male cash earners gaining more authority at the expense of the senior official 'household head'. Third, it changes people's attitudes and perceptions, leading to a mixed rural-urban culture, causing changes in both areas; this element is strengthened by the ubiquitous presence of mobile phones. Fourth, it has different impacts on women: in some cases, women gain more authority, in others they simply end up doing a lot more work, taking on men's tasks, such as terrace rehabilitation, ploughing and building tasks, while authority remains with a more or less distant male relative.

Agriculture remains a major occupation for millions of Yemenis, male and female, despite the fact that, even including livestock, it only contributed about 20% of Yemen's GDP in the mid-2010s; this is also partly due to the fact that GDP is not an accurate reflection of productive economic activity and the oil export sector distorts the balance. However, despite massive imports of basic staples, local produce contributes about 25% of the food consumed in the country: prior to the war the country was self-sufficient in fruit, vegetables, chicken and fish, and to a large extent other meats. As 55% of the population earn much of their income from agriculture, it is a major contributor to employment, particularly in the areas with high concentrations of poverty. But the returns are low: per capita annual GDP from agriculture was a mere USD 133 in 2005 (a fairly typical pre-crisis year) by comparison with USD 1100 in Tunisia (Dorte Verner ed., 2012, p. 166).

Only about 3% of the country's land is suitable for agriculture, including broadly defined pasture. Of the 1.6 million ha of agricultural land, prior to the crisis, 405 000 ha (or 25%) was irrigated by wells, though the data make no distinction between shallow and deep wells, 255 000 ha (or 16%) by flood or spate irrigation and 105 000 (or 7%) by other means, including springs and dams.[5] Rain-fed crops still cover between 50 and 60% of cultivated land, depending on the year's rainfall. Only one agricultural census has ever been held in Yemen, so no data are available for comparisons over time, particularly with respect to changes in tenure or in cropping patterns. Held in 2002, it found 1.2 million landholders in the country, 58% of whom owned a total of 8% of cultivable land in holdings of less than 0.5 ha, a further 15% owned another 8% in holdings of 0.5 to 1 ha, while 20% owned 28% in holdings of 1 to 5 ha, and a mere 7% of owners controlled 56% of the land in holdings of more than 5 ha (Lackner, 2017a, p. 281). These figures demonstrate the already very skewed distribution of agricultural land at that time and also ignore the different potential income from varying climatic conditions, quality of soils, or types of access to water. But at least they give a sense of the overall rural situation, which has since worsened. This is the result of the concentration of ownership due to worsening social differentiation which has affected the rural sector, particularly the skewed distribution of irrigation potential. The census also recorded 770 000 landless rural livestock holders. The remaining 2.5 million rural households included sharecroppers, casual agricultural labourers, artisans, shopkeepers, as well as government employees such as teachers and medical staff and security/military personnel.

Rain-fed agriculture remains the main form of agriculture for smallholders in the mountainous western highlands extending to the southern mountains, i.e. all the areas which benefit from the monsoon rains (Varisco, 2021). The main crops are cereals (sorghum, wheat, maize and millet), with small areas of fruits and vegetables in the best-watered areas, as well as coffee and *qat*, both of which grow best at altitudes ranging from 700 metres above sea level (masl) to 1800 masl.

There are two main types of irrigation in Yemen: spate and well. Spate irrigation has two models: annually rehabilitated traditional structures, and modern cement 'permanent' structures as found in the main wadis. Since the 1970s, these were subject to 'improvement' projects with loans from the World Bank and other international financiers, but more than half these investments barely last five years (World Bank, 2014). This raises the question of their actual value, since they increase the state's hard currency indebtedness in addition to primarily benefitting wealthier landowners. Smallholders in the catchment areas of these projects complain that their fields are not irrigated, as the water is diverted to the wealthier landowners (Bonzanigo and Borgia, 2009; World Bank, 2007, section 6; Lackner, personal communication re. Tuban).

There are also two models of well irrigation, though nowadays all use motorised pumps to extract the water: shallow wells exclusively using annual recharge, and built at low cost, and therefore accessible to most smallholders; the other type is deep tube wells, many of which access non-renewable fossil aquifers at depths usually greater than 100 m. Only wealthier farmers can afford to pay the initial investment, the subsequent regular deepening costs, and the ongoing operational costs (for diesel and electric pumps), as the water table drops becoming more difficult to reach. In view of the cost, these are mainly used for high value crops, namely *qat*, vines, vegetables and sometimes coffee in the highlands, and bananas, mangoes and other vegetables in the coastal plains. The last decade has seen the emergence of solar pumping which requires expensive initial investment but then has almost no running costs, until expensive parts need to be replaced. Deep tube wells are responsible for most of the unsustainable over-extraction of the country's scarce water resources.

Many crops can be cultivated both rain-fed and under irrigation, such as wheat, *qat*, almonds, figs, coffee, though they obviously have higher yields with more water. Therefore, annual production depends on a number of factors, some related to the political situation, such as availability of fuel (for irrigation, input acquisition or marketing), financial incentives, competition from food aid, and others on climatic factors (timing and quantities of rain, drought). While sorghum remains a favoured staple for local consumption, thanks to its drought resistance and ability to grow in difficult environmental conditions, its production has decreased under war conditions, falling from 459 000 metric tons (mt) in 2012 to a mere 164 000 mt in 2017. Overall national production of cereals dropped by about one third in 2012–2017, from 910 000 mt to 358 000 mt, and the area cultivated with wheat dropped from 9.2% to 5.7% (Republic of Yemen, Ministry of Planning and International Cooperation, 2018, p. 1). Although the above-mentioned factors partly explain this drop, at the same time the area under *qat* has increased from 11.3% in 2013 to 15.4% of cultivated land in 2017. The vast differential in income between *qat* and other crops, including coffee, is an issue which is inadequately addressed by the anti-*qat* lobby and promoters of increased production of alternative crops, who generally over-emphasise the negative aspects of *qat* while ignoring its economic and social importance.

Wheat is the main cereal consumed throughout Yemen, and by far the one most imported, it is a good indicator of the country's food crisis. In 2014, representing the pre-war situation, the country imported 3.4 million mt, and produced 192 000 mt, i.e. 5% of imports. Self-sufficiency has dropped from 7.8% in 2012 to 2.8% in 2017 (Republic of Yemen, Ministry of Planning and

International Cooperation, 2018, p. 4). While monthly wheat requirements are estimated at 350 000 mt, the level of imports since 2015 has been well below that amount, due to foreign exchange and blockade constraints, as well as the increased poverty and lack of income of consumers, thus partly explaining the food emergency experienced by Yemenis since the war started.

Official agricultural policies have contributed to this dismal record. Given Yemen's water scarcity, the obvious priority should have been to focus on improving rain-fed subsistence and cash-crop potential. Yemeni policy makers and their international 'development aid' financiers, with the World Bank in the lead, have neglected this sector. Agricultural research since unification has focused on export-oriented irrigated crops, thus encouraging Yemen to export its water as per the 'virtual water' concept, leading to a remarkable rise in the production of mangoes and bananas, both thirsty crops, contributing to the enrichment of the few who could afford the major initial investments. Much of this produce ended up being held up at the Saudi border while the fruit deteriorated and 'paper work' was processed. There was a complete absence of research or investment in rain-fed crops, staple, high value or other.

In the early years of this century (Lackner, 2022, p. 183) a single project, the Rainfed Agriculture and Livestock Project (RALP), jointly funded by the World Bank and the International Fund for Agricultural Development (IFAD) included USD 3.4 million or 8% of its total cost for a component for 'farmer based system of seed improvement and management' (World Bank, 2013). Neither research into new varieties of staples nor of potential new high value crops was included. No other effort has been made to address the issue except for numerous labour-intensive 'cash for work'community projects to help the reconstruction of terracing, which positively but indirectly impact water management, but is hardly a substitute for a serious agricultural development policy to improve Yemen's economy.

Yemen's fisheries sector is mainly based in dozens of small settlements along the 2000 km Arabian and Red Sea coasts, operated by artisanal fisher communities, some of whom benefitted from various internationally funded projects providing engines, cold storage and marketing facilities. About 200 000 men are involved in actual fishing, but the sector is responsible for a mere 3% of the country's GDP, providing jobs for about 3% of the country's labour force. Production has fluctuated wildly over the decades, as seen in Table 3.4, largely due to unsustainable over fishing which has almost led to extinction of some species, such as high value lobsters. This has happened through non-enforcement of international and national fisheries regulations, disrespect of maritime exclusion zones, and other actions which prioritised short-term profits. National large fishing vessels whose owners had good relations with the ruling clique are partly responsible for this, but the bulk of the culprits are different foreign fleets, whose nationality has varied according to political alignments over the past half century. All of them fished with complete disregard for the sustainability of the resource. These contributed to the problems of the sector to the detriment of the small-scale artisanal fishers.

Table 3.4 Fish production (metric tons)

Year	*Production*
1990	77 310
1995	114 750
2010	163 861
2011	157 261
2012	230 516
2013	235 342
2014	219 672
2015	180 813
2016	154 450

Source: data.worldbank.org/indicator/ER.FSH.CAPT.MT?locations=YE, accessed 28 January 2021.

Significant periods of recovery are essential to enable restocking; in the long run, good management would enable a profitable fisheries sector to operate satisfying both the national and international markets.

The war has a major impact on the economy: agriculture has lost much of its irrigation potential due to the lack of fuel for transport of inputs or produce to markets, though many, particularly the wealthier, have installed solar pumping in their irrigation for high value crops. By end 2019, irrigated land had shrunk by 11% (FSTS, December 2019, p. 4) and the number of livestock decreased by 9% between 2014 and end 2019. Fisheries installations and equipment were destroyed mostly by direct bombing on the Red Sea coast by the blockading states who also attacked and killed many fishermen, on the assumption that their small boats might be smuggling weapons to the Huthis. This problem has been more acute in the Red Sea but also affected the Arabian Sea. In addition, fuel shortages and distribution problems have affected marketing.

The urban sector and industry

The country's major cities have a primarily urban economy, with numerous workshops, a few large factories and thousands employed in the private services sector, as well as in government, both civil service and military/security institutions. In the absence of recent figures, even the World Bank had to resort to data from the 2004 population census in its study of economic potential in 2015. The data on the number of private enterprises is indicative of the situation, though it can be safely assumed that the number of enterprises grew up to 2010, possibly remaining static for the following five years and diminishing since the full-scale war started in 2015. In 2004, the overwhelming majority (92%) of the 301 000 private enterprises employed fewer than five people, while a further 13 000 (or 4%) employed five to nine.

This situation can be examined further through recent employment data, but the first thing to notice is that the number of enterprises in 2004 is larger than the total number of employees in 2017 suggesting either an extreme level of shrinkage or inaccuracy.

By 2017, the industrial sector had already shrunk from its 2015 level, with a total of 203 000 employees, of whom 186 000 were in the private sector. As is the case internationally, the oil and gas sectors provided few jobs, a mere 1%, or 2400 jobs but, even here, there was a drop from 2015 due to the interruption of oil and gas production. Of the 85% of workers employed in manufacturing, 24% were in food processing or production, 18% in construction and metalwork, 15% in furniture manufacturing and 6.5% in water. Although there is no information on the total number of enterprises involved, 45% of private sector employees were in small enterprises, 19% in medium ones and 36% in large ones, though the latter had a higher income than the previous two: the 36% of employees in large enterprises earned 64% of the total income in the sector, the 45% working in small enterprises only earned 21% of the income, while the 19% in medium enterprises earned 14% of the income; all of them showing a drop from the 2015 situation. These data indirectly confirm that the main non-agricultural sector is construction, mainly of homes, followed by food production and water distribution, the latter including the numerous small water purification shops found throughout the towns and cities, selling potable water to the population.

There are many reasons for the limited development of industry in Yemen prior to the war. A 2013 survey found that the main constraints to development for industry were, first and foremost, political instability experienced by 86% of surveyed companies, with 79% complaining of power cuts, 75% of corruption and 67% of insecurity. Other reasons include access to credit as well as taxation, let alone corruption, with 59% of companies stating that they were expected to pay 'gifts' to tax inspectors. As the survey was done before the war, it is interesting to note how prominently insecurity featured among the problems listed, confirming that instability and insecurity have been lasting characteristics of life in Yemen. It is also likely that insecurity here was perceived in a broader sense than mere military action, also covering exactions and extortion as well as pressure on successful companies to involve regime cronies in companies. In addition, free trade policies have made it difficult, if not impossible, for local manufacturing to compete with imports, thus discouraging initiatives at the local level and the emergence of national manufacturing enterprises.

Regardless of one's views on World Bank policies, it is difficult to disagree with its conclusion that government-to-business services suffer a serious implementation gap 'whether it is business registration, licensing, inspection, taxation or customs, Cross cutting issues prevent this, primarily the lack of rule of law, poor government accountability and weak state capacity' (World Bank, 2015, p. 42).

Employment

The 2013–14 Labour Survey provides the only available indicator of the employment situation in Yemen, despite its figures on unemployment in particular being widely considered to be vastly underestimated. With comparative data from earlier sources, it indicates a small drop in the percentage of people involved in agriculture to 41% (compared to 44% in 1999), and a significant rise in the industrial labour force from 5.6% in 1999 to 12.2% in 2014, despite industry remaining a minor component of the country's economy. Services was the largest sector in 2014, providing 47% of employment (a rise of 5% from 1999), with the top two occupations for men being agriculture and shop work. Women do not feature in shop work for cultural reasons and instead, the three main occupations they practise are livestock husbandry, crop cultivation and tailoring, followed by education.

Sectoral definitions used in this ILO-implemented survey are not always appropriate to the Yemeni context, estimating that half the labour force are employees, while the other half are employers or working on their own account. But it also indicates that 73% of the labour force, more than 3 million people, are in the informal sector. Its definition of the informal sector is extremely broad including people in enterprises without official formal registration and operating outside government labour regulations. It found that only 350 000 people work in the larger companies. These definitional issues also explain the difference about the role of agriculture and other rural activities between this report and others.

More recent unemployment data are more realistic, though in the view of this author, still underestimates: they give rates of more than 30% (33.8% in 2016, 31.9% in 2017, 29.9% for 2018, and 32% for 2019) (Republic of Yemen, Ministry of Planning and International Cooperation, 2020a, p. 13). One thing is clear, though unlikely to be reflected in official statistics: the main sector of employment today for men are the various armed militias operating in the country. They attract youth for a number of reasons, the main one being their reliable and reasonable incomes.

Corruption, the predatory/nepotistic economy

Corruption in Yemen has been a major theme for decades and is often blamed for the lack of development. There is no doubt that Saleh's crony capitalism played an important role in preventing the emergence of an equitable economy giving equal opportunities to all according to qualifications and ability; the same can be said of many states. A brief examination of the role of corruption in Yemen's economy not only helps understand the country's weak economy prior to the war but also explains numerous features of the war economy which is basically an expansion of the earlier system.

Defined by Transparency International as 'the abuse of entrusted power for private gain', corruption has emerged and worsened in Yemen since the establishment of the RoY. According to the Sana'a Centre for Strategic Studies,

> the country has witnessed decades of state capture, in which a political elite has distorted the basic legal framework in order to extract state rents … The country's informal elite networks have become more influential than formal state institutions, another hallmark of state capture. State capture and lower level administrative corruption, characterized by everyday bribery and favouritism, have been underpinned by informal institutions and a tacit cultural acceptance in Yemeni society that the abuse of power in business and politics is simply 'how things are done'
>
> (SCSS, 2018, p. 8)

Saleh's patronage system gave priority, in order of importance, to his close kin, Sanhan tribesmen (i.e. the branch of the Hashed tribal confederation in his home area), followed by other northern tribesmen, and others throughout the country according to expediency. These overlap with professional sectors according to a similar order of priorities, military/security personnel taking the first place, followed by tribal leaders and commercial/industrial families. There was a clear cross-cutting mechanism, whereby senior military/security personnel from Sanhan might well become major industrialists or traders, or obtain senior positions in existing enterprises through formal or informal pressure.

Sources of income were numerous and varied, including the multiplicity of 'ghost' soldiers, contracts in the petroleum industry after oil production started in 1984, telecommunications and import licences. The Yemen Economic Corporation was a favoured mechanism which incorporated different elements, imports, local trade and manufacturing in particular. Originally the Military Economic Corporation, its name was changed in 1993 under IMF pressure to 'privatise', but it remained under the control of Saleh's closest associates. While financing for the patronage system was initially based on oil-related activities, once that income started to decrease in the early 2000s, the main external source became foreign aid. The reduced resources limited the amounts available for redistribution and particularly for the purchase of local loyalty from community leaders, worsening social tension. The main mechanism to ensure popular support had been Saleh's personal distribution of cash and projects during his visits to communities throughout the country, a process by which he ensured political support not only among the community leaders but the population.

Capital flight is a particularly blatant form of corruption, as it deprives the country and its people of resources needed for development, particularly since most of the funds exported were originally intended to finance development investments. Between 1990 and 2008, USD 2.70 left Yemen illicitly for every USD 1 received in aid (UNDP 2019, p. 23) adding up to a total of USD 12 billion. It is also interesting to note that no study has been carried out since, thus demonstrating relevant institutions' lack of concern for this major loss to Yemen and other developing countries.

Opposition to corruption was a fundamental theme of the 2011 uprisings, but the situation did not improve during the transitional period. The most prominent attempt by Hadi to demonstrate cleaner politics was the rescinding of the contract with Dubai Ports World (DPW) for the management of Aden's container port; the original agreement favoured Saleh family members at the expense of the Yemeni economy. Its mismanagement was demonstrated by the fall in port activity and the lack of the promised investment (Lackner, 2017a, p. 269). Cancellation of the contract came at a price as the state had to pay expensive compensation. Another attempt, the renegotiation of export contracts of Liquified Natural Gas (LNG) was less successful: the main contractor, the French Total, refused to renegotiate while the contract was in force, and the Hadi government only managed to improve the contract with the Korean company (see p. 81).

Other corrupt practices continued pretty much 'as normal' during Hadi's transitional government, with the political parties in government vying with each other to increase benefits for their relatives and political supporters. As the allocation of ministries was done on a factional basis, each minister tried to strengthen his position by filling his ministry with actual or potential supporters, regardless of competence or commitment.

Although Yemen has been a party to the United Nations Convention against Corruption for decades, it has ranked among the most corrupt states in different institutions' scoring systems, with no improvement: in 2020, it was 176th out of 180 in the Transparency International's corruption index, and had dropped by eight points since 2012, merely emphasising the situation that corruption has increased since the war started. It was also the most fragile state in the world in the Fragile States index, which includes the functioning of security, the role of elites, legitimacy and others.

The emergence of the war economy

The main change brought by the war has been a modification in the identity of profiteers from corruption. While many earlier beneficiaries continue to operate, new ones have emerged from the ranks of new political and military powerful forces, mainly the Huthis but also local warlords and other powerful individuals on all sides. Once the Huthis had taken control of government, their anti-corruption rhetoric sounded increasingly hollow as prominent Huthis were seen to acquire a multiplicity of wealth indicators (cars, houses, etc.) and also filled the civil service with their supporters. The financial constraints imposed by the sanctions and international banking issues mean that, unlike colleagues in other countries, their wealth is staying within Yemen, rather than exported to international money laundering havens.

Soldiers are obviously important in the war, and the multiplication of 'ghost' soldiers comes as no surprise, but it certainly does not contribute to military achievement. This phenomenon is particularly acute in the forces of the IRG and benefits commanders who obtain salaries, rations and weapons for non-existent troops, allowing them to sell these for their own profit (SCSS, 2018, p. 29). In a similar vein, some soldiers manage to get paid twice by being on the roster of different military groups, something which is easier in the South where they can be simultaneously members of the UAE-supported Security Belt militias and other forces, as well as the official government of Yemen army. Corruption in the military concerns not only salaries and maintenance costs of soldiers, but also military materiel. Occasional scandals emerge when US or European military hardware is found to be in the wrong hands, given international end user regulations. Such sales also reflect the extent of commitment of the different fighters.

> There are also many instances in which individual soldiers themselves sell heavy weapons and military vehicles provided by either the internationally recognized Yemeni government or the Saudi-led coalition to anyone who meets their asking price. According to several independent sources, senior commanders and their subordinates reportedly sell weapons to interested buyers either directly, through intermediaries, or via the local arms market.
>
> (SCSS, 2018, p. 31)

Trade, import and export of fuel, primarily diesel, has been a major source of income for senior corrupt individuals since the Saleh period, and continues to be so. Main beneficiaries have partly changed as well as the direction of travel of the fuel, with a reduced role for Ali Mohsen and an increased one for Ahmed al Issi and Jalal Abdu Rabbu Mansour Hadi (SCSS, 2018, p. 35–36). Not only do these deals affect the price and availability of essential fuel to Yemeni citizens and traders in basic commodities, but they also illustrate the cooperation between supposedly enemy groups, as individuals close to President Hadi have, in exchange for cash, enabled the Huthis to import and distribute fuel. The blockade on Hodeida port is also used and manipulated by the Huthis to create shortages of fuel, and a highly profitable black market when these occur.

In addition to profiteers, the war economy has basically had a fundamental impact on all Yemenis' living standards, primarily through the increased cost of basic necessities at a time when incomes were collapsing. In February 2015, just before the internationalised war started, the basic minimum monthly survival food basket for seven people cost YR 17 366, By June 2021, it was YR 70 000 in the IRG area and YR 46 000 in Huthi-controlled areas, the 52% differential due to the collapse of the riyal in the IRG areas (FAO, August 2021, p. 4). Other basic necessities have seen the following increases: between 2014 and end December 2020, the price of a litre of diesel increased from YR 150 to YR 450, petrol from YR 158 to YR 400, and cooking gas from YR 19 925 to YR 5580 per cylinder (Republic of Yemen, Ministry of Planning and International Cooperation, 2021a, pp. 9–10). These are averages with considerable local variations. For those who still managed to find work and earn an income, unskilled daily wages were YR 4400 for unskilled labour, YR 7500 for semi-skilled and YR 4300 for agricultural labour in February 2020. Inflation between December 2014 and August 2020 was 145% according to the consumer price index for necessities (Republic of Yemen, Ministry of Planning and International Cooperation, Economic Studies and Forecasting Sector, 2020a, p. 12). The mechanisms used by ordinary people to cope with market instability are numerous and vary between the areas under the control of local authorities, the IRG and the Huthis (Huddleston and Wood, 2021).

Poverty

Unsurprisingly, the outcome of this multiplicity of problems is an extremely high poverty rate. Yemen's population has more than trebled since the state was created in 1990 when it had 12 million people. Its hydrocarbon resources are limited and, in any case, insufficient to finance high employment development policies, its education system is unable to encourage the skills necessary for a modern economy, its smallholding agriculture has forced thousands to rely on casual labour locally as farm labourers or sharecroppers. It is therefore unsurprising that Yemen had one of the world's highest poverty rates even before the current war.

The number of poor people doubled between 2005 and 2014, i.e. before the war started, reaching 12.6 million people or 49% of the population, though in 2012 the World Food Programme assessed the poverty level at 54%. Since then, figures have increased to a frightening level of 80% in 2020 (Republic of Yemen, Ministry of Planning and International Cooperation, 2020a, pp. 4–5), though in 2019 the World Bank's Macro Poverty outlook estimated a poverty rate of over 90% for 2020.[6] Given that the 1.25 million civil servants (supporting about 6 million household members) have only occasionally received their salaries since September 2016, and the collapse of most economic sectors, alongside the rise of the war economy, estimates over 80% are reasonable. There is a close overlap between poverty and humanitarian needs, and in 2021, the UN assessed that 20 million people were in need of some form of humanitarian aid, so certainly suffer poverty. By August 2021, OCHA stated that 'today, about 5 million people are just one step away from succumbing to famine and the diseases that go with it. Ten million more are right behind them' (OCHA, 2021).

Conclusion

Despite widespread popular opposition to the current war, there are two economic/military factors which enable it to continue: first, the emergence of a new class of war profiteers on all sides who would lose their sources of enrichment if it ended. Second, the financial desperation of millions of families whose legitimate sources of income have vanished and are compelled to allow or encourage their young men to join in the fighting, the main new source of fairly reliable salary payments.

The inability or unwillingness of the international community to prioritise development investments which would enable people to build a sustainable economy needs to be added to the list of failures. Humanitarian aid uses temporary employment, calling it 'cash for work' as a mechanism for conditional transfers rather than simply providing salaries for work. In addition, the activities financed replace basic services, such as waste disposal, or repair infrastructure like buildings, roads and bridges, rather than contributing to new economic enterprises or activities. This is partly due to the administrative constraints and procedures of both multilateral and bilateral funding agencies which separate humanitarian assistance from development activities, only permitting limited 'early recovery' economic activities within the humanitarian portfolios, thus perpetuating both financial and psychological dependence on outsiders to solve problems. One strategy which would simultaneously contribute to speeding up the end of the war and rebuild the economy would be immediate financial and technical support for development activities (Lackner, 2020b).

By the time the war ends, those in charge of whatever is left of the country will have to face enormous reconstruction costs to repair the destroyed infrastructure (roads, bridges, buildings, water and electricity networks) and build a productive economy. There is little doubt that the destitute citizenry will not be able to finance this. Since 2015, a succession of reconstruction conferences has been held under the auspices of the World Bank and other IFIs, providing estimates of billions of dollars of reconstruction costs, with the numerous international construction and consultancy firms licking their symbolic lips at the prospect of massive profits. All these operated on the assumption that these costs would be financed by the GCC states, primarily Saudi Arabia and the UAE. However, such financing depends on a number of factors, first of all the politics of those who control all or parts of the country: the GCC states are unlikely to finance infrastructure for the Huthi movement, which is also unlikely to be able to access much financial support from an Iran which has suffered decades of international sanctions. With notable exceptions, the GCC states are increasingly focused on their own financial development problems in an age when the international importance of hydrocarbons is diminishing and their own national populations are increasing. While the West may expect them to finance the reconstruction of Yemen (financially supporting Western companies in the process), the amounts made available will be significantly below what is needed. They are also unlikely to support strategies which challenge the neo-liberal agenda to which their own elites are fully committed.

While a return to previous economic policies is likely to produce the same results as in the past, namely poverty for the majority, a microscopic kleptocratic group of elite rulers, and a variety of endless more or less localised conflicts, this outcome is not inevitable. Yemen has impressive resources which can form the basis to build an equitable future: a young, talented and dynamic population, a wonderful and beautifully varied environment with a rich cultural heritage suitable for ethical tourism development, a long coast with fisheries potential, sun and wind for renewable energy, among others. To enable Yemenis to stay at home, the future regime must have an effective water management policy focused on domestic supplies, allowing supplementary irrigation in agriculture while serious investment in developing high value rain-fed crops is essential for rural Yemenis to enjoy their environment. With the development of high-quality education, and expansion of social and other services within the country, multiple SMEs and some industries, millions of Yemeni households could achieve reasonable living standards. For the country to remain viable, these policies must be complemented by its GCC neighbours welcoming Yemeni workers at all levels. None of these approaches alone is sufficient to solve all the country's problems due to population increase and limited natural resources, but between them they offer a positive outlook.

An ideal regime giving priority to the needs of the citizens, run in a democratic manner, implementing an equitable economic agenda would probably need to prioritise a high level of self-sufficiency. Beyond hopes for the discovery of new natural resources, a massive investment in education, in particular, will be essential to a prosperous future.

Notes

1 For more on water, see Lackner (2020a), (2020c).
2 All figures in this paragraph calculated from data from CSO annual statistical yearbook 2017.
3 See World Bank (n.d.a).
4 See World Bank (n.d.b).
5 These figures are for 2012; the debatable nature of all figures is illustrated by the fact that for 2004, the FAO website gives 540 000 ha irrigated with ground water and 254 000 with surface water (FAO Aquasat website, accessed 5 June 2019).
6 The World Bank's Macro poverty outlook 2020 edition simply gives no figure, just repeating its values of 2014!

4 International Relations

Yemen has never been isolated and has long had very active relations beyond its borders, both politically and through centuries of migration of its people. This chapter examines its formal political international relations and the impact on its internal politics of dependence on the world for development and humanitarian aid. Yemen's geographical position has also played an important role in determining its geopolitical constraints, as well as its earlier relationships with world powers, the Ottomans in the imamate and Britain in what became the People's Democratic Republic of Yemen during the Cold War, and in the twenty-first century dealing with dominant, unbridled, globalised capitalism. Recent history and current issues of Yemen's relations with the world will be discussed in an expanding circle, starting with the region. Rather than attempt to be comprehensive, the chapter will focus on the most significant relationships.

Some of the most important aspects of international relations for the people, namely migration and remittances, are discussed in the previous chapter. Remembering that remittances are as significant financially as any foreign aid agreements, the big difference is that the remittances go directly to households and are therefore of immediate benefit and use to families without mediation of institutions, and the recipients decide on their use according to their personal priorities and economic strategies. They are therefore largely independent of political relations between states but are far more influenced by the receiving states' labour migration policies. By contrast, the overwhelming majority of international aid assistance goes through state institutions and therefore is subject to the quality of governance, and vagaries of government policies.

The Arabian Peninsula and surroundings

Saudi Arabia

Relations with Saudi Arabia have dominated Yemen's internal and international politics since the establishment of the kingdom in 1932: a mere two years later the war between the kingdom and the imamate led to Yemen losing

DOI: 10.4324/9780429059315-5

the provinces of Asir, Najran and Jizan, on a series of 20-year renewable agreements, permanently enshrined in the 2000 border settlement between the Republic of Yemen and the Kingdom of Saudi Arabia (KSA). The seven intervening decades saw the replacement of the imamate by the YAR and the firm support of the KSA for the imam's forces during the civil war in the YAR in the 1960s, when the KSA initiated its policy of supporting and strengthening Zaydi tribal leaders in the far north of Yemen. This policy continued after the defeat of the imam's forces, and was designed to ensure that the Sana'a based state remained weak thanks to the presence of a rival tribal power based further north; the KSA also supported the state in Sana'a itself, to ensure it retained influence on all fronts. Thus, the KSA effectively set up its own 'divide and rule' mechanisms in the YAR. During the 23 years of existence of the PDRY, Saudi hostility to the 'communist' regime only mellowed slightly after 1976 when diplomatic relations were established, having spent years supporting military incursions and other hostile actions against the PDRY regime. The KSA did not welcome Yemeni unification in 1990, and in the 1994 civil war, it encouraged the secessionist faction it had actively opposed as 'communists' only a few years earlier. Contrary to statements of support in advance, it then failed to recognise the separatist state declared by Ali Salem al Beedh in Aden in May 1994. Such international recognition might have helped it to survive, but instead the separatists were soundly defeated by Saleh's forces within weeks.

Having achieved a final border agreement with the unified Republic of Yemen in 2000, the Saudi regime continued with ambiguous policies in relation to the Saleh regime until the current war started. Basically, regardless of its leadership, the KSA wants Yemen to be simultaneously strong enough and weak enough not to be a threat. Some may wonder how Yemen can be perceived as a threat to Saudi Arabia, but the rise of Huthis provides an element of an answer to this question. The two states have similar populations, around 30 million people and are largely arid, with two notable differences. First, in the KSA a substantial proportion of the population are migrant workers at all levels. Migrant workers are officially estimated at about 30% of the total, probably an underestimate until recently and, in the 2020s becoming an overestimate with the current draconian Saudisation policy being implemented by the regime of Mohammed bin Salman. Yemen's population is almost entirely Yemeni, with an insignificant migrant population, other than refugees from the Horn of Africa, most of whom are trying to migrate beyond Yemen to the GCC states and are only in Yemen due to the difficulties in crossing the borders. The second fundamental difference between the two states is the contrast between the wealth of Saudi Arabia, with its vast petroleum-based resources (more than 10 million b/d oil production) and that of Yemen, with hardly any natural resources (at its peak in 2001 of 400 000b/d oil production). Added to socio-cultural factors, these fundamental economic differences underlie the complex relationship between the two states as well as between their people.

Saudi influence in Yemen is political through the direct funding of the state and earlier the northern tribal leaders, thus affecting Yemeni domestic and international policies. The population is influenced through two main mechanisms: first, the large numbers of Yemenis working and living in Saudi Arabia depend on the KSA for their livelihoods; second, until recently, they were also ideologically influenced on a daily basis by living in the cultural constraints imposed by Wahhabi culture. Ideological influence also came, first in the YAR and later in the RoY, through Saudi financing and support of the Yemeni educational system implemented by Egyptian and Sudanese teachers; throughout the 1970s and 80s, teachers were recruited among their national Muslim Brotherhood communities and expected to spread Islamist culture in the towns and villages where they worked. In addition, religious cadres trained in Saudi universities operate throughout Yemen, not only in the majority Sunni areas but even in Zaydi areas where the famous Dar al Hadith was established in 1980, creating a hub of Sunni fundamentalism in the heartland of Zaydism (Bonnefoy, 2011). Regardless of changes in official Saudi ideology, it will take time for decades of promotion of fundamentalist Islamism to cease being a relevant political and cultural factor in Yemen as, indeed, in many other countries.

The Saleh regime, like its predecessors, maintained a complex relationship with Saudi Arabia, combining financial dependence with attempts to maintain political independence. Saleh had to balance between financial support for his government and the competing Saudi support to powerful tribal leaders who challenged his authority. Saudi ambiguous attitude to Saleh was best illustrated in 2011 when, seriously wounded by a bomb in Sana'a, he was flown to Saudi Arabia for treatment. But, two months later, he was able to slip back into Yemen, re-assert his authority, and continue to frustrate KSA and other efforts to finalise the GCC Agreement. Eventually, with the help of the UN Security Council, Saleh was forced to sign the agreement and to abandon the presidency of the country. Saudi authorities could have left him to die in Yemen or ensured unsuccessful medical treatment in Riyadh, thus solving their problem with the Yemeni leader. Care for this guest would probably have been different after 2015 when the effective ruler of Saudi Arabia, Mohammed bin Salman (known as MBS), had no hesitation to have senior Saudis imprisoned in luxury hotels or assassinated in the country's consulate in Istanbul.

Until his death in 2011, Saudi policy towards Yemen was under the control of Prince Sultan bin Abdul Aziz who managed the Special Office for Yemeni Affairs from which he selected beneficiaries for Saudi subsidies. Its annual budget reached USD 3.5 billion in the 2000s (Lackner, 2017a, p. 75). In the following years, with different princes in charge of the Yemen file, King Abdullah's regime reduced its detailed involvement in Yemeni affairs so that, when Salman became king in 2015, no senior leader in the KSA was well informed of the intricacies of Yemeni politics. While there is little doubt that the Saudis would intervene in the conflict between the Hadi regime and the Huthis, the form this intervention took came as a surprise to many. In previous eras, the KSA was careful to act indirectly and through proxies in Yemen, rather than take open military action. Its limited intervention in the Huthi war of 2009 on behalf of Saleh had demonstrated Saudi military weakness, confirming widespread international belief regarding the overall capacity of Saudi forces.

Throwing caution aside, Mohammed Bin Salman, newly appointed as minister of Defence, decided to launch the Decisive Storm operation in March 2015 believing that victory would be easy and speedy thanks to the KSA's expensive and sophisticated weaponry. Clearly, if he was aware of it, he had given no credence to his grandfather's warning in 1934 that Yemen 'is mountainous and tribal; no one can control it … the Ottoman state was the last of the failed invaders. I don't want to embroil myself or my people in Yemen' (al-Gosaibi, 2013, p. 20). The coalition led by Saudi Arabia, in its seventh year in 2021, has achieved very little, other than the death of about 100 000 Yemenis from directly war-related activities, and a further 250 000 or more from indirect causes due to the blockade, the humanitarian crisis, damage to much of Yemen's medical infrastructure, as well as other destruction. For the KSA it has worsened an already blemished reputation and is estimated to cost USD 5 to 7 billion per month.

The ostensible reason for the intervention was to restore to power the Hadi regime created by the 2011 GCC agreement and expelled from Sana'a in 2015. Spending on military equipment has been a major expenditure: as 73% of Saudi arms are purchased from the US and 13% from the UK, the total spent is staggering. Between 2011 and 2015, 'US arms transfers to Saudi Arabia amounted to $3 billion; between 2015 and 2020, the US agreed to sell over $64.1 billion worth of weapons to Riyadh, averaging $10.7 billion per year' (Riedel, 2021). With respect to both the US and UK's roles in the war, arms sales are only one element: the involvement of their nationals in maintenance of aircraft, supply of spares, etc. are essential to the KSA's ability to continue its military activities in Yemen. Ending arms sales would not have an immediate impact, stopping technical support and training would. With fluctuating oil prices, the Covid-19 pandemic, the cost of extravagant projects, and other demands on Saudi finances, the drain on state resources is an increasing concern. In 2021, MBS is finding it more difficult than expected to extricate his country from the war.

Post-war, regardless of anyone's wishes, by the nature of geopolitics, Saudi Arabia will be the country with which Yemen has the closest relations. It is unlikely that Yemen will be able to dispense with financial support from Saudi Arabia, or that it will stop exporting labour there, though with the changes in the world and its own economy, Saudi support will certainly be far less than Yemenis may hope. How relations are managed and to what extent they become more balanced and/or cooperative and friendly remains to be seen, and will depend on the nature of the regimes in both countries. What is clear is that the relationship will remain important and that the perceptions developed by Yemenis on all sides in the last decade will affect it. It is also clear that the financial expectations of some Yemenis (including the Huthis) as well as the international community will be disappointed: the amounts the KSA invests in Yemen will be far below any of the figures mentioned in the last few years. Should water management in Yemen continue its current unregulated course, it is also likely that, within a generation or less, many thousands, if not millions of Yemenis might cross the border into Saudi Arabia having been driven out of their country by the lack of water.

The United Arab Emirates

Established in 1971, the United Arab Emirates (UAE) is composed of seven small emirates and only became prominent on the regional and world stage thanks to the financial clout brought by the export of hydrocarbons. Dominated by Abu Dhabi, the wealthiest and most populated emirate, the UAE's early relations with Yemen were based on Shaykh Zayed bin Sultan al Nahyan, its founder-leader, believing his ancestors came from Marib. As a result, the UAE financed the reconstruction of the historic Marib dam in the 1980s, which never fulfilled the high expectations of Yemen's agriculture due to land tenure issues among others. He also invited many Yemenis originally from that area to live in Abu Dhabi, giving them nationality, so the UAE has a significant national population of Yemeni origin. Through separate processes, thousands of Socotrans settled in Ajman, one of the emirates. Saleh visited the UAE in December 1987. While relations between the PDRY and the UAE were marked by similar tensions to those with other GCC states, those of the YAR were good and the Saleh regime fully supported the GCC states in the 1980–88 Iran–Iraq war.

After the formation of the RoY, relations with the UAE were mostly positive and the country was increasingly dependent on financial and development aid from the UAE and other GCC states, mostly through their development-financing institutions. Until its involvement in the current war, the UAE did not publicise its support for Yemen and therefore figures for the above are difficult to access.[1] Politically there were no significant issues once the question of Yemen's support for Saddam Hussein's Iraq ceased to be relevant.

After decades of focusing on its own internal socio-economic construction, the UAE developed an active and forward moving foreign policy roughly since the war in Yemen started in 2015. Abu Dhabi's financial power enables this small state of 10 million people (close to 90% of whom are foreign workers without rights to settlement) to take initiatives attempting to position itself as a significant actor on the world geopolitical map. Thanks to military and other cooperation with the US and to retaining a close relationship with the UK, while also hosting a French military base, its international military ventures started with participation in the Western coalition in Afghanistan and, on its own initiative, more recently expanded in Yemen and Libya. Crown Prince

Mohammed bin Zayed (known as MBZ), the effective ruler of the UAE due to the medical condition of his brother Khalifa, the official ruler is trying to promote the UAE as a 'medium' level world power and taking regional and international initiatives to establish this status.

Other than its involvement in Yemen, the UAE was the initiator of the UAE-KSA attempt to marginalise Qatar in the conflict between 2017 and early 2021, a clash which MBS's Saudi Arabia was only too happy to leave behind but remains an issue for MBZ's UAE. In addition to historic family feuds, the main rationale for this hostility is a very different perception of the role of political Islam. The Gulf monarchies were firmly opposed to the flagship calls for democracy of the 2011 'Arab Spring', but Qatar was the only one to support popular movements, while the rest of the GCC responded with varying degrees of bribery or repression, including massive social benefits for nationals in KSA and the GCC police/military intervention in Bahrain in March 2011. The UAE under MBZ considers political Islam and, in particular the Muslim Brotherhood, to be the greatest threat facing its autocratic system, and actively undermines and attacks anything which its regime considers to be even remotely connected with this group.

The UAE is the second most important state in the coalition in Yemen, and the only one alongside Saudi Arabia involved in decision making. It had more troops in the country than Saudi Arabia (including on a number of front lines), and it initiated and led the 2018 offensive on Hodeida. When this was halted under international pressure resulting in the Stockholm Agreement, it became clear that the coalition had no alternative military strategy to defeat the Huthis, other than continuing with skirmishes on multiple fronts. Consequently, the UAE decision to formally withdraw was logical. As relations deteriorated between the IRG and the STC and the latter expelled the former from Aden in August 2019 (see Chapter 2, pp. 66–68), the UAE's announced withdrawal left the Saudi regime with all the problems of the Yemen war. Moreover, the UAE continued to support the STC thus seriously undermining Saudi efforts to solve this problem, and in particular to implement the Riyadh Agreement between the STC and the IRG. The early decision officially describing the coalition as 'Saudi-led' has also enabled the UAE to avoid being associated with the abysmal international public perception of the war, despite its extremely active role, including its operating of secret prisons and torture centres (Amnesty International, 2018; Roston, 2018), as well as its undermining the Hadi government by its persistent support for southern separatism and other forces which refuse to align with the IRG.

UAE policy in Yemen has a number of objectives. First, as just mentioned, the elimination of political Islamism, in this case the Islah party which it equates with the Muslim Brotherhood. Second, increasing its maritime power throughout the Indian Ocean, Arabian Sea and stretching into the Mediterranean Sea. Yemen has a very long coast, three major ports and control over the Bab al Mandab strait leading to the Suez Canal, all of which are important to the UAE's determination to dominate maritime routes in the region and ensuring the commercial primacy of its own ports over others. Third, it supports factions in Yemen which help promote the first two objectives, and in this context, it sponsored and assisted the development of the Southern Transitional Council (STC) enabling it to gain prominence over other factions. It also supports the military groups operating elsewhere, mostly on the Red Sea coastal Tihama region, which are not affiliated with the IRG, namely the Guardians of the Republic led by Tareq Saleh, as well a local forces and Salafi brigades, including significant numbers of southerners.

These priorities have, among others, led to two surprising consequences: first, the support of Salafi groups, who are far more extreme Islamists than Islah, including both so-called 'quietist' Salafis and more militant ones with connections to terrorism; second, the UAE rejection of Islah-connected institutions mean that it has a tense relationship with President Hadi's government where Islah has a strong presence. This government is officially supported by the international community, the UN and the Saudi-led coalition, including obviously the Saudi regime; Riyadh is the base of President Hadi and many of his ministers. Consequently, the competing support of Saudi Arabia for the IRG and that of the UAE for the STC is increasingly putting the two allies on opposite sides. As other elements of competition between them emerge under a Saudi regime actively engaged in shifting away from a hydrocarbon-based economy, including, for example, demanding that foreign companies move their regional HQ to Saudi Arabia, tensions are likely to increase in the coming period. Although this is most visible in Yemen, other elements will emerge with equal or greater importance over time. The Saudi determination to lead the Arab and Muslim world is already being challenged by UAE moves to position itself as a leader of the Arab world, for example in its open and public relationship with Israel, starting in mid-2020. While the KSA is the 'big neighbour' to the UAE, the latter's diversification of alliances can be seen as a form of insurance against the renewal of ancient problems and rivalries between the two states, control of the seas surrounding the peninsula being another element of that strategy.

As of late 2021, the UAE continue to have a significant direct presence in Yemen. it has military forces controlling the Mukalla airport at Riyan, the gas export port in Balhaf in Shabwa governorate, the Bab al Mandab through air facilities on Perim island, and has a strong presence in the Socotra archipelago. Its diplomatic, political, financial and military support to the STC and to Tareq Saleh's forces remain significant features of the internal fragmentation of the anti-Huthi forces.

Oman and other GCC states

Oman has a particular place in Yemen's foreign relations. After a period of hostility between the PDRY and the Sultanate during the early 1970s, due to the PDRY's active support for the People's Front for the Liberation of Oman which was defeated by the sultan's forces in the mid-1970s, relations gradually improved. Oman's relations with the YAR were peaceful and did not include any particularly notable features as the two states did not share a border.

Oman became important for Yemen after unification. The Omani policy of neutrality and non-involvement in internal conflicts first enabled the two states to finalise a border agreement in 1992. As tension rose between Sana'a and Aden in 1993, Sultan Qabus visited Sana'a trying to prevent the outbreak of intra-Yemeni hostilities. His and other efforts having failed, Oman remained unaligned in the 1994 civil war and gave refuge to southern leaders provided they did not involve themselves in politics. In 2009, when former leader Ali Salem al Beedh took up a position in the southern separatist movement, he had to leave and relinquish his Omani passport, thus enabling Oman to remain neutral.

In the war which has raged since 2015, Oman maximised the potential of its position as a possible mediator. Since the closure of Sana'a international airport in 2016, Muscat is where Huthi negotiating teams can meet visiting international delegations and travel to other locations. Oman has also assisted the freeing of hostages kept by the Huthis movement. Its position as a potential mediator is assisted by decades of neutrality and good relations with states supporting each side in the Yemeni conflict. The sultanate's close relations with the shah's Iran (overthrown in 1979 by the Islamic revolution) were maintained with the Islamist regime, while the numerous problems between Oman and its immediate neighbours, Saudi Arabia and the UAE, have largely been swept under the carpet but remain underlying issues. Close relations with the US, UK and other European states further facilitate its possible role as a mediator.

Oman's economy has been in crisis for years. Sultan Haytham bin Tareq acceded to the throne in early 2020 just weeks before the Covid-19 pandemic worsened GCC economies and has taken a number of measures to address political, economic and social problems. These included a more active approach to the Yemeni crisis, at the instigation of all the international parties involved, from the USA to the KSA, and has also increased economic relations with the Saudi regime. For the first time, an Omani delegation spent a full week in Sana'a in June 2021, and since then all international negotiators have included Muscat and discussion with its senior officials, in attempts to find a solution to end the war. The only missing element is willingness on the Yemeni side to find a solution.

Oman has, in the past, supported Yemen's membership of the GCC, and post-war cooperation between Yemen and Oman could prove very fruitful in manufacturing, cultural tourism and other socio-economic sectors, contributing to solving both countries' economic woes.

Yemeni relations with Kuwait were good until the 1990 crisis over Iraq's invasion, and it took many years for Kuwait to forgive Yemen for its position, particularly as it had been very generous with development aid to both states. Although formally a member of the Saudi-led coalition, Kuwait has done its best to mediate the current war. In particular it hosted many months of negotiations between the parties in 2016, and has since expressed willingness to do so again.

In the first decade of the century, Qatar's foreign policy of attempting mediations in other conflicts was applied to the Huthi conflict with the Saleh regime. This led to a cease-fire in June 2007 and an agreement in February 2008 involving significant Qatari financial aid for reconstruction in Sa'ada. Eventual failure of this attempt was due first to Saleh's resistance to investment support in Sa'ada outside of his control and second, probably, to Saudi Arabia's unhappiness at the involvement of a 'rival' state so close to its borders. Yemen kept out of the conflict between the KSA and the UAE on the one hand, and Qatar on the other in 2014, but the Hadi regime enthusiastically and immediately 'joined' the anti-Qatar boycott in 2017 and then welcomed the reconciliation in early 2021.

Throughout the boycott period, Qatar provided considerable humanitarian aid via the UN system and directly through its Red Crescent organisation. Its post-war involvement will depend on the political outcome of the Yemeni crisis and there is little doubt that Qatari investment would be welcome by Yemenis in different sectors, if only to reduce Yemen's dependence on other GCC states. In 2021, Qatar was, once again, trying to revive its role as potential mediator in regional conflicts, particularly between Iran (with whom it shares the major South Pars/North Dome gas field) and the rest of the world. Insisting on an independent foreign policy, it is likely to continue supporting political Islamist parties in Yemen, as its leadership has a more open approach to political pluralism than others in the GCC.

Iran

While the PDRY had relatively friendly relations with the Iranian revolutionary regime, as both considered themselves progressive, even though in widely different ways, the YAR's alignment with Iraq in the Iran–Iraq war of the 1980s clearly put the two Yemeni states in opposite camps, and Saleh's visit to Baghdad in 1988 merely confirmed this situation. Although the Iraqi and YAR regimes were very different, and Saleh's regime in Yemen far less oppressive than that of Saddam Hussein, Saleh supported Saddam and this was certainly one of the reasons Yemen took the position it did at the UN in 1990, as the PDRY had been a firm opponent of the Iraqi regime. In the following years, Iran did not feature prominently in Yemeni affairs, though the Huthis started their ideological links and sent family members and others for religious training in Iran, something which did not seem particularly significant at the time.

In the twenty-first century, the situation changed: in May 2003, Saleh received a large delegation led by President Khatami, and numerous agreements were signed. With the emergence of the Huthi rebellion against his regime in 2004, the state's relations with Iran deteriorated and by 2009 Saleh closed the Iranian-supported hospital in Sana'a. His efforts at that time to persuade Saudi Arabia and the US that Iran was supporting the Huthis failed (see Lackner, 2017a, p. 81; Vatanka, 2020, p. 151).

Huthi relations with Iran started early but remained insignificant until the current war, though Husayn al Huthi brought back the Huthi slogan from Iran after his studies there. Increasing tension between Saudi Arabia and Iran under the US Trump administration contributed to worsening the situation in Yemen and increasing Iranian involvement in support of the Huthis militarily and politically. Internally the Huthi movement itself has deepened religious and political relations with Iran and is implementing a shift towards Iranian-Shi‘i rituals partly to distinguish itself ideologically from traditional Zaydism. Twelver (Iranian Shi‘a) religious celebrations have been introduced and promoted in Huthi-controlled Yemen, while mutual statements of political support multiply and both have resident ambassadors in their respective capitals.

The military support from Iran and Lebanese Hizbollah which is widely publicised internationally is largely an exaggeration as can be seen by a careful, rather than biased, reading of the annual reports of the UN-established sanctions committee. However, starting from nothing, by 2021 there were clear indications that Iran is providing Yemen with advanced technological support in the development of missile and drone technology as well as other weapons. This has enabled the Huthis to target sites deep into Saudi Arabia, and particularly the capital, though some of the main Huthi claims have been disproved. For example, the serious and remarkably effective missile attack of September 2019 on Saudi Arabia's major oil producing and export facilities at Abqaiq and Khurais was claimed by the Huthis, giving them a great propaganda boost internally. Forensic examination soon demonstrated that these missiles had come from the north and north-east, whereas Yemen is located south-west of Saudi Arabia. This is a clear case of collusion between the Huthis and the Iranian regime, allowing the former to take credit for a significant military action, actually performed by people geographically closer to the latter.

Internationally, it is often claimed by officials and others that the Huthis are no more than Iranian 'proxies'. This deliberate misinformation is dangerous, as misunderstanding of a situation leads to inappropriate policies which are bound to fail. The relationship between the two has intensified since 2015, but the Huthis do not take orders from Tehran, and it is only when both parties have concordant objectives that their actions are in step. For Iran, the Huthi movement in Yemen is a cheap opportunity to create problems for the rival Saudi regime. As stated by Vatanka, 'Iran was not the cause of the Yemeni conflict, nor did it have the capacity to end it. What Tehran set out to do from the outset was exploit the Yemeni conflict to its benefit as part of a broader competition for regional power, vis-à-vis the Saudis in particular' (Vatanka, 2020, p. 149). Within the context of discussions to re-establish cooperative relations between Iran and the rest of the world, Yemen and the Huthis are no more than a marginal element. The significant development of an emerging direct dialogue between Iranian and Saudi leaders in 2021 may contribute to easing regional tensions in the peninsula, but it remains essential to remember that the Huthis have their own interests and objectives and will not abandon them to please the Iranian regime.

Post-war relations between Yemen and Iran will obviously depend on the role of the Huthi movement in the Yemeni state. It is, however, unlikely that Iran, even freed from the stranglehold of current sanctions, would be in a position to provide Yemen with much more support than it already does by providing cheap or free oil. Its ideological influence through the Huthi movement is likely to remain significant and possibly even expand in the future, but after decades of sanctions, Iran is unlikely to provide significant amounts in development financing.

Across the Red Sea

Yemeni relations with its neighbours across the Red Sea and the Gulf of Aden have always been important and varied. The PDRY had close relations with the revolutionary Ethiopian regime and its relations with Somalia varied according to who was in charge and Ethiopian–Somali relations, so the PDRY broke off relations with President Siyadh Barre when Ethiopian–Somali relations broke down. Relations were also closely connected with the positions of the USSR at the time, and the PDRY formed a tripartite pact with Libya and Ethiopia in 1981 (Halliday, 1990, pp. 172–173), a grouping of radical states in which Libya was expected to provide financial and economic support to the other two, but the PDRY was also concerned with control over the Red Sea and challenging conservative states in the area.

The intricacies of Horn of Africa politics would require pages to merely describe the changing alliances and deals between Sudan, Ethiopia, Eritrea and Somalia (see de Waal, 2020, pp. 195–208). The RoY did its best to keep out of them, but its control over the Bab al Mandab and presence in the Red Sea demand involvement in this region and also gives it an important strategic role. A variety of meetings of states bordering the Red Sea have taken place over the decades, including one in 1977 in Taiz when President Hamdi tried to strengthen his position vis-à-vis Saudi Arabia. With the end of the Cold War and with Yemeni unification, the area saw many changes, mostly focused on the strategic importance of the Bab al Mandab, including the fundamental transformation of Djibouti from a French base watching the entrance to the Red Sea, to the site of bases belonging to numerous states, including the USA, China, Japan and Saudi Arabia. In 2003, a series of meetings known as the Sana‘a Forum for Cooperation brought the RoY together with Ethiopia and Sudan, later joined by Somalia, obviously to the great irritation of the excluded Eritrea. The last such meeting took place in December 2008, with Sudan, Yemen, Ethiopia, Somalia and Djibouti, many of them in dispute with each other.

After Eritrea regained its independence in 1993, it was initially welcomed by the new RoY, but relations soon deteriorated when it occupied the Hunaysh

Islands in 1995. Yemen went to arbitration at the International Court of Justice in 1998–99 which ruled in its favour, confirming Yemeni ownership of these islands, and Eritrea respected the ruling. Since then, Eritreans have frequently arrested Yemeni fishermen, keeping them hostage for long periods, ensuring constant tension. Eritrea, now largely a pariah state in the region, has worked to mend its relations with the main financiers of the area through the handover to the UAE of significant areas in Assab, where the UAE built a large base to replace Djibouti from where it had been expelled.

The last decade has seen a renewed involvement of Horn states with Yemen, partly through the rise of intra-GCC rivalries with different states expanding relations with Horn entities in the hope of outdoing each other. Qatar initially attempted to mediate between different conflicting parties according to its foreign relations policy in the first decade of the century, for example in Sudan between different internal factions in Darfur. Turkey was also very active in Somalia, where it eventually ousted the UAE, leading the UAE to support the separatist Somaliland where it turned Berbera port into a military base. The UAE also expanded the port of Bossasso in Puntland, the first claiming independence from Somalia and the second merely autonomy. In both cases UAE involvement was not welcome by Mogadishu authorities. Wherever it succeeded, the UAE included contracts with Dubai Ports World (DPW), emphasising its long-term strategy of controlling maritime routes and gaining significant income from commercial shipping.

The Yemen war has deepened the relationships between the Horn states and Yemen: the Eritreans ended their cooperation with the Huthis when the UAE and Saudis made better financial offers, leading to further frequent and regular attacks on Yemeni fishermen. The UAE–Eritrean agreement on Assab turned it into a base used in its operations in Yemen, for training of Yemeni troops, aerial and surveillance attacks, but also as a secret detention centre (de Waal, 2020, p. 202). Eritrea benefitted from its involvement, thus breaking its previous isolation and eventually, thanks to Saudi and UAE support as well as the change of regime in Addis Abeba, largely solving its problems with Ethiopia. The war which started in Ethiopia in November 2020 is another complicating factor for the future of the Red Sea region.

Sudan became the main provider of ground troops to the coalition; having failed to involve both Pakistan and Egypt in the ground war in Yemen, the coalition has relied on Sudanese troops, under direct contract between their leader, the notorious Mohammed Hamdan Dagolo (known as Hemedti), the UAE and KSA. As leader of the Janjaweed militias his troops had terrorised people in Darfur for decades, so they were renamed the Rapid Support Force and deployed in Yemen from 2015 onwards, operating under both Saudi and Emirati command. Up to 30 000 Sudanese troops fought in Yemen (Amin, 2019), according to Hemedti, giving a figure twice that found elsewhere over the period (Abdelaziz, 2019), and many were killed. Like the majority of Yemeni fighters, most Sudanese volunteering to fight in Yemen do so out of financial necessity at a time of deep economic crisis in their own country. With the significantly reduced Emirati military involvement in Yemen since mid-2019, and the emerging crises in Sudan, their numbers in Yemen have dropped.

In January 2020, after two years of negotiations, Saudi Arabia formally launched the Council of Arab and African Coastal States of the Red Sea and Gulf of Aden which includes Saudi Arabia, Sudan, Djibouti, Somalia, Eritrea, Egypt, Yemen, and Jordan (Arab News, 2020; see also Bagnetto, 2020). Its responsibility is to address 'the threats and challenges facing our region, and safeguard the security of the Red Sea and Gulf of Aden' according to the Saudi Foreign Minister. Its real role is as a mechanism to increase KSA influence in the Red Sea; the absence of the UAE is particularly notable given its own numerous bases in the region, let alone the issues and problems within Somalia, and the rising rivalry between the UAE and the KSA. Whether this turns out to be more than a paper organisation remains to be seen.

Regardless of inter-state political relations, given the proximity of the Horn and many other factors, there have been for centuries considerable population movements in both directions between Yemen and the Horn of Africa. Communities of Yemeni origin are found throughout east Africa. In the 1970s, the Sana'a regime took many initiatives to encourage Yemenis to return to Yemen from these countries, largely so they would bring back their skills and material assets (see Bezabeh, 2016). Many of the men had married locally and returned with African wives; their children are known as *muwalladeen* and suffer discrimination within Yemen, though some of them are privileged with respect to employment with foreign agencies (embassies, international agencies, as well as NGOs) thanks to their mastery of English, an important selection criterion for these organisations.

The broader Middle East

Egypt

Egypt's relations with Yemen have been long and tempestuous. As discussed in Chapter 1, Nasser's Egypt lost thousands of troops in the Yemeni mountains in the 1960s civil war. Throughout the Saleh period, relations were cordial and largely to the benefit of Egypt which sent teachers who staffed the education system in the YAR for decades, most of them financed by Saudi Arabia and selected for their affiliation to Salafi Islam, which they spread throughout the country. The PDRY's relations with Egypt were significantly more negative: after Sadat signed the Camp David Accords with Israel in 1978, the YSP regime expelled all Egyptians, except leftist exiles, from the country. As a result, Egyptian teachers disappeared from the PDRY and were replaced by Yemeni secondary school graduates sent on two-year 'national service' stints throughout the country to teach. Relations remained cool for the remaining years of the PDRY.

Saleh's closeness to Saddam Hussein's Iraqi regime contributed to the formation of the Arab Cooperation Council in 1989, which included Yemen,

Iraq, Egypt and Jordan, following visits to Sana'a by Mubarak (1988) and Saddam (1989). Short lived as it was, the council was ostensibly intended to create a common market and alliance between the states excluded from the GCC. It was widely perceived, in Saudi Arabia in particular, as a group of republican anti-monarchical states surrounding Saudi Arabia and threatening it. Egypt's participation in this grouping was also the 'excuse' for the expulsion of Yemenis and Egyptians from GCC states when Iraq invaded Kuwait in 1990.

The RoY's relations with Egypt remained cordial without any significant features other than the continued presence of numerous Egyptians in the Yemeni educational system. This largely reflects the reduced significance of Egypt on the international Arab scene after the GCC states, thanks to their financial clout, achieved greater international political prominence, though Egypt remains a reference for many Yemenis, both politically and culturally. During the 2011 uprisings, many foreign observers suggested that Yemenis were following the Egyptian example, promoting a vision of Egyptian superiority and primacy. In reality, this was certainly not the case as the Yemeni uprising, like others, had its own roots and rationale and had actually been active prior to the Egyptian one, though the overthrow of Mubarak did give a boost of hope and optimism to an already strong anti-Saleh movement in the country.

Institutional military memory certainly contributed to persuading Egypt to avoid sending ground troops when the current war became internationalised in 2015. This resulted in stress with both Saudi Arabia and the UAE which are the main financiers of the Sisi regime as they had expected Sisi to comply with their requests. So, although Egypt is explicitly part of the coalition, its military involvement has been minimal and restricted to naval support in the Red Sea and diplomatic backing. To compensate for its refusal to send ground troops it has been particularly indulgent towards other Saudi demands. In particular, it handed over islands in the Tiran straits to Saudi Arabia despite considerable Egyptian opposition from groups normally in support of the regime. For exiled Yemenis, Cairo has been welcoming to many, including senior current and former members of government, while also being a place where politicians can meet each other and international politicians and diplomats, though Islah members are definitely less welcome than people with other affiliations. For exiles, the low cost of living in Egypt is also an attraction.

Palestine

On the Palestinian issue, both pre-unification regimes had strong pro-Palestinian policies though the Saleh regime favoured the PLO in the 1980s while the YSP in Aden was more supportive to the movements emerging from the Movement of Arab Nationalists, the People's Front for the Liberation of Palestine (PFLP) and the Democratic Front for the Liberation of Palestine

(DFLP). Both Yemeni states gave asylum to thousands of PLO troops when they were expelled from Lebanon in 1982, while senior PLO politicians moved to Tunisia.

Since its establishment, the RoY maintained good relations with the PLO and recognised Palestine as a state, with a Palestinian embassy opened in Sana'a. The current war has put the issue of Palestine very much on the back burner. Though the Huthi movement considers Israel a prime enemy and asserts support for the Palestinians at every opportunity, it is more focused on denouncing Israel. The 2020 establishment of diplomatic relations between Israel, the UAE and other states, led to a flurry of support statements from STC leaders which have aroused considerable hostility from most Yemenis, let alone the Huthis for whom it merely confirmed their view of Israel is a main enemy closely linked to the coalition. Whether this will lead to Israeli actual military and surveillance facilities in Yemen will clearly depend both on how relations develop with the UAE and the outcome of the war in Yemen.

Asia

Asia has been a main destination for Yemeni migration, particularly India, Malaysia and Indonesia, since the nineteenth century. Political relations with South-East Asian countries are influenced by the presence of senior officials of Yemeni descent, particularly high status *sada* who achieved important positions in their countries of migration. Trade has also been important. Yemen has kept out of local conflicts in South Asia, for example between India and Pakistan. In India itself, other than formal diplomatic relations and some trade, the main lasting connection is that of the Yemeni Ismaili community with its mother community in the Indian subcontinent. Under the Hindu nationalist Modi regime, these links are not particularly helpful to Yemen.

In recent decades, for Yemen as for so many other countries, the Far East has become extremely important, mainly as a source of imports for items of daily life. Vehicles in Yemen are almost exclusively from the Far East with a strong dominance of Japanese Toyotas, though Chinese and Korean vehicles have started appearing this century and are gradually increasing their share. East Asian imports have contributed significantly to the collapse of local artisanal production of goods of daily use while also preventing the emergence of locally industrial manufacture, thanks to the internationally imposed so-called free trade system. Korea participates in the Yemen LNG company and is likely to purchase some of Yemen's main export when operations resume.

China had 'friendly' and supportive relations with both the PDRY and the YAR, contributing to their development and infrastructure investments in the 1970s. These were influenced by the 1960s and 1970s Sino-Soviet dispute when both these states competed for political support in different third world countries and China claimed its solidarity with third world countries. With its change of policy and efforts to become a major world power, the nature of its relationship with Yemen accordingly shifted from solidarity between developing countries, to the prioritisation of commercial gains and interests: Chinese exports to Yemen grew from USD 911 million in 2000 to USD 4 billion in 2010 (Chang, p. 98).

However, Yemen's poverty and limited natural resources of interest to China means that it remains low on the Chinese political agenda, though its large population means it retains relevance as a potential market. China has been involved in petroleum exploration in Yemen and by 2014 Chinese companies produced 20 000 b/d of Yemen's petroleum, about 15% of its production at the time. The relationship was of greater importance to Yemen, and President Saleh visited Beijing in 2006, hoping for more Chinese investments. Like many other autocratic rulers in the world, Saleh appreciated China's willingness to provide assistance without any preconditions, and particularly preconditions connected with human rights and democratic reforms.

After decades of support to Saleh, as representative of a permanent member of the UNSC, the Chinese ambassador was one of the group of ten ambassadors involved in assisting the transition from the Saleh regime in 2011. China followed the lead of the Western states, a situation which contrasted with Beijing's position on Syria for example, where China and Russia formed a bloc opposing US/UK/French positions. China was determined to retain its potentially good commercial relations with any future regime and received President Hadi in a state visit in 2013, officially supporting the transition and planning a number of investments in energy and transport.

Yemen's importance for China remains limited despite its position at the entrance of the Red Sea which still controls the majority of Chinese trade with Europe and other parts of the world. Relations with Saudi Arabia and the UAE clearly take priority over those with Yemen. China's involvement in maritime affairs in the region started in 2008 with an anti-piracy operation, and in 2015, it sent its own naval force to evacuate Chinese citizens when the war started, but it was only in 2017 that China opened its first international base in the region in Djibouti which guarantees it reliable access to the Red Sea and the Suez Canal.

While China might wish to include Yemeni ports among the 'pearls' of the Belt and Road Initiative, as of 2021, most Yemeni ports are under UAE influence or Huthi control and therefore their access depends more on Chinese–UAE relations, while Saudi Arabia is a major supplier of oil. Hence China is unwilling to take any position on Yemen which might risk its relationship with either of these two states. This explains why it voted in favour of resolution 2216 at the UNSC and has continued with good relations and mutual visits with Saudi Arabia.

Since the war started, China's position on Yemen has remained one of non-involvement, supporting the UNSC and the special envoy, making pious statements on the occasion of the more outrageous military attacks, while demonstrating its presence at the international level. Chinese priorities in the region are focused on maintaining equitable relations with both Saudi Arabia and Iran in the context of the US extreme pressure policy against Iran. Its own relations with Iran have bilateral dynamics while also being a tool in the increasing rivalry with the US. Yemen is not sufficiently important to China for it to jeopardise other regional relationships. As neatly summarised by Chang, Chinese objectives in Yemen were 'to work with and support regional and international efforts to achieve a ceasefire and open channels of humanitarian aid to the Yemenis; remain neutral on the Saudi-Iranian rivalry but yield to Saudi Arabia's national security interests on Yemen; and invest in Yemen's mineral wealth and oil resources, while positioning itself to play a role in post-war development and reconstruction' (ibid., p. 107). This post-war role is most likely to prioritise economic benefits to China, so it is likely to seek construction contracts for infrastructure, as well as mechanisms to expand exports to the country. Again, following its usual current policies, China is very unlikely to take any principled position on human rights or other issues or, indeed, to even care what type of regime rules Yemenis.

The North

Yemen receives limited attention by powerful states, despite its strategic importance. During the Cold War, its division between two states, one aligned with the West and the other with the USSR, meant that it was a front line, in addition to its geographic position in control of the Bab al Mandab strait leading to the Suez Canal. After unification, the RoY rapidly lost significance for powerful states, particularly as it had taken the 'wrong' side in the Iraq–Kuwait conflict and was effectively ostracised by the West which, then and thereafter, saw Yemen as a secondary issue, relegated to being the responsibility of its immediate neighbours, Saudi Arabia in particular, who could call on Western support if needed and were important thanks to their hydrocarbon reserves and resulting financial strength. The large sums they spent in Western countries, primarily on advanced and expensive weaponry, ensured their views were prioritised.

The emergence of the jihadi movement changed this situation and re-established some big power interest in Yemen. Since the 1990s, the primary concern of world powers was never the needs and welfare of the Yemeni people. Instead, their 'aid' focused on 'security' issues and was invested in counter-terrorism activities supporting the regime's military and security institutions, giving far less attention to governance, corruption, socio-economic development or poverty alleviation. Thus, most support actually, if indirectly, contributed to the country's instability and worsening poverty. This situation persists to this day in the international community's response and involvement in the war which has destroyed much of the country.

RoY–USA relations

Yemeni–US relations have varied over time. The YAR was close to the USA and got significant development and military support, but its rulers also made sure the country retained diversified sources for both, leading to the possibly apocryphal ironic situation where the US and the USSR both trained the Yemen air force at different ends of the same landing strip in Sana'a in the 1970s. After the 1990 setback of the Iraq–Kuwait crisis, Saleh systematically asserted his support for the US, even when his actions suggested otherwise, so he rushed to express support for the USA's 'war on terror' after the 11 September al Qaeda attack on the US.

Yemen was the site of one of the earlier deadly al Qaeda attacks in October 2000 when jihadis successfully struck the USS Cole in Aden port killing 17 US personnel and wounding more. Investigation in this incident was an example of Saleh's skilful manoeuvring and ambiguity in relations with the US. He was fully aware of the importance of having active jihadis operating in the country, as it was the main rationale for US military support to his regime. He allowed US investigators to come but once they were in the country, he systematically prevented them from carrying out their tasks as discussed in detail by then US Ambassador Edmund Hull (Hull, 2011, p. 9). Saleh's prompt support for Bush after 9/11 was intended both to compensate for unsatisfactory cooperation with investigators of the USS Cole incident and to ensure favourable response to his numerous demands for equipment and training, which increased in the following years.

One outstanding disappointment was the USA's unexpectedly changed position during Saleh's official visit to Washington in 2005. Despite his expectation following earlier negotiations, he was informed that Yemen would not be included in the Millennium Challenge funding due to the regime's corruption and lack of democratic practices. Saleh had looked forward not only to the cash benefits of inclusion in this programme but also to the kudos it would have given him by endorsing his regime as a rising democracy. The previous year, Yemen had hosted a widely publicised international conference on 'Democracy and Human Rights in the Broader Middle East, Fostering Democratic Change' attended by numerous international personalities. The Saleh regime thought it had successfully presented Yemen as a leading democratic progressive state and that its democratic credentials were unarguable. The rejection of the Millennium challenge was a real shock.

Despite this set-back, US aid to Yemen continued and strengthened the military security apparatus led by Saleh's close relatives, his son Ahmed and his nephews Tareq and Ammar. The elite units were well trained and well equipped; when the 2011 uprising forced Saleh to give up the presidency, the US administration reluctantly supported President Hadi's transitional regime plan to restructure the military/security sector. As the US was directly involved in 'supporting' this element of the transition, it bears some responsibility for the failure of this absolutely crucial and essential component of the transition. Can a state without control over its security services implement any other reform, particularly when it is unpopular?

According to Day, 'three factors obstructed the military reform process' (2020, p. 57): Yemeni commanders more interested in cash benefits than national interest, lower ranking officers retaining their loyalty to Saleh even when senior commanders were replaced, and weak state capacity. US ambassador Feierstein attributed Hadi's failure to restructure these institutions to the Saleh–Huthi alliance whose main purpose was to undermine Ali Mohsen and the sons of Shaykh Abdullah Husayn al Ahmar. US officials were concerned about Ali Mohsen's closeness not only to Islah but also to jihadis.

By contrast, after 2012 Hadi, persuaded the US that the Huthis were not a threat, despite serious concerns about their anti-US slogans. This position persisted well into 2014 though then US Ambassador Tueller believed that the Huthis, in alliance with Saleh, were the main threat to a successful transition. Day's analysis, based on detailed interviews with US ambassadors to Yemen and other senior staff, indicates that the Obama administration feared being 'entrapped' in Yemen, as it had been in Syria and did not perceive the Huthis to be Iranian proxies, by contrast with the embassy staff in Sana'a, who did.

When the Saudi-led offensive started in March 2015, the Obama administration refused to participate in military operations to avoid entrapment.[2]

> Obama authorized US commanders at the major-general level to participate in a 'joint planning cell' in Saudi Arabia, yet … disallowed Americans from selecting bombing targets in Yemen. US commanders could only assist their Arab colleagues by providing intelligence reports drawn from US satellite data. Likewise, American pilots flew mid-air refuelling missions for GCC fighter jets, yet they were not allowed to engage targets in Yemen. No restrictions were placed on the sale of US weapons to Saudi Arabia.
>
> (Day, 2020, p. 64)

He argues that the JCPOA agreement with Iran took priority and that the US administration was unwilling to take any action in the Yemen war which would jeopardise it. Disturbed by accusations that US weaponry was being used against civilian infrastructure, Obama tried to persuade the Saudis to 'help relieve Yemen's growing humanitarian crisis' (ibid., p. 65). Whether this was the reason for Saudi significant financing for humanitarian relief remains to be demonstrated. The contradiction between impressive financing of the war and the simultaneous support for humanitarian efforts to relieve its impact is not lost on many.

The US was also directly militarily involved in counter-terrorism activities, mainly through drone and air strikes, the first of which occurred in 2002, followed by a long gap. But starting in 2009, drone and other air strikes became increasingly frequent, as per Table 4.1. The frequency of strikes varied over the years: the first period, when Saleh was still in charge, was followed by the transition when President Hadi claimed to have given blanket authority to the US to launch strikes at will while simultaneously asserting that he had authorised each individually (Lackner, 2017a, p. 86). The third period covers

Table 4.1 US drone and other strikes on Yemen

Confirmed strikes	*2009–11*	*2012–14*	*2015–20*	*Total*
Strikes	16	80	229	325
Minimum killed	111	386	405	902
Maximum civilians killed	132	535	544	1211

Source: Bureau of Investigative Journalism website July 2020.

the full-scale war from 2015 onwards, which began with an increasing number of strikes (58) in the last two years of the Obama administration, followed by a spike in the early days of the Trump administration in 2017. On 29 January 2017, merely days after Trump became president, there was a strike on Yakla (al Baydha Governorate), a debacle, as the US lost a marine as well as a helicopter, in the process of killing 25 civilians including children. That year saw the largest number of strikes (127) and they diminished significantly in 2018 (36) and 2019 (8), while none took place in the first half of 2020. Interestingly, the US was also involved in a total of ten land operations during this period which killed more than 120 people including 83 civilians.

The issue of weapons sales to Saudi Arabia and their use in Yemen was a focus of struggle between the US Congress and President Trump. After years of efforts by some Congress members to control US arms sales to Saudi Arabia, each of which achieved more votes but was eventually defeated in the Senate, the situation changed once US Congress members on all sides were shocked by the Saudi assassination of Jamal Khashoqji in October 2018. As a result, in 2019 success was within reach when both Houses of Congress approved resolutions which would prevent the US from selling weapons to Saudi Arabia and the UAE. However, Trump vetoed them, and the Senate was unable to achieve the two thirds majority needed to overturn the veto. Meanwhile arms and ammunition sales continued apace to the greater profit of the US arms manufacturers.

Immediately upon taking office, the Biden administration put a halt to ‘offensive’ arms sales to Saudi Arabia. In his first major foreign policy statement, on 4 February 2021, Biden declared:

> We’re also stepping up our diplomacy to end the war in Yemen – a war which has created a humanitarian and strategic catastrophe. I’ve asked my Middle East team to ensure our support for the United Nations-led initiative to impose a ceasefire, open humanitarian channels, and restore long-dormant peace talks … And to underscore our commitment, we are ending all American support for offensive operations in the war in Yemen, including relevant arms sales. At the same time, Saudi Arabia faces missile attacks, UAV strikes, and other threats from Iranian-supplied forces in

multiple countries. We're going to continue to support and help Saudi Arabia defend its sovereignty and its territorial integrity and its people.
(www.whitehouse.gov/briefing-room/speeches-remarks/2021/02/04/remarks-by-president-biden-on-americas-place-in-the-world/)

This statement was linked to the appointment of an experienced diplomat as US special envoy to Yemen. By end 2021, despite the envoy's numerous trips to the region, little had been achieved, and new arms sales were confirmed. The Biden administration's effort to improve US–Iranian relations by re-establishing the JCPOA or something similar remains embroiled in internal US complications; contrary to the belief of many in the US, this would not significantly impact the Yemen crisis. Loud statements concerning the Saudi regime's breaches of human rights have prevented direct contact between the US president and the KSA's de facto ruler, Mohammed bin Salman; but the US–Saudi relationship has not been fundamentally changed.

I share Day's conclusion that US policy in Yemen, under both Obama and Trump, was concerned with US national security and counter terrorism, neglecting '[Yemen's] vastly greater need for short-term humanitarian relief and long-term economic development' (ibid., p. 67). Economic aid 'would have given Yemenis a greater stake in the transitional government's success' (ibid., p. 67). A year of Biden's presidency and the prospect for changes during the 2022 mid-term elections in the US suggest that the US is unlikely to profoundly affect the situation in Yemen. It cannot 'end the war in Yemen', both because it is fundamentally a civil war and because US policies prioritise other issues in the Gulf region.

Western Europe

Differences between US and European policies with respect to Yemen are more than merely cosmetic, but do not indicate intrinsically different objectives. France is the only country which has a major economic investment in Yemen through Total's large share of the Yemen LNG company (discussed in Chapter 3); although it is the largest Yemeni investment, it is of far lesser significance for Total than it is for Yemen. Most European Union states and the UK share a priority concern with counter-terrorism when focusing on Yemen, and on trade and arms sales with other Arabian Peninsula states, positions which are similar to those of the US.

All these states had working political relationships with the Saleh regime and did little to challenge the regime's autocratic tendencies, accepting its claims to democracy, which were facilitated by the presence of opposition parties and an elected parliament. In development, they provided financial and technical support in different sectors, reflecting socio-economic marginal advantages: the Netherlands were deeply involved in water management and in rural development, Germany worked in all economic and social sectors, while France and Italy focused on cultural support. The UK was closely involved in training security personnel and in education, while all participated jointly in a wide range of projects through the European Union, as well as financing all sectors through their contributions to the international financial institutions.

European states' counter-terrorism priorities must also be compared to those of the US. France suffered a series of terrorist attack starting in 2015 when a group claiming to have been trained in Yemen carried out attacks against the satirical magazine *Charlie Hebdo*. This was followed by terrorist incidents elsewhere which, although not related with Yemen, keep its regime seriously concerned with the issue. Its diplomats are active on the Yemeni scene but have not taken a leading role, nor has France reduced its arms sales to Saudi Arabia and the UAE. For France, its relationship with Saudi Arabia and other GCC states remains a priority over that with Yemen, as Saudi Arabia 'ranked as the second largest client of French military companies, settling more than US $12 billion worth of contracts between 2008 and 2018' (Bonnefoy, 2020, p. 72). The UAE is another major client as well as the site of the first new French military base in the world opened in 2009.

Germany is particularly active in Yemen. In addition to its development support, it has hosted many Yemeni leaders, whether in power or dissident, members of the Saleh family, Huthi movement leaders and others. This gives it opportunities for political influence thanks to its easy access to Yemeni politicians of all stripes. During the war it has established strong 'back channel' opportunities through the numerous NGOs it funds. Activities have included a series of discreet meetings between Yemeni politicians over a period of years. Germany also continues to have a physical presence in the country through GIZ, its development technical assistance institution. While civil society pressure failed to prevent continued arms sales from the UK, Germany and other European states officially stopped selling arms to Saudi Arabia and the UAE, though this ban seems to have a limited effectiveness. German humanitarian contribution to the UN's annual humanitarian response plan, has been quite generous coming in fourth position, after the USA, Saudi Arabia and the UK: in 2021, USD 268 million (or 10% of total funding), in 2020, USD 173 million (or 9% of total funding), in 2019 USD 184 million, 2018 USD 154 million, and 2017 USD 204 million. As the third financier in 2021, Germany took this place due to lower contributions by the UK and the UAE (UNOCHA, 2021).

Other than humanitarian issues and efforts at 'peace making', arms sales have been the most prominent elements of European attention to Yemen. One reason Yemen has failed to get the attention it deserves in Europe is, of course, that unlike Syria, it does not present the immediate 'threat' of thousands of refugees arriving into the European Union space. Europe-wide state activities for the past few years have concentrated on preventing the arrival of thousands of war refugees from Syria, Afghanistan, West Africa and other conflicts, as well as that of other migrants seeking to come and work in Europe. Although the EU as an institution has been relatively generous in humanitarian aid since the war started, it is still way behind some of its member states, having contributed USD 176 million in 2021, USD 106 million in 2020, USD 163 million in 2019, USD 135 million in 2018 and USD 132 million in 2017.

Institutionally, the EU has been involved in Yemen through training in security-related activities, investment in rural and urban development, and political exchanges. Its overall impact has been limited by a number of factors: first that in the already complex EU bureaucracy, Yemen is situated in a number of different departments, making coordinated and cohesive intervention difficult. Second the need to get unanimity for all decisions and investments has ensured a particularly slow decision-making process, combined with highly complex and demanding reporting procedures from beneficiaries (Evaluation of EU-Yemen cooperation, 2002–12). Involvement in a multiplicity of projects, including some very small ones, has not helped. Between 2002 and 2012, the EU invested a total of EUR 287 million in Yemen, a fairly modest sum given the needs of the country and the size of its population, distributed as follows: 57% for economic development, 25% on social development and 14% on governance (Evaluation, annex 8, p. 52).

The inability of the EU and its member states to act in unison is a missed opportunity; such an approach would have given it a louder voice on the world scene and possibly greater influence on Yemeni politics. However, as Bonnefoy put it,

> while it is relevant to note the obvious limitations of Europe acting as a global power, the lack of coordination between EU institutions and member states can also serve as an asset. In times of conflict, it helps to generate a division of labor that can multiply the number of diplomatic initiatives. The lack of coordination and even competition between member states can foster creative solutions that may be needed to tackle the complex issues in a country like Yemen.
>
> (Bonnefoy, 2020, p. 79)

More significantly, due to its own decision, the EU has been unable to act independently as an entity bringing its own perspectives and possible initiatives; it is relegated to merely 'supporting' UN efforts, despite the fact that the UN and its special envoy's own initiatives are constrained to impotence by the text of UNSC 2216.

The UK had a special place in Yemen due to its role as the former colonial power in the then 'Aden and Protectorates' which preceded the PDRY (see Chapter 1). In the Saleh period of the RoY, this had a double conflicting impact: southern separatists expected British support for their ambition to return to a state within the former southern borders, while Saleh himself and his close associates were suspicious of British motives for the same reason.

British policy has been, throughout the RoY period, and since the war started, to support the Yemeni state within its current RoY borders

Discussing Western states' involvement in Yemen tends to be repetitive given that most had little interest in Yemen *per se* but instead focused on counter terrorism. Yet again this is the case for the UK which, after years of neglect from the time of unification, revived its interest in Yemen when the threat of jihadi activism became prominent. Hence, like other states, British 'support' to the RoY focused on strengthening its security institutions. Taking a slightly broader perspective, Britain hosted a donor conference in 2006 which, a precursor to what happened six years later, produced ambitious promises and pledges followed by very limited actual investment. The UK itself, in 2007–8, spent GBP 12 million in Yemen (precisely the amount it had promised the PDRY at independence and failed to provide), an impressively modest amount given the country's population, increased to GBP 20 million the following year. In 2010, in response to the December 2009 'underpants bomber' incident, it initiated the 'Friends of Yemen', primarily motivated by security issues. This grouping was active under joint Saudi-UK chairmanship until overtaken by events a few years later; yet again, it was mainly concerned with security issues but also intended to fund development activities insofar as these were considered to help calm security issues.

Since 2015, Britain consistently boasts of the massive amount of humanitarian aid it provides to Yemen avoiding comparison with the profits British companies make from arms sales to Saudi Arabia and the UAE, the main belligerent states. Between 2015 and 2020 inclusive, Britain contributed USD 1.35 billion in humanitarian aid through the UN system. During the same period, BAE alone earned GBP 17.5 billion from its sales to the KSA Ministry of Defence and Aviation under a range of types of licenses. Thanks to deliberate obscurantism in data production, the Campaign Against Arms Trade estimates the total value of arms sales to be more than GBP 20 billion since 2015 (Campaign Against Arms Trade, 2021).

East Europe and Russia

Eastern Europe and the USSR had close relations with the PDRY and also reasonably friendly ones with the YAR as the latter signed a treaty of friendship with the USSR in 1984. With the demise of the Soviet Union and the socialist bloc coinciding with Yemeni unification, most of these states sank into deep political and economic crises, and their relations with Yemen did not feature in their priorities. Russia alone, intent on maintaining great power status, remained seriously involved, keeping a large embassy in Sana'a throughout the Saleh period and well into the current war. Saleh visited Moscow three times in 2002, 2004 and 2009, and Yemen continued to buy Russian weapons including Scud missiles and 30 MiG aircraft of different types, paying cash. Relations between the two states were not entirely smooth as Yemeni Islamist leaders expressed support for Chechen separatists, upsetting the Russian authorities.

Russia had to balance its historic involvement in Yemen with its new post-Soviet priority of improving relations with the wealthy GCC states: their main shared interest is the price of hydrocarbons, but trade is also relevant. Relations with Saudi Arabia are the most crucial, and mutual visits and agreements have increased, marked by the recent visits to Moscow of King Salman in 2017, MBS in 2015 to St. Petersburg, and Putin to Riyadh in 2019. The establishment of OPEC + in 2016 included Russia in determining world oil prices. Clearly Saudi Arabia is the most powerful country locally, but Yemen controls the Bab al Mandab, leading to access to the Red Sea and the Suez Canal, ensuring its continued strategic importance.

The uprisings in 2011 were an opportunity for Russia to join other states as a member of the group of ambassadors pushing Saleh to accept the GCC initiative, and its ambassador witnessed its signing on 23 November 2011 in Riyadh. President Hadi visited Moscow in 2013. During the transition, in the distribution of assistance responsibilities among the members of the ambassadors' group, Russia was assigned to support NDC outreach, its public relations element, an interesting choice. This unified international approach on the Yemeni crisis compared favourably with the situations in both Syria and Libya in the early years of that decade. However, cooperation was breached over UNSC resolution 2216 which Russia did not support, and abstained. At that time, not only was Russia still close to Saleh, it was more aware of Huthi strength than the states which supported it, and realised that demands for their surrender, the real meaning of 2216, was unrealistic. Russia maintained its dialogue with the then Huthi–Saleh alliance, through the presence of its embassy in Sana'a until Saleh's killing. Russia strongly argued against the coalition's air strikes.

Since 2017, Russia has been more cautious in supporting the US and others at the UNSC, not so much due to disagreements about Yemen, but to distinguish its positions from those of other northern states and demonstrating its distrust following developments in Syria and Libya. Russia also continues to receive delegations from all factions in Yemen including Huthis, STC and IRG. Moscow's attempts to position itself as a potential mediator have had limited success, for a number of reasons: first, it has insufficient power and weight locally; second, its wish to play this role in Yemen is not trusted by the powerful states with which it is competing elsewhere in the region, particularly Syria and Libya; third, rising tensions with the US and UK elsewhere in the world further discourage them from encouraging a Russian role in Yemen despite the fact that it might prove useful. On the positive side, Russia's good relations with Iran enable it to access the Huthis. Further assets are its good historic relations with President Hadi and some of his government, as well as members of the GPC whether 'independent' or aligned with others, let alone the southern separatists who don't hesitate to try and call upon any past allies. Needless to say, Yemeni factions' unwillingness to seek a solution, contribute to Russian powerlessness.

Should international and Yemeni circumstances change, Russia has put itself in a position where it might be able to play a useful role.

International organisations

The Republic of Yemen recognised all the international commitments approved by both the YAR and the PDRY and is a party to more than 80 international agreements. It is a member of the Arab League and all the UN's specialised institutions, as well, of course, as the UN itself. It has approved a wide range of international treaties and agreements, some of which it implemented with greater fervour than others prior to the war. It is particularly notable that it has participated in the Committee for the Elimination of Discrimination Against Women (CEDAW), though this is an example of a situation in which inconsistencies remain between the clauses of CEDAW and the Yemeni constitution. These were not addressed prior to the conflict, and will remain contentious thereafter: although full equality is asserted in Yemen's constitution (see Chapter 1), other articles deny it. Yemeni participation in the regular meetings concerning women has been an opportunity for Yemeni women to struggle for improvements, without much evidence of success.

An international agreement on which Yemen has taken a different position from all other Arab states is the 1951 Refugee Convention, which Yemen has signed and which has contributed to its more positive treatment of refugees from the Horn of Africa, Somalia in particular. Its participation in this convention means that officially recognised refugees have access to the same services as Yemenis, specifically health and education services. This does not protect them from social discrimination, a phenomenon which has worsened alongside the crisis. It is also relevant to note that while Somalis are recognised as refugees on arrival, the same is not the case for Ethiopians, who are not.

Participation in UN and UN institutions has given Yemen access to funding and technical support over the decades and Yemenis broadly perceive it positively. It has not prevented the emergence of significant tensions with the UN and particularly its political elements. As discussed above, the 1990 crisis at the UNSC over Iraq's invasion of Kuwait led to very serious economic and financial difficulties for the new state, which also encouraged the regime to regard the UN as an instrument of the big powers, and not an independent entity. In the current conflict, the UNSC has been unable to take a stand independent of the influence of Saudi Arabia and the UAE, mediated by the UK and US, and this has contributed to its inability to help bring the crisis to an end as discussed above (Chapter 2).

The Arab League

The imamate was a founder member of the Arab League, and all Yemeni states have been part of it ever since. However, this membership has not been particularly useful to Yemen throughout its history though, alongside other fora, it was the site for disagreements between the YAR and PDRY, particularly when the relationship was at its most tense, in 1978.

Overall, the Arab League has been as powerless in solving the Yemeni conflict as it is elsewhere. For most of its history it has been dominated by the most powerful states though its secretary generals have all been Egyptian and its headquarters are in Cairo, reflecting the dominance of Egypt in Arab politics in the twentieth century. This remains the case despite the fact that Arab decision-making has shifted to the Gulf states. It would therefore be unwise to expect the League to even attempt to act as an independent mediator to bring the current conflict to an end.

Yemen and the Gulf Cooperation Council

Of far greater importance and relevance to Yemen is the Gulf Cooperation Council (GCC). Established in 1981 as a response by the Arab Gulf monarchies to the threat of the Iranian Islamic Revolution, it is a club of wealthy states which joined a security-focused organisation aimed at protecting themselves, under US umbrella, from the perceived threat of the Iranian revolution. Internally, they share certain characteristics, including considerable wealth and small national populations. Their labour forces are mostly migrant at all levels, from domestic servants, construction workers and other infrastructure activities to senior professionals throughout the economy and administration. In its first decade, a fair number of these were from both Yemeni states but (as discussed in earlier chapters) this situation changed in 1990–91 with the Iraq–Kuwait crisis. The return of many migrants in the past two decades has taken place under very different and tougher conditions, far less profitable for the migrants without easing their living conditions where they work.

Yemen's leaders have systematically attempted to get close to the GCC and, ideally, to join it, but have faced a wall of rejection. Membership of the GCC would solve many of Yemen's problems, particularly its economic and financial ones, as its nationals could then freely move and work in other GCC states, earning far better incomes enabling them to support their families at home. This would create an integrated economic space beneficial for all. It would also create an institution with a greater social and economic rationale by integrating a peninsula whose states have complementary potential resources, creating a larger internal market for manufacturing and other industries. Certainly, a GCC including all the peninsula states would make a lot more sense than the 2011 GCC invitation to Jordan and Morocco to join, obviously a response to the 2011 popular uprisings, and equally clearly an attempt to bring together unelected monarchies in an anti-democratic movement. An Arabian Peninsula with a single collective strategic institution would control both the Straits of Hormuz and the Bab al Mandab, and therefore be able to organise security of these major marine passage ways more effectively and systematically.

The leading GCC states are firmly opposed to Yemeni membership for the following reasons. First, it is a republic (however flawed), and therefore perceived as a threat by the monarchies, particularly Saudi Arabia and the UAE whose repressive autocratic systems brook no opposition or allow any freedom of speech, and firmly oppose anything with the slightest hint of democratic politics. Second, Yemen is the poorest state in the Arab world, and therefore would be in a position to claim considerable financial and economic support from the wealthier GCC members. Third, they perceive Yemen as a source of insecurity and jihadism. Finally, of course, they feel threatened by the demographic imbalance: Yemen alone has a larger national population than all the GCC states put together.

In practice, Yemen applied to join the GCC in 1996 at the Doha summit and was rejected. As Yemen's conditions deteriorated and under pressure to help its counter-terrorist activities following 9/11, the GCC summit of 2002 included Yemen in four of its groupings: the Health Ministers' Council, the Gulf Education Bureau, the Council of Ministers of Social and Labour Affairs and the GCC football tournament. As is obvious from their titles, this was no more than a sop to Yemeni demands and excluded them from all key decision-making bodies, though inclusion in the football tournament certainly caused some satisfaction among the millions of football enthusiasts in Yemen and beyond. Other than this, as I put it elsewhere, 'in Yemen this was viewed as a first step towards inclusion. The GCC saw it as a palliative measure to silence further demands for Yemeni membership' (Lackner, 2017a, p. 78).

The current war has changed the relationship in many ways, with both Saudi Arabia and the UAE perceived as aggressor states by many Yemenis, while others have benefitted from the relationship. Socotrans have migrated to Ajman (in the UAE) for decades and this presence is facilitating domination of Socotra by the UAE, while the thousands of UAE citizens of Yemeni origin have a variety of more or less ambiguous feelings about the current situation. Yemeni migrant workers without UAE national family members are fewer. By contrast in Saudi Arabia, most Yemenis are migrant workers, and only a few have Saudi family members. Saudi Arabia also hosts the largest number of Yemenis despite the changes resulting from the Saudisation policies (discussed in Chapter 3). Oman is, as in other aspects of the crisis, providing some assistance, but is certainly not in a position to host large numbers of refugees, whether political or climate related. It is also the only state which has supported Yemen's membership application.

The GCC itself is in deep crisis, and its own future is in question in the early years of the third decade of the century. The blockade and siege of Qatar by the UAE, Saudi Arabia and Bahrain lasted three and a half years, and its ending in early 2021 took place without any significant achievement for the blockading states. While the Saudis are effectively reconciled with Qatar, and were not at the origin of the spat, the UAE only reluctantly accepted ending the siege and tensions between the two ruling families remain lively.

The UAE's hostility to political Islam continues to see Qatar's international policies as a major challenge.

The main long-term impact of this problem is the destruction of any trust between GCC members, leaving future cooperation to be based on an exclusively transactional basis serving any shared interests or concerns. Moreover, both Kuwait and Oman fear similar strong-arm tactics against themselves when their policies deviate from those shared by the UAE and Saudi Arabia. In the coming decade increasing international and internal divergences in the UAE–Saudi alliance are the best security for the other GCC states. In addition, all the GCC states face economic and political challenges with the diminishing role of hydrocarbons in world energy supplies, rising populations and economic problems. Their individual and collective confidence in the security umbrella provided by the USA for decades has been shattered, first by the lack of US response to the September 2019 attack on the major Saudi oil facilities in Abqaiq and Khurais and second the 2021 debacle of the US departure from Afghanistan. These are factors encouraging the GCC states to smother their internal differences, but tensions remain in the background. It is worth remembering that there were frequent conflicts in earlier centuries which have only been kept at bay thanks to all of them becoming wealthy from hydrocarbon exports.

Conclusion

Yemen's relations with the outside world have always been crucial to its development politically and socially. Migration in all directions has taken place for a range of reasons but mostly due to need and the inability of the country to provide sustenance for its population, as well as, in some cases to promote trade or proselytise. Since the formation of the RoY, its relations have focused on its neighbours in the GCC and the powerful Western world powers, the US, UK and European Union member states. The trend towards increasing Far Eastern involvement has not been as important for Yemen as for the GCC, not so much because of Yemeni policies but more because of those of China and other Far Eastern states.

Certain features of Yemen's international relations remain stable under war conditions primarily that, except for the GCC states, Yemen remains a remote country of limited importance and concern. It manages to attract attention thanks to negative factors, specifically the presence and action of jihadis and the 'world's worst humanitarian crisis'. Saleh successfully played the threat of international terrorism card to obtain financial and military support from the US and its allies. This is still one of the reasons the international community supports Hadi, as he was willing to allow the US to strike at will against the jihadis during the transition. Even today, it is the 'threat' posed by the presence of a few AQAP militants in remote rural regions which is the justification, if not the real reason, for UAE and US continued military presence in parts of southern Yemen.

With the doors firmly closed to Yemeni labour migration in most northern countries and the very reduced Yemeni migration to the GCC states, combined with the sad situation arising from the country's environmental, humanitarian and political/military crises, it is unlikely that its relations with the outside world will actively contribute to solving its problems. Whether external financial, development and humanitarian support is likely to have a positive outcome is a subject worthy of serious debate. What remains unarguable is that different aspects of Yemen's future will depend considerably on its relations with the Kingdom of Saudi Arabia, the United Arab Emirates and other GCC states. Neither the KSA nor the UAE is likely to favour a democratic regime, even a flawed one, nor do they want to see a flourishing and stable Yemen. More likely than not, their strategy will be to have Yemen neither too strong nor too weak to present a threat, which has been their policy for decades. Both are currently behaving in a way which is unlikely to lead to stability in Yemen, or to alleviate its long-term problems, be they environmental or political.

Yemen's desperate need for a regime focused on the social, economic and environmental concerns of its population, is not just an issue for Yemenis. Unless its neighbours help achieve this, there is a considerable likelihood that, in coming decades, millions of Yemenis will be forced to migrate due to the water crisis, other climate change aspects, or economic and political considerations. A simple look at a map and basic knowledge of the situation in the Horn of Africa make it clear where they will go, into Saudi Arabia, Oman and the UAE.

Notes

1 See Salisbury (2017).

2 The rationale and debates on US policy concerning Yemen throughout the Obama and Trump administrations is discussed in forensic detail by Robert Malley and Stephen Pomper (2021).

5 Conclusion

Writing in late 2021, with no immediate prospect of the war ending or any clarity as to the likely endgame in Yemen, conclusions are necessarily speculative. There are, however, a number of trends which have emerged in the past decade and continued throughout the war, which suggest some directions and possible outcomes. Regardless of when the war ends, by the time it does, Yemen will be in a very sad state, simply worse than it is at the moment.

Socio-economic impact of the war

In brief, outside the Huthi-controlled areas, central government will have disappeared, the country's remaining administrative structures will be at the local level of communities, districts and in some cases governorates, lacking finance from the centre and largely reliant on locally collected incomes. Some areas will be better able to cope than others, specifically those controlling oil and gas resources and pipelines, ports, the few industrial zones and those with commercial agriculture. The country's physical infrastructure will need comprehensive rehabilitation, and its social infrastructure significant financial and human inputs to return education, medical and other services to an acceptable functioning state.

Younger people emerging from the universities or who have been unemployed for years will be ready to take up positions but lack a work culture, while the thousands of militia and other security personnel will need serious interventions to ensure their demobilisation, disarmament and training. This will be essential if they are to be integrated into a constructive economy. Millions will be in need of psychosocial support to recover from the multiple traumas they have suffered and which have pervaded their world views. The lifelong potential and health of hundreds of thousand children will have been lastingly impaired by severe malnutrition in their early years, and they will be in desperate need of support if they are to, partly at least, compensate for this loss and become able adults. The humanitarian crisis and hunger will not disappear overnight, and intervention on this front will be essential for at least half a decade while basic rural and urban economies are restored to some kind of operational level.

DOI: 10.4324/9780429059315-6

Years of fighting have deeply fragmented Yemeni society throughout the country. Not only have the tensions between the different ascribed social status groups worsened during this period but fighting of all kinds has led to thousands of deaths; families and wider groups will be calling for retribution and justice, if not revenge. By end-2021, the total death count is estimated at 377 000. Avoiding an endless cycle of killings will be an essential political move, which should get the full attention it deserves. The calls for transitional justice which have remained a dead letter since the 2011 uprisings must finally be addressed through effective legal intervention.

The intensification of fragmentation at the regional level has also been a major outcome of the current war and will be difficult to repair. The crude and common oversimplification which divides the country in two along the borders that existed until 1990 ignores the multiplicity of both historic and current divisions and conflicts throughout the country. For example, the Huthis are relying on fighters and support from the tribes in the far north of the country, tribes whose allegiance was, not so long ago, to Saleh and his regime, as well as to the al Ahmar family leadership of the Hashed tribal confederation. They were dependent on the Saudi regime for subsidies for generations and are now divided between supporters of the Huthis, the IRG, Islah and other factions. Similarly, the rivalry, not to say open struggle, between the IRG represented by Hadi and his supporters on the one hand, and the STC on the other, is largely a continuation of the internal conflict in the PDRY. which blew up in the short but bloody civil war of 1986. The current STC leadership are the direct descendants and heirs of the group which won that conflict, while Hadi was a member of the defeated faction which then went into exile in Sana'a and joined Saleh's GPC. There are numerous other examples, within and between most governorates (to use modern administrative terminology), each of which covers diverse earlier cultural and political entities and rivalries within its borders. These rivalries will re-emerge as soon as the national struggle ends. Many fail to realise this and consequently misrepresent the situation, leading to inappropriate interventions.

Two other forms of social fragmentation have deepened and changed in the course of the war, in some places they have been more or less dormant while elsewhere they have revived in the last decade during and after the 2011 uprisings and since the war started. The first form originates from the transformation from earlier ascribed statuses into emerging social differentiation based on wealth due to changes in economic circumstances. As a result, a minority of formerly low status groups and others connected with the security/military have achieved great enrichment, while many people of varying statuses are suffering gradual impoverishment. Overall, the mercantile group's status has risen dramatically, largely through the adoption of its activities by members of other groups. This shift from a social structure based on ascribed status to a modern class-based society will continue.

The second form is sectarian, both in the Zaydi and the Shafi'i areas. In the first, it is prompted by Ansar Allah's policies exacerbating and emphasising the distinctions between their version of Zaydi Islam and all other forms in the country, including both 'traditional' Zaydism and Shafi'ism whose practical similarities have long characterised Islamic practice in the country. In the second, the role of Salafi and Muslim Brotherhood Sunnism is playing a comparable role. Sectarianism is therefore likely to become increasingly ingrained and irreparable with time and worsen the fragmentation between Huthi-dominated areas and the rest of the country. This would add another major cause of tensions and conflict to those caused by other socio-economic problems.

Political entities

The various social, economic and historical divergent interests are not now, and have not been in the past, directly reflected in the country's political organisations. With the exception of the now small parties established on ideological bases, such as the Baath, the Nasserists and the Yemeni Socialist Party, political organisations were created more on patronage than ideological bases. The Islah was formed in response to the establishment of a multi-party state at the time of unification, to create a formal opposition which would not actually challenge Saleh's policies. It was, and remains, an uneasy conglomerate of conservative northern Zaydi tribal membership with a more standard Islamist component based in the rest of the country and including mostly Shafi'i Sunnis. Its founder and original leader, Shaykh Abdullah bin Husayn al Ahmar was the leader of the Hashed confederation at the time, and until the current war started, the most cohesive and influential tribal confederation in the country. The last decade has seen its leadership transferred to the Islamist section of the party, both due to the absence of such an influential figure within the al Ahmar family but also to the reduced power of the fragmenting Hashed confederation, sections of whom have joined the Huthi movement. So, although today Islah membership and leadership are both closer to Islamist Muslim Brotherhood ideology, it remains fairly mixed and its programme has not been significantly modified since the 1990s.

Unless one defines 'support to the president' as a political programme, Yemen's largest political organisation, the General People's Congress (GPC) was not established on the basis of an ideology and programme. It included many defectors from other parties, in particular from the YSP as a result of internal struggles in the YSP while it ruled the PDRY. Among others, its membership included everything from those who simply sought material benefits to people who hoped to found a genuine 'social-democratic' or maybe more accurately a 'Muslim-democratic' party on the model of Christian democrats in Europe. The succession of conflicts in the country and changes of allegiances has resulted in even greater fragmentation at the political level with, for example, GPC members and groups aligned with the Huthis' Ansar Allah in Sana'a, while others are part of the Hadi Government and yet others forming individual or group tendencies in exile, primarily in Egypt, the UAE and Oman.

For years Yemeni politicians have allowed this organisational, rather than ideological, diversity (or chaos if one prefers) to continue throughout the various military and other debates of the war. In 2021, a tendency is emerging to develop new 'political' entities: in March, Tareq Saleh, the main military leader of the anti-Huthi front in Tihama, added a political title to his group, establishing a political bureau, though at the time of writing, it has neither a new name, nor a programme. There is talk of the formation of a National Salvation Front, bringing together elements of the GPC and others (Horton, 2021). Between these overlapping groupings, there certainly will be scope for a wide membership for future proposed peace negotiations to sit on one side facing the, as yet, single Ansar Allah on the other.

Negotiations for a 'peaceful' settlement

As discussed above, UN efforts to end the war have achieved little. The systematic calls from numerous sources to include the 'new forces of 2011', namely women, youth and civil society in negotiations to reach a political settlement, all fail to address the nature and composition of these groups on other than demography (age and sex) while 'civil society' is a loose concept. Despite years of discussion and meetings, many taking place under the auspices of the office of the UN Special Envoy for Yemen, there appears to have been no public discussion of the practical or political issues involved in this demand: half of Yemenis are women, about 70% are under 24 years of age (and include 50% females) and, in addition, some members of both these groups are also participants in existing political parties. As for civil society, although not excluding political action, such as human rights defenders, the term most commonly describes primarily non-political groups involved in a broad range of activities of common interest to communities and groups, such as football clubs. The fact that these issues have not been addressed is indicative of the lack of seriousness from the politicians, national and international, who call for the inclusion of these groups in discussions to end the war. This is confirmed by the women invited to participate, who systematically complain of being marginalised and refused access to influential politicians. Of course, this would only become important if serious negotiations were taking place.

Another constantly repeated notion is that 'there is no military solution to the crisis, only a political one'. Again, repeated thoughtlessly, it defies reality: for more than seven years now, Yemenis on all sides have been actively seeking a military solution, and have not ceased to do so. Historically, in Yemen as elsewhere, political agreements are reached after military means have either achieved their end (for one side at least) or a stalemate unacceptable to all participants has been reached and the participants have come to recognise that they cannot break it. As long as combatants see possible benefit or success from military action, their presence in political discussions is little more than camouflage to avoid publicly asserting their real choice and keep mediators on their side. The last three decades in Afghanistan are a good example of the pitfalls of claiming that a war has 'ended' when the reality is nothing of the sort.

A further issue is the widespread belief, among Yemenis in particular, that the intervention of the 'international community' is essential to force a solution on the combatants. Openly contradicting the counter-belief that Yemenis want to be responsible for their own fate and oppose foreign intervention, these assertions have not been challenged. This is partly because the international community, in practice represented by the UN system at large, is itself caught lacking, given on the one hand its fundamental mandate to solve world problems and on the other its actual impotence to achieve this aim demonstrated on a weekly base, in many conflicts including in Yemen.

Constant bickering within the UNSC and the refusal of the permanent five members to reform it to make it more demographically and politically representative are compounded by the UN's inability to act independently from the supposedly most powerful states in the world. The five permanent members of UNSC include some whose current global influence has diminished considerably over the decades and refuse to relinquish this last remaining symbol of historical power. Financial contributions to the UN also contribute to increasing influence for others. So, the gap between UN capacity and ambitions worsens as each new crisis further weakens the institution, but the myth of the power of the 'international community' persists throughout the world. As far as Yemenis are concerned, it is time they, as a nation, cease to try and manipulate this ineffective system and realise that the solution to the Yemeni crisis actually has to be found by Yemenis, that the 'international community' is not able to solve their political problems even if its various institutions can participate in different sectors.

Appeals to this 'international community' rarely refer to the neighbouring states, the KSA and UAE, both of whom have far more impact on what happens in Yemen than the rest of the world, and whose influence is less welcome by most Yemenis, probably even including some who are currently clients or implementers of those states' policies and strategies. Yemenis should think again before calling for intervention by the 'international community'. Yemenis are not alone in this; most people throughout the world, call for 'the international community', 'the world', to help whenever they are faced with disasters, whether climatic or environmental, or even political upheavals, coups and unacceptable oppression from state or other authorities. The lack of response to multiple appeals for humanitarian and political assistance reflects the current forms of governance at the global level, whether in response to climatic disasters or breaches of either international humanitarian law or universal human rights.

Possible outcomes

There is no certainty that there will be a single Yemeni state by the time this conflict ends. The actual balance of power between the multiplicity of political and military groupings within Yemen is unclear, though it is likely that Ansar Allah will remain a dominant, if not exclusive, force in the northern highlands. While at the moment the Huthis fully control their area, once fighting against the 'forces of aggression' ends, divisions within their camp will intensify, both within the core of the Ansar Allah movement between hard liners and others more willing to compromise, as well as between the movement and the tribal groups which have fought on its behalf. So even the 'stability' which prevails within the Huthi-controlled area may well not outlast the war.

In the rest of the country, there are a range of politico-military groupings whose ideological differences are few, but who are determined to promote their own interests. They include the various elements which originally formed the GPC as well as sections of Islah and other groupings. The part-Islamist Islah is likely to become enmeshed in a struggle against other forces but is probably the strongest rival to Ansar Allah, given the divisions within the GPC. In view of their relative strengths, it is possible that Yemen in the future might be ruled by two competing Islamist fundamentalist organisations, Ansar Allah and the Islah. Despite deep theological disagreements, in practice their policies are remarkably similar, as they demonstrate daily in the behavioural norms they impose on society and women in particular. Islah includes moderates, but has the full range of Islamists, including people close to the jihadis. Political and possibly military struggle between competing forces is likely.

Regional rivalries are also relevant for the future. Conflict in the area of the former PDRY must be addressed. UAE promotion of its creation, the Southern Transitional Council, has transformed this small group of southern separatists into an internationally recognised force which has now, on paper at least, been included in the IRG and therefore may potentially be involved in a government negotiating team for discussions with the Huthis. Other groups, with comparable or greater popular base, are still excluded, but have been trying to have their voices heard for years. They include both other southern separatists and southerners who believe in Yemeni unity.

The re-division of Yemen along the pre-1990 borders is unlikely to provide a solution: as in the case of Sudan, southerners are quite able to fight effectively among themselves without any involvement from the North: the divisions within the South remained unresolved for decades and persist today. In addition to those prevailing in the south west between the STC and its local rivals, the people and leaders of Hadhramaut and al-Mahra are extremely unlikely to take orders from an Aden-based political authority. Their calls for autonomy, if not independence, have been as loud as others and, moreover, would benefit from support of their diaspora in the GCC states, in particular in the KSA in the case of Hadhramaut, and Oman and the UAE for al-Mahra. The Saudi regime would, of course, be promoting its own long-term interests rather than those of Yemenis. Their push for access to the Arabian Sea, avoiding the constraints of both the Hormuz straits and the Bab al Mandab, has been an active political objective for decades, and their actions in al-Mahra during the war were a strong step towards achieving that aim until they reached agreement for a shorter pipeline to Oman's major new port Dukum. Therefore, southern unity is an unlikely outcome.

Millions of Yemenis live in areas which are formally under Huthi control but have no allegiance to the movement, and are politically and culturally more liberal, with different religious affinities. Those who envisage a re-establishment of the pre-1990 borders ignore the fact that the most densely populated areas, Ibb and Taiz, as well as others such as Dhamar, al Baydha and much of the Tihama, are currently reluctantly under Huthi control as well as having characteristics which would encourage the Huthis to abandon them, specifically high population densities and few natural resources. Here the political debate is likely to be fierce as some of these areas have been the birthplace of many political movements during the past century. State wise, attempts to restore earlier borders would, more likely than not, lead to political and armed struggle against rulers in Sana'a.

The international community, and here this description is correct in its most literal sense, is unlikely to accept the division of Yemen into two or more states, which would almost certainly end up including statelets comparable to those of the Federation of South Arabia of the 1960s. Other than the UAE, opposition to any division of the country is pretty much universal. Should the country end up with a single state, federalism which emerged formally in official discussions during the 2012–14 transition, would be the most reasonable response to help heal the current fragmentation. It is a realistic option, as it would allow significant autonomy to the different socio-cultural regional groups while ensuring economic and political cooperation, thus increasing the state's financial and international viability. However, contrary to what happened in the 2014 proposal, the number and delimitation of the boundaries of each region within this federation must be defined on equitable and rational criteria, ensuring as much balance as is possible. This would balance access to natural resources (water, agricultural land, hydrocarbons), population size, existing levels of development and socio-political criteria, in particular ensuring that groups within a single region have tribal and other social compatibility and a historic record of cooperation.

The future 'new' Yemen

The type of regime which emerges will unavoidably be influenced by the external states most concerned with Yemen, namely the KSA and the UAE; although Oman would certainly want to have a positive influence, it is too small and too poor to have as much say as either it or Yemenis might wish. Given their commitment to and enforcement of autocracy, together with their opposition to freedom of expression and other basic human rights, neither the UAE nor the KSA regimes is likely to accept a truly open and democratic regime in Yemen. Their leaders reluctantly put up with the republics in the past and know that it would be impossible to restore a formal monarchy; indeed, the only ones suspected of such an aim are the Huthis! Therefore, although the post-war Yemeni regime is likely to have the word 'Republic' in its title, it is unlikely to implement and concretise the hopes of the 2011 revolutionaries. A quick reminder: the overwhelmingly popular movement was seeking to bring about a regime which would address the needs of the majority, provide employment and adequate social services, and promote a 'national' economy. The more ambitious among them looked forward to political, economic and social equity, the absence of massive differentials in wealth and the final definitive removal of the corrupt and kleptocratic elites who controlled the country in the past.

It is therefore likely that the future regime will be formally democratic, despite being in the environment of the GCC autocratic monarchies. However, the issue of the amount of power held by ordinary citizens in such a regime is a major challenge, not only for Yemen but throughout the world in an age when authoritarian regimes are increasing both in numbers and influence and where many of the human rights and other concepts traditionally associated with democracy are increasingly challenged by *elected* as well as inherited authoritarian leaders. Lack of respect for supposedly 'universal' values of human rights and equality is rising; regime change throughout the world, including through voting, is increasing the number of right-wing authoritarian regimes each year; socialism has become a 'dirty' word.

Any future regime in Yemen, regardless of how democratic it is or its willingness to allow popular will and demands to determine its actions, will have to confront and address a number of objective constraints. These include water scarcity and climate change, both of which must be addressed by strong state action to avoid disaster. With respect to water, without firmly enforcing policies prioritizing human domestic needs over all others, followed by livestock and industry, significant populated parts of the country will become uninhabitable within a generation. Rising sea levels will create very considerable problems, not only for two of Yemen's largest cities (Hodeida and Aden) but also for medium ones such as Mukalla as well as the hundreds of fisher communities and agricultural areas along the coast. Between them, if not rapidly addressed seriously, these issues will turn at least half the country's population into forced migrants. While a few may head west to the Horn of Africa, even after years of war, thousands more are still heading in the opposite direction and only a few hundred Yemenis are travelling west across the sea. The majority will force their way into the neighbouring states, however hostile their immigration policies might be. This prospect should be sufficient to encourage the KSA and the UAE to help Yemen to have an effective state that addresses the basic needs of its people.

New economic development policies are essential ingredients for long-term viability, maximising the sustainable use of the country's limited natural resources. They should prioritise equitable distribution of material and technical support, concentrate on poverty reduction and employment creation, addressing the needs of ordinary Yemenis, whether rural or urban. Unless a totally new approach is taken to economic development, the fundamental problems underlying the current conflict will eventually lead to its resumption.

More specifically, the creation of a labour force able to be productive in a twenty-first-century economy must be a basic element of any strategy; this implies a complete renewal and massive improvement in the quality of the country's education system at all levels. The multiple vocational training centres built with GCC financing in past decades throughout the country could, at last, be used to provide training relevant to the semi-skilled and skilled labour requirements of both Yemen and the neighbouring states. In particular, access to the GCC for Yemeni labour would significantly alleviate the country's financial constraints, giving opportunities to thousands who could contribute to their families' survival without further depleting Yemen's scarce natural resources. This would produce a 'win-win' situation throughout the Arabian Peninsula.

Investment will be essential in all sectors. In particular, agriculture which currently employs half the population, must be re-designed to support smallholders by providing good incomes from both staple and high-value rainfed crops, reserving irrigation as a supplementary element in the areas where water availability permits. This will be a crucial element of the water management policy. Fisheries, which currently occupy only about 3% of the labour force, have suffered enormously from the lack of enforcement of national and international regulations: some species have completely disappeared as a result of the predatory and environmentally destructive fishing techniques of uncontrolled foreign ships. Restoring catch potential will be a slow but essential component to improve living conditions and the Yemeni economy. Modern industries will hopefully emerge from the improved skills of the labour force, while peace and stability would enable the development of a well-managed tourism industry, protecting the environment and the country's rich natural and cultural heritage. All these depend on the provision of good medical services and physical infrastructure essential to support a modern economy and the lives of Yemenis.

Hopefully such a regime will be able to build upon the work which has started in various locations throughout the country, where local communities have started to build their citizens' technical and managerial capacities, partly with the assistance of various projects. The process involved in creating a new citizenry committed to their communities and promoting altruistic and caring values has started in some places and needs material and moral support while fighting is ongoing, as that is the main hope for a better future. Meanwhile Yemenis can work at the local level to achieve these aims and hope that a new generation of politicians will be less self-serving.

Bibliography

Abdelaziz, K. (2019), 'Sudan says it has reduced troops in Yemen to 5,000', 8 December. Available at: www.reuters.com/article/uk-sudan-politics/sudan-says-it-has-reduced-troops-in-yemen-to-5000-idUKKBN1YC0HX?edition-redirect=uk.

ACAPS (2021), 'Yemen, effects of the fuel embargo at al Hodeidah port on fuel supply dynamics and fuel prices'. Available at: www.acaps.org/country/yemen/special-reports.

Aklan, M. and Lackner, H. (2021), *Solar-powered irrigation in Yemen: Opportunities, Challenges and Policies*, Rethinking Yemen's Economy, Sana'a Center for Strategic Studies.

al Eryani, A. (2020), 'Remittances, abundant capital and labour shortages: the North Yemeni economy of the 1970s', *British-Yemeni Society Journal*, 28: 20–27.

al-Gosaibi, G. (2013), 'A memoir of Yemen', *British-Yemeni Society Journal*, 21: 19–22.

Al-Hamdani, R. and Lackner, H. (2020), 'War and pieces: political divides in southern Yemen', European Council for Foreign Relations. Available at: www.ecfr.eu/publications/summary/war_and_pieces_political_divides_in_southern_yemen.

Al-Manar (2020), 'A press briefing for the Yemeni Armed Forces spokesperson on the outcome of five years of Yemeni aggression and steadfastness', 20 March. Available at: www.almanar.com.lb/6431394.

al-Qubatee, W., Hellegers, P. and Ritzema, H. (2019), 'The economic value of irrigation water in Wadi Zabid, Tihama Plain, Yemen', *Sustainability*, 11, 6476. DOI: 10.3390/su11226476.

Alwaday, H. and Shuja Al-Deen, M. (2021), 'Sectarianism, tribalism and the rise of the Huthis' in al Soswa, A. and Brehony N. (eds) *Building a New Yemen: Recovery, Transition and the International Community*, London, IB Tauris, pp. 51–71.

Amin, M. (2019), '30,000 Sudanese forces fighting in Yemen: official', 22 June. Available at: www.aa.com.tr/en/africa/30-000-sudanese-forces-fighting-in-yemen-official/1512989#.

Amnesty International (2018), *'God Only Knows if He's Alive': Enforced Disappearance and Detention Violations in Southern Yemen*, London, Amnesty International.

Ansar Allah (2020), 'Statement on fifth anniversary of "decisive storm"'. Available at: www.almanar.com.lb/6431394.

Arab News (2020), 'Saudi Arabia and 7 countries form council to secure Red Sea and Gulf of Aden', 6 January. Available at: www.arabnews.com/node/1609121/saudi-arabia.

Awlaqi, W., al-Hada, S. and al-Shawthabi, Y. (2019), *Yemen's Expatriate Workforce Under Threat: The Essential Role of Remittances in Mitigating Economic Collapse*, Sana'a, Sana'a Centre for Strategic Studies.

Bagnetto, L.A. (2020), 'New Red Sea alliance launched by Saudi Arabia, but excludes key players', 10 January. Available at: www.rfi.fr/en/africa/20200108-new-red-sea-alliance-formed-saudi-arabia-notable-exclusions.

Bezabeh, S.A. (2016), *Subjects of Empires, Citizens of States, Yemenis in Djibouti and Ethiopia*, Cairo, American University in Cairo Press.

Bidwell, R. (1983), *The Two Yemens*, London, Longman.

Biswell, A. (2020), *The War for Monetary Control Enters a Dangerous New Phase*, Sana'a, Sana'a Centre for Strategic Studies.

Bonnenfant, P. (ed.) (1982), *La Péninsule Arabique d'Aujourd'hui*, vol. 2, Paris, CNRS.

Bonnefoy, L. (2011), *Salafism in Yemen, Transnationalism and Religious Identity*, London, Hurst.

Bonnefoy, L. (2020), 'The European Union's role in the Yemen crisis' in Day, S. and Brehony, N. (eds) *Global, Regional and Local Dynamics in the Yemen Crisis*, Cham, Palgrave Macmillan, pp. 69–80.

Bonnefoy, L. (2021), 'Yemen and the international community, fragmented approaches' in Alsoswa, A. and Brehony, N. (eds) *Building a New Yemen: Recovery, Transition and the International Community*, London, IB Tauris, pp. 21–35.

Bonzanigo, L. and Borgia, C. (2009), *Tracing Evolutions of Water Control in Wadi Siham, Yemen*, MSc Thesis, Wageningen University.

Brandt, M. (2017), *Tribes and Politics in Yemen, a History of the Houthi Conflict*, London, Hurst.

Brandt, M. and Weissenburger, A. (2022), 'Huthis' in Madelung, W. and Daftary, F. (eds in chief) *Encyclopaedia Islamica Online*. Available at: http://dx.doi.org/10.1163/1875-9831_isla_SIM_062041.

Brehony, N. (2011), *Yemen Divided, the Story of a Failed State in South Arabia*, London, IB Tauris.

Campaign Against Arms Trade (2021), 'Open? The UK's secret arms sales', 14 July. Available at: www.caat.org.uk/publications/open-the-uks-secret-arms-sales/.

Carapico, S. (1998a), *Civil Society in Yemen: The Political Economy of Activism in Modern Arabia*, Cambridge, Cambridge University Press.

Carapico, S. (1998b), 'Pluralism, polarization and popular politics in Yemen' in Korany, B., Brynen, R. and Noble, P. (eds) *Political Liberalization and Democratization in the Arab World, Vol 2: Comparative Experiences*, London, Lynn Rienner Publishers, pp. 241–266.

Chang I-wei, J. (2020), 'The Chinese perspective on the Yemen crisis' in Day, S. and Brehony, N. (eds) *Global, Regional and Local Dynamics in the Yemen Crisis*, Cham, Palgrave Macmillan, pp. 97–111.

Chelhod, J. (1984), *L'Arabie du Sud, Histoire et civilisation, vol 2, La société Yéménite de l'Hégire aux idéologies modernes*, Paris, Maisoneuve et Laros.

Closas, A. and Molle, F. (2016), 'Groundwater governance in the Middle East and North Africa', IWMI project, Report no. 1.

Cook, J. (2022), 'AQAP and governments in Yemen: post-conflict considerations' in Alsoswa, A. and Brehony, N. (eds) *Building a New Yemen: Recovery, Transition and the International Community*, London, IB Tauris, pp. 73–96.

Day, S. (2020), 'America's role in the Yemeni crisis' in Day, S. and Brehony, N. (eds) *Global, Regional and Local Dynamics in the Yemen Crisis*, Cham, Palgrave Macmillan, pp. 51–68.

Day, S. (2022), 'The future of the Yemeni State' in Alsoswa, A. and Brehony, N. (eds) *Building a New Yemen: Recovery, Transition and the International Community*, London, IB Tauris, pp. 37–49.

Day, S. and Brehony, N. (eds). (2020), *Global, Regional and Local Dynamics in the Yemen Crisis*, Cham, Palgrave Macmillan.

de Waal, A. (2020), 'The Horn of Africa and the Yemen crisis' in Day, S. and Brehony, N. (eds) *Global, Regional and Local Dynamics in the Yemen Crisis*, Cham, Palgrave Macmillan, pp. 195–208.

Detalle, R. (1995), 'Esquisse d'une sociologie électorale de Sanaa' in Grandguillaume, G. Mermier, F. and Troin, J.F. (eds), *Sanaa hors les murs: une ville arabe contemporaine*, Paris, Sanaa, Centre Fancais d'Etudes Yemenites, UNESCO URBAMA.

Disclose, (2019), 'Cartographie d'un Mensonge d'Etat', Paris, 15 April. Available at: www.made-in-france.disclose.ngo/fr/chapter/yemen-papers.

Dorte, V. (ed.) (2012), *Adaptation to a Changing Climate in the Arab Countries: A Case for Adapting Governance and Leadership in Building Climate Resilience*, Washington DC, World Bank.

Douglas, L. (1987), *The Free Yemeni Movement, 1935–1962*, Beirut, American University of Beirut.

European Union (2015), 'Evaluation of EU-Yemen cooperation 2002–2012, final report ADE/COWI'.

European Union Election Observation mission (2006), 'Yemen presidential and local council elections, 20 September 2006, final report'.

FAO (2021), 'Yemen, quarterly food security report April–June 2021'.

Gavin, R.J. (1975), *Aden under British Rule 1938–1967*, London, C. Hurst and Company.

Halliday, F. (1990), *Revolution and Foreign Policy, the Case of South Yemen 1967–1987*, Cambridge, Cambridge University Press.

Hamidaddin, A. (ed.) (2022), *The Huthi Movement in Yemen: Ideology, Ambition and Security in the Arab Gulf*, London, Bloomsbury.

Hanna, T., Bohl, D.K. and Moyer, J.D. (2021), 'Assessing the impact of war in Yemen: Pathways for recovery'. UNDP. Available at: www.undp.org/publications/assessing-impact-war-yemen-pathways-recovery.

Hart-Davis, D. (2011), *The War That Never Was, the True Story of the Men Who Fought Britain's Most Secret Battle*, London, Century.

Holden, D. (1966), *Farewell to Arabia*, London, Faber.

Horton, M. (2021), 'Yemen's emerging political coalitions, a first step towards de-escalation', *Terrorism Monitor*, 19(6).

Huddleston, R.J. and Wood, D. (2021), 'Functional markets: Yemen's war economy', *Journal of Illicit Economies and Development*, 2(2): 204–221. DOI: doi.org/10131381/jied.71.

Hull, E. (2011), *High Value Target: Countering al-Qaeda in Yemen*, Washington DC, Potomac Books.

Ismael, T.Y. and Ismael J.S. (1986), *PDR Yemen, Politics, Economics and Society*, London, Frances Pinter LTD.

Kendall, E. (2021), 'Twenty years after 9/11: the Jihadi threat in the Arabian Peninsula', *CTC Sentinel*, 14(7): 63–75. Available at https://ctc.usma.edu/twenty-years-after-9-11-the-jihadi-threat-in-the-arabian-peninsula/.

Kingdom of the Netherlands, Ministry of Foreign Affairs (2019), 'Climate change profile Yemen'. Available at: www.government.nl/documents/publications/2019/02/05/climate-change-profiles.

Lackner, H. (1985), *PDR Yemen, Outpost of Socialist Development in Arabia*, London, Ithaca Press.

Lackner, H. (2016a), 'The change squares of Yemen: civil resistance in an unlikely context' in Roberts, A., Willis, M.J., McCarthy, R. and Garton Ash, T. (eds) *Civil*

Resistance in the Arab Spring: Triumphs and Disasters, Oxford, Oxford University Press, pp. 141–168.

Lackner, H. (2016b), *Yemen's 'Peaceful' Transition from Autocracy: Could it have succeeded?*, Stockholm, International Institute for Democracy and Electoral Assistance.

Lackner, H. (2016c), 'Understanding the Yemeni crisis: the transformation of tribal roles in recent decades', Durham Middle East, Paper no. 17, Durham University.

Lackner, H. (2017a), *Yemen in Crisis, Autocracy, Neoliberalism and the Disintegration of a State*, London, Saqi.

Lackner, H. (2017b), 'Hadhramaut: social structure, agriculture and migration' in Brehony, N. (ed.) *Hadhramaut and its Diaspora: Yemeni Politics, Identity and Migration*, London, IB Tauris, pp. 67–84.

Lackner, H. (2017c), 'The People's Democratic Republic of Yemen: unique socialist experiment in the Arab world at a time of revolutionary fervour', *Interventions*, 19(5): 677–691.

Lackner, H. (2017d), 'Climate change and security, major challenges for Yemen's future' in Sternberg, T. (ed.) *Climate Hazard Crises, in Asian Societies and Environments*, London, Routledge, pp. 103–119.

Lackner, H. (2019a), 'Extreme environmental challenges in the context of lasting political crisis: the case of Yemen' in Pouran, H. and Hakimian, H. (eds) *Environmental Challenges in the MENA Region, the Long Road from Conflict to Cooperation*, London, Gingko, pp. 108–126.

Lackner, H. (2019b), *Yemen in Crisis: Autocracy Neoliberalism and the Disintegration of a State*, London, Saqi; US edition, *Yemen in Crisis: The Road to War*, New York, Verso.

Lackner, H. (2020a), 'Community-based water practices in Yemen' in Dubois, M. (ed.) *Water and Conflict in the Middle East*, London, Hurst, pp. 121–150.

Lackner, H. (2020b), 'No security without development in Yemen, a community-based approach towards long-term sustainable peace' in Vogt, A. and Schmid, S. (eds) *Navigating the Regional Chessboard: Europe's Options to Address Conflicts in the MENA Region*, Beirut, Friedrich Ebert Stiftung.

Lackner, H. (2020c), 'Global warming, the environmental crisis and social justice in Yemen', *Asian Affairs*, I(4): 859–874.

Lackner, H. (2020d), 'The role of the United Nations in the Yemen crisis' in Day, S. and Brehony, N. (ed.) *Global Regional and Local Dynamics in the Yemen Crisis*, Cham, Springer, pp. 15–32.

Lackner, H. (2021a), 'Tribes in the Neo-liberal Era: transformation of Yemen's social structure' in Brandt, M. (ed.) *Tribes in Modern Yemen, an Anthology*, Vienna, Austrian Academy of Sciences Press.

Lackner, H. (2021b), 'Revisiting the People's Democratic Republic of Yemen in its international context', *Jemen Report 2021*: 37–42.

Lackner, H. (2021c), 'The future of Yemen's agriculture and water' in al Soswa, A. and Brehony, N. (eds) *Building a New Yemen*, London, IB Tauris, pp. 175–190.

Malley, R. and Pomper, S. (2021), 'Accomplice to carnage: how America enables war in Yemen', *Foreign Affairs*, March/April. Available at: www.foreignaffairs.com/articles/united-states/2021-02-09/how-america-enables-war-yemen.

Moench, M. (1999), *Yemen: Local Water Management in Rural Areas: A Case Study*, Washington, World Bank.

Moench, M. and Lackner, H. (1997), *Decentralized Management Study*, Sana'a, World Bank.

Moyer, J.D., Bohl, D., Hanna, T., Mapes, Brendan R. and Rafa, M. (2019), *Assessing the Impact of War on Development in Yemen*, UNDP.

Mundy, M. (2018), 'The strategies of the coalition in the Yemen war: aerial bombardment and food war', Tufts University, World Peace Foundation. Available at: https://sites.tufts.edu/wpf/files/2018/10/Strategies-of-Coalition-in-Yemen-War-Final-20181005-1.pdf.

Mwatana and Global Rights Compliance (2021), 'The use of starvation by warring parties as a method of warfare', Sana'a, The Hague, pp. 386. Available at: https://mwatana.org/en/the-use-of-starvation/.

Mwatana (2021), 'Civilians in Yemen remain stuck between the warring parties and waiting for justice'. Available at: mwatana.org/en/civilians-in-yemen-remain-stuck/.

National Democratic Institute for International Affairs, (n.d.) 'Report on the 2006 presidential and local council elections in the Republic of Yemen'.

Obermeyer, G.J. (1982), 'La formation de l'Imamat et de l'Etat au Yemen: Islam et culture politique' in Bonnenfant, P. (ed.) *La Péninsule Arabique d'Aujourdh'ui*, vol. 2, Paris, CNRS, pp. 31–46.

OCHA (2021), 'Under-Secretary-General for Humanitarian Affairs and Emergency Relief Coordinator Mr. Martin Griffiths statement briefing to the Security Council on Yemen', 23 August. Available at: www.reliefweb.int/report/yemen/under-secretary-general-humanitarian-affairs-and-emergency-relief-coordinator-mr-martin.

Peterson, J.E. (1982), *Yemen, the Search for a Modern State*, London, Croom Helm.

Peterson, J.E. (2021), 'Tribe and state in the Arabian Peninsula', *Middle East Journal*, 74(4): 501–520.

PDRY, Central Statistical Organization (1989), 'Statistical yearbook 1988', p. 47.

Phillips, S. (2008), *Yemen's Democracy Experiment in Regional Perspective, Patronage and Pluralized Authoritarianism*, New York, Palgrave Macmillan.

Republic of Yemen (2002), 'Poverty Reduction Strategy Paper (PRSP) 2003–2005', p. ix.

Republic of Yemen, Central Statistical Organization (2015), 'Yemen labour force survey 2013–14'.

Republic of Yemen, Ministry of Planning and International Cooperation, Central Statistical Organisation (2017), *Statistical Yearbook 2017*.

Republic of Yemen, Ministry of Planning and International Cooperation, FSTS (February and April 2020; December 2019), 'Update on the food security situation in Yemen'.

Republic of Yemen, Ministry of Planning and International Cooperation, Economic Studies and Forecasting Sector (2018), 'Yemen socio-economic update', (38), pp. 1, 4.

Republic of Yemen, Ministry of Planning and International Cooperation, Economic Studies and Forecasting Sector (2020a), 'Yemen socio-economic update', (51), pp. 2, 4–5, 12, 13.

Republic of Yemen, Ministry of Planning and International Cooperation, Economic Studies and Forecasting Sector (2020b), 'Yemen socio-economic update', (53), p. 5.

Republic of Yemen, Ministry of Planning and International Cooperation, Economic Studies and Forecasting Sector (2021a), 'Yemen socio-economic update', (56), pp. 9–10.

Republic of Yemen, Ministry of Planning and International Cooperation, Economic Studies and Forecasting Sector (2021b), 'Yemen socio-economic update', (60), p. 1.

Rethinking Yemen's Economy (2019), 'Yemen's expatriate workforce under threat, the essential role of remittances in mitigating economic collapse'. Available at: www.devchampions.org/publications/white_papers/Yemens_Expatriate_Workforce_Under_Threat/.

Riedel, B. (2021), 'It's time to stop US arms sales to Saudi Arabia', Brookings Institution, 4 February. Available at: www.brookings.edu/blog/order-from-chaos/2021/02/04/its-time-to-stop-us-arms-sales-to-saudi-arabia/.

Roston, A. (2018), 'A Middle East monarchy hired American ex-soldiers to kill its political enemies. This could be the future of war,' Buzzfeed, 16 October. Available at: www.buzzfeednews.com/article/aramroston/mercenaries-assassination-us-yemen-uae-spear-golan-dahlan.

Salisbury, P. (2017), *Aiding and Abetting, the GCC States, Foreign Assistance and Shifting Approaches to Stability*, New York, Carnegie Centre for the Middle East.

Sana'a Centre for Strategic Studies (2018), 'Beyond the business as usual approach: combating corruption in Yemen'. Available at: www.sanaacenter.org/publications/main-publications/6614.

Sana'a Centre for Strategic Studies (2021), 'When aid goes awry', October. Available at: www.sanaacenter.org/reports/humanitarian-aid.

Sarkar, A. and Hamdani, S. (2022), '"Once we control them, we will feed them": mass starvation in Yemen' in Conley, B., de Waal, A., Jordash W. and Murdoch, C. (eds) *Accountability for Mass Starvation: Testing the Limits of the Law*, Oxford, Oxford University Press.

Schmitz, C. and Burrowes, R.D. (2018), *Historical Dictionary of Yemen*, Lanham, Rowman and Littlefield.

Schwedler, J. (2006), *Faith in Moderation, Islamist Parties in Jordan and Yemen*, New York, Cambridge University Press.

Shuja al Deen, M. (2021), 'Yemen's war-torn rivalries for religious education' in Wehrey, F (ed.) *Islamic Institutions in Arab States: Mapping the Dynamics of Control, Co-option, and Contention*, Carnegie Endowment for International Peace, pp. 33–52. Available at http://carnegieendowment.org/2021/06/07/yemen-s-war-torn-rivalries-for-religious-education-pub-84651.

South 24 (2020), 'Al-Zubaidi vows to protect the institutions and people of South Yemen', 6 May. Available at: https://south24.net/news/newse.php?nid=567.

Southern Transition Council (2019), 'President Al-Zubaidi delivers speech to Southern people on 52nd anniversary of Independence Day', 1 December. Available at: https://en.stcaden.com/print/8903.

Statista (2017), 'Number of mobile cellular subscriptions in Yemen from 2000 to 2016', July. Available at: www.statista.com/statistics/501168/number-of-mobile-cellular-subscriptions-in-yemen/.

Stookey, R. (1978), *Yemen, the Politics of the Yemen Arab Republic*, Boulder, Westview Press.

UK Gov (2013), 'Friends of Yemen: questions and answers'. Available at: www.gov.uk/government/news/friends-of-yemen-q-a.

UNDP (2019), 'Yemen Country Programme framework 2019–21'. Available at: www.yemen.un.org/en/17382-country-programme-framework-cpf.

UNOCHA (2021), 'Yemen Conference 2020: financial announcements', 1 March. Available at: www.unocha.org/sites/unocha/files/20210103-YemenHLE2021_AnnouncementsResults.pdf.

UN Security Council (2020), 'Welcoming mass prisoner swap in Yemen as "airlift of hope", speakers urge Government, Houthi rebels to negotiate durable peace, during Security Council briefing', 15 October. Available at: www.un.org/press/en/2020/sc14328.doc.htm.

UN Security Council (2021), 'Final report of the Panel of Experts on Yemen', 25 January, S/2021/79. Available at: www.reliefweb.int/report/yemen/final-report-panel-experts-yemen-s202179-enar.

UN Secretary General (2021a), 'As famine looms in Yemen, Secretary-General calls on donors to fund $3.85 billion humanitarian appeal, describes recent aid decline as "death sentence"', 1 March. Available at: www.un.org/press/en/2021/sgsm20607.doc.htm.

UN Secretary General (2021b), 'Disappointing outcome of Yemen funding conference mere "down payment" to prevent famine, Secretary-General says, asking donors to boost pledges', 1 March. Available at: www.un.org/press/en/2021/sgsm20609.doc.htm.

USAID (2016), Available at: www.climatelinks.org/resources/climate-change-risk-profile-yemen.

Varisco, D.M. (2021), 'Qabilah, Jirbah and Tanmiyah: tribes and agriculture in the northern highlands of Yemen' in Brandt, M. (ed.) *Tribes in Modern Yemen: An Anthology*, Vienna, Austrian Academy of Sciences, pp. 79–94.

Vatanka, A. (2020), 'Iran's role in the Yemen crisis' in Day, S. and Brehony, N. (eds) *Global, Regional and Local Dynamics in the Yemen Crisis*, Cham, Palgrave Macmillan, pp. 149–164.

WFP (n.d.), Available at: www.reliefweb.int/report/yemen/wfp-appeals-solution-yemen-fuel-shortages-threaten-worsen-widespread-food-insecuritywe.

World Bank (n.d.a), 'GDP (constant 2015 US$) – Yemen, Rep'. Available at: https://data.worldbank.org/indicator/NY.GDP.MKTP.KD?locations=YE.

World Bank (n.d.b), 'Personal remittances, received (current US$) – Yemen, Rep'. Available at: https://data.worldbank.org/indicator/BX.TRF.PWKR.CD.DT? locations=YE.

World Bank (2012), 'Climate Investment Funds, Strategic Program for Climate Resilience for Yemen', Meeting of the PPCR sub-committee, 17 April.

World Bank (2014), 'Future of climate change is visible now in Yemen'. Available at: www.worldbank.org/en/news/feature/2014/11/24/future-impact-of-climate-change-visible-now-in-yemen.

World Bank (2019), 'Migration and remittances, recent developments and outlook', Migration and development Brief, April, 31.

World Bank (2020), 'Pupil-teacher ratio, primary', various years. Available at: https://data.worldbank.org/indicator/SE.PRM.ENRL.TC.ZS?locations=.

World Bank, Republic of Yemen (2010), 'Assessing the impacts of climate change and variability on the water and agricultural sectors and the policy implications', Report no. 54196-YE.

World Bank, Republic of Yemen (2015), 'Unlocking the potential for economic growth', Report no. 102 151-YE.

Yemen Data Project (various dates), Available at: www.yemendataproject.org/.

Index

Note: Page numbers in **bold** refer to tables